Realizing the
American Dream

To: Maria
Enjoy
Feb 2, 2018

Realizing the American Dream

The Personal Triumph of a Guyanese Immigrant

Yuvraj Ramsaroop

.

To order additional copies of this book, contact:

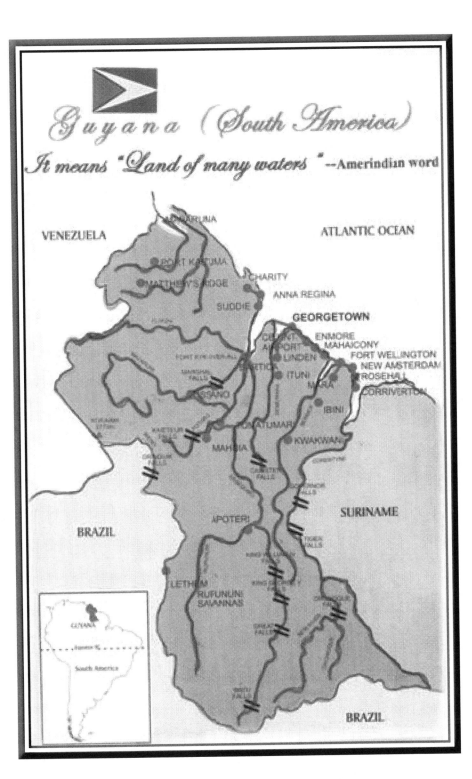

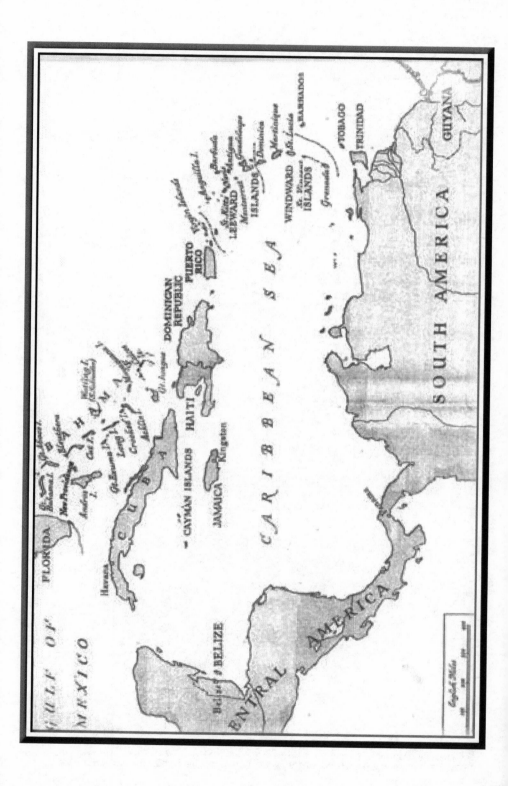

To my daughters Nanda and Sharda

"Truth is liberating, regardless of how painful it is."

I am not sure where or when I had heard that statement, but it amplifies the purpose of this book.

It is exactly as I remembered it.

CONTENTS

CHAPTER 1

Some Youthful Indiscretions

*Always tell the truth. That way you don't have to remember
what you say.*

—Mark Twain

There are some events of my childhood years that stand out firmly
in my mind even after all these years. It is doubtful that I could erase these
memories, and in an inviting way, I really don't want them to ever fade
away. They have remained a part of me and of the person I have become.
Their traces are present in many of the things I did later in life. Although
there was nothing unusual about them, they were experiences of uninhibited
innocence and an almost carefree spirit in the way I grew up as a boy. Now,
I have found them amusing in many ways, and I often marvel at the mere
adventure and the indiscretions I displayed.

I am not sure what impact they may have had on me in later years.
However, I still look back upon those days with reverence and with an almost
frightening disbelief that I had done some of those things. It has been more
than four decades, a throwback in time, and it was certainly a different era.
Everyday life seemed simple and without complications in comparison to
today's world. Many times I wonder if such activities have become extinct
for youths growing up in this age of advanced electronic equipments.
Space-age technologies of virtual reality video games, computerized toys,

and the revolving communication gadgetry enable instantaneous comfort. It is sad to realize that the simplicity in which a boy grew up in my days has changed so much in so short a time.

At ten years of age, I had never given any thoughts to the things I did. Growing up amid a large family of thirteen with seven brothers and four sisters presented its problems. Although we were poor, that did not seem to matter. We accepted the daily rigors and the constant struggles to survive as if it were normal. There was no clear direction in my life, and I found myself passing each day lazily between attending primary school and performing the melee of the household chores that I inherited at this young age. At home, there was always something that I was called upon to do. I can still hear some of the commands that vibrated from wherever my parents stood and shouted out toward me.

"Boy, go fetch in the wood before the rain com down."

"Boy, go wata dem plants . . . dem roots look like dem dry."

"Boy, go clean the lamp shade before it get dark."

"Boy, go mek some smoke before dem masquita start bite."

"Boy, go bring some boosie from de rice mill."

Weekends were different in many ways. I always looked forward to them with all the misguided endeavors that so engaged my abundant free time. My best friend Laxie and I would get together early in the morning at the culvert by the street corner near our house. He lived only two houses down on my street. Being of similar age and an unexplained inclination for wickedness, we had developed a strong friendship for as long as I can remember. We were together most of our free time, and we always engaged in mostly useless, idle conversations that spelled trouble down the road. Sometimes, an idea would come up, and if our confidence levels were high, we acted upon it.

One Saturday morning, I met Laxie soon after I had completed my chore of cleaning the chicken coop. We met at the culvert at the end of the street. I was often found here, hanging out and just plain loafing. The sun was sharp in the clear blue sky, and the dew had already evaporated from the grasses. Shortly after some idle talk, we started to meander slowly down the main Canje road. We were accustomed to the red-brick road in its poor condition, and we avoided the large ankle-deep holes created by the constant wash of the rains. We headed toward John Sawh's rice mill in the next village. Lingering on the bridge over the drainage canal, we kept an eye out to collect some *boosie* from the rice mill nearby. We had to wait until the engines stopped and it was safe to get under the turbine belt, where the boosie fell into a mound, like grains of sand on a dune. The boosie was just the waste product of ground up paddy shells mixed with broken grains of rice, which were an excellent source of feed for our chickens at home. Gathering some boosie usually gave me an excuse when my mother would question me about my whereabouts. She would be pleased if I brought home some boosie for the dozen or so chickens we raised in the backyard.

We were just passing time and idly watching everyone involved in their affairs. A few older men were playing cards on the corner of the road across the street. They were drinking rum mixed with coconut water, and every few minutes, some form of a loud argument ensued with cursing and name-calling in the process. We were sure they were drinking the illegal *bush rum*, as the bottle was always returned among the tall grasses and kept hidden after each one had taken a quick sip.

"Man, you na know wa de hell you talking about." One elderly man frowned. He briskly walked away in disgust, throwing up his hands in the air and mumbling some curses. The others laughed, and then the game was over as they all left in different directions. By noon, the Adelphi market, a short distance down the road, was beginning to get crowded. Housewives armed with straw baskets in hand hurried to make their purchases of fresh fish and vegetables. Factory workers were rushing home to eat lunch. Riding on bicycles, they staggered along the red-brick road, being careful to avoid the large potholes. With the *rice mill* operating, the humming sounds of the engines deafened the ear. In one corner, some men were constantly kicking over the water-soaked and smelly paddy on the hot concrete floor to dry before the milling process could begin.

John Sawh's house was diagonally across the road from the rice mill. Its mansion-like design and large manicured lawns were symbolic of the very few rich and upper class business owners. The high wire fence that surrounded the house kept everyone out. Perched on the bridge, we stared at the mango tree across the drainage canal or sideline as it is often called. We pondered our next move. It was not an especially tall tree, but half of the branches leaned lazily over the drainage canal. There were mangoes on every branch. There were mangoes in bunches of three and bunches of four. There were green mangoes and ripe mangoes, and scattered around the trunk were rotting mangoes that had fallen to the ground.

Prominently displayed, we could see two large ripe mangoes on the second branch overhanging the drainage canal, which were within easy reach from inside the yard. They looked juicy, delicious, and inviting. Something inside me prompted my next move.

Laxie had the same idea, and no words were necessary. We understood each other. I was determined to get my hands on them. It was a sure thing that some other youngster from the neighborhood would make an effort to get them soon enough. After all, it seemed such a waste to just let them fall in the murky water below. The water was filthy with raw sewage and was a dumping ground for dead dogs, dead chickens, and other debris. Both sides of the drainage canal were overgrown with weeds and tall bamboo grasses in thick clusters in the mostly stagnant water. Only a narrow stream in the middle kept the broad-leafed *mucka mucka* plant from over-growing it completely. Sometimes it was common to see everyone with their hands over their noses to shut out the stench when they passed the canal. We assumed that the owner did not seem to care much for the mangoes since none of them were picked from the tree. We were certain that the owner had no children, and it was evident that no one picked the ones that had fallen to the ground. Those that fell in the drainage canal were no good to eat.

We had to crawl under the barbed-wire fence to get into the yard, and I was careful not to get my shirt caught on the sharp twisted rivets. Laxie was not so lucky. I could see through the big tear on his shirt that left one side of the sleeves on his shirt barely hanging on threads. His brown shoulders were visible from my vantage point on top of the mango tree. He crouched on one knee to pick up the mangoes I had thrown down, and he seemed engrossed in his efforts to keep them together.

"Hey, Laxie," I whispered to get his attention, my hand covering my mouth to muffle the sound. There was no response, not a stir.

"Run." My voice was louder now. "An old man coming," I blurted out in haste, looking down at him from on top of the mango tree. Startled, Laxie turned and gazed up in my direction. His expression looked puzzled.

"Wa wrang?" he asked as he fumbled to keep the mangoes from falling out of the bosom of his shirt, which he had knotted at the waist. Both of his pants pockets were also bulging with a mango stuck halfway on each side. It pleased me that he had gathered up all the half dozen or so mangoes I had thrown down so far. Straddling two branches with my feet and holding on tightly to another above, I spotted the old man limping toward us from the little rusted one-story zinc house. It was no more than a stone's throw away from the mango tree. We may have disturbed him from his sleep or whatever he was doing caused by the rustle of the branches and the little gasps of excitement we made as Laxie caught the mangoes one at a time.

"Look!" I shouted and pointed to the back door of the house from where the old man had emerged. He had appeared suddenly, for there were no signs of anyone in the dilapidated little zinc house when we sneaked into the yard.

The place looked deserted, and I was surprised that anyone would be living in this little run-down shack, tucked away under a clump of tall trees. It tilted on one side as if it could topple at any time with a sudden rush of a strong wind. Coconut husks littered the ankle-deep muddy pools of water that surrounded it on all sides. He had a stick in one hand and walked with a limp on one foot as he hurried in our direction. I could hear him swearing feverishly and waving the stick in the air in rapid succession. As he got closer, his frail husky voice became stronger and distinctly alarming.

"You goddamn bastards," I heard him yell out. "You goddamn bastards." He panted and continued to curse repeatedly.

His tone of voice was becoming louder with a sternness that certainly put a chill on my spine. I wasted no time in starting to descend the mango tree. The branch that I was standing on hung over the drainage canal. There was no time to lose, and I may have underrated the danger. If I moved down limb by limb in the same manner I had climbed up, it was apparent that the old man would get to the tree in time to grab me. He was almost near the tree trunk now. Laxie was already on the move without any hesitation. Trying to keep his balance, he had tiptoed down the steep slope into the drainage canal to cross over.

"Come on," Laxie called out to me as he was almost halfway across. He was desperately hugging the mangoes in his bosom to keep them from falling out. "Jump quick," he yelled again. "It's not deep, see," he assured me and pointed to where the water had reached just past his knees. "Hurry up," were the last words I faintly heard him say.

With one swift motion, I held on tightly to the branch and hung on for no more than a second or two. The branch started to bend with my weight, and it was a sure six to eight feet drop into the drainage canal below. Seeing Laxie already in there boosted my confidence to let go of the branch. I heard two thumping sounds in rapid succession, and my eyes followed the disturbance in the dirty water below. Two ripe mangoes had broken off from their stems with the sudden shaking of the branch from which I was now hanging. For a flashing second, a degree of disappointment crossed my thoughts. These were the mangoes I had climbed up the tree to get in the first place. It did not take long for me to convince Laxie that we had to get them before anyone else. He was just as eager to get his hands on them. They were two of the juiciest mangoes I had ever laid eyes on. When we looked at them from the bridge that day, they appeared ripe to the eyes and the blend of their golden color glistened in the bright sunlight. A touch of crimson red surrounded the base near the stem that made them even more appealing. Eyeing them for more than a glance made small bubbles of saliva appear on the corners of my mouth. They were the irresistible *Buxton Spice* mangoes. They were sweeter than the *Long mangoes* and other varieties. When they were not yet ripe, a touch of salt and pepper camouflaged the tart taste. The spectacle of these two mangoes were too great to pass up, and between Laxie and me, we had to get our hands on them.

"Oh, shucks," I cussed out loudly, letting go of the branch and falling feet first into the drainage canal. It was no more than about knee-deep as expected. I sank a little into the soft mud, water splattering to soak my pants up to the waist, and I quickly scampered off to the other side. Glancing back, I could see the old man under the tree now. He was still waving his stick over his head and cursing in a fury.

"You f—ing bastards. You f—ing bastards."

His voice could be heard all the way to the main road by now. We did not care, and there was no way that this limping gray-haired old black man could catch us. He had no shirt on, and his exposed dark skin and his frail scrawny features posed no definite threat. I was almost certain that he would not dare to cross the drainage canal and chase after us. Laxie was right in front of me as we scampered across in a hurry. The knot on his shirt had come apart, and all the mangoes from under his bosom slipped into the dirty water. The two mangoes in his pockets had fallen out also, and mud covered his pants up to his waist.

A small group of housewives on their way to the market had stopped to watch the commotion. Almost everyone from Reliance knew us very well.

"Ah, who picnee dem da?" I faintly heard one woman asked. Panic gripped me instantly. I feared that we would be recognized and my parents would be told about this. In their eyes, this was stealing, and this would not be tolerated. I knew I would get a good beating if they could catch me. The usual punishment was a few slaps behind the head and some extra chores to do. Then I will be the object of recrimination, and a flurry of insults would follow indiscriminately for the next few days. Soon it would be forgotten, and no one would pay close attention to me anymore until the next incident. Of course, I would deny being near the rice mill or that mango tree area. I would swear left and right that it was not me, and I was relying on Laxie to back up my story. After all, I did not view this as stealing. I did not understand what the big deal was all about. It was only a few mangoes anyway. I had already stolen fruits many times before from the neighbors, especially guavas, cashew, pears, papayas, and other fruits that I laid my eyes on. It would have been different if the old man or whoever owned the tree was at least picking the mangoes and selling them at the market. This would rob his efforts to make a few cents and earn a living. This was my rationalization, but at ten years of age, I did not know any better. It was one of my wicked ways of convoluted thinking.

However, I knew exactly what my parents would say. It was not the stealing of mangoes that they were concerned about, although this was by no means inexcusable. It was the danger in which I was putting myself. Then I could almost hear exactly what insults and tongue-lashing that awaited me when I got home.

"Suppose something bin happen to you," my mother would say. Then she would reach for any stick near her and fire a few harmless blows wildly to show her disapproval. If I was close enough, a slap over the back of the head would find me instantly. The usual warnings would follow, accompanied with varied comments by my other elder brothers and sisters or anyone else who happens to be there. The remarks were always the same although they never seemed to register in my thick skull.

"You a play big man now, eh."

"What you need is some good lash on you backside."

"One of these days, all you manish-man gonna com out of you backside."

"Don't let me hear you thief mango again."

"And stop hanging around with all dem nat-a-ras."

"You only follow all dem loongera boys."

"How com you na water dem plants and clean de fowl pen yet?"

"How many times we got to tell you the same thing?"

"Dis boy hard ears."

I would whine my way through it all, denying everything, and in a few minutes, all the day's activities would be forgotten.

"Dat was na me," I would argue fiercely. "Ask Laxie if you na believe me."

It was the same treatment like always, and I had been through it many times before. My father used to say, "Boy, me na know when you go learn some sense. Everything a go in one ear and come out the other ear."

In the meantime, we had reached the other side and were running very fast. Laxie was panting close behind and following my every stride. I could feel my heart pounding as we followed the narrow beaten pathway that served as a back route to the burial ground. The tall saw grass and black sage bushes that lined the dam made it easy for us to disappear from view. In the background, we could still hear the faint cries of the old man cursing away. We never looked back until we reached the canal bordering the burial ground and slowed to a brisk walk. We were safe now as no one followed.

"So where all dem mangoes dey?" I asked.

"All gone." Laxie was almost inaudible. "Lost dem all," Laxie whispered, breathing heavily.

"All of dem?" I pouted in disbelief.

"All." He shrugged.

"What about dem ones you had in your pocket?" I inquired.

"Fell out somehow," he said with resignation and tapped his pockets to make sure.

"Shucks," I said whimpering and shaking my head.

Feeling disgusted, my thoughts raced to the two mangoes that fell right in front of my eyes. They were within easy reach. I did not even get to touch them. I was so close to them. I kicked the dirt to display my anger and started to throw small rocks in the canal to ease some of the disappointment.

"If it was not for that stupid old man," I said softly now, "I could be lapping up sweet mango juices from my fingers by now."

"Yeah," Laxie replied. There was pity in his tone of voice.

"Where the dickens he com from anyway?" I asked.

"I think he live in that zinc house," Laxie remarked.

"Well, he is just a bull poop," I sucked on my teeth lightly to dismiss the whole situation.

"Well, let's go back tomorrow," Laxie suggested. I did not answer right away, just to ponder the situation as we panted lazily along.

"I wonder if anyone recognized us." I asked. I was visibly worried, but it soon vanished as Laxie began to squint his nose.

We were a mess. Something was stinking all around us. It was the stench of the nasty water on our soaked pants and the mud on our feet. Laxie kept murmuring how he lost them all, shaking his head. The late afternoon sun was bearing down on our backs, and a layer of mud was beginning to dry to the bare skin from the legs down. We had reached the cross canal near the burial ground. This was the watering hole for the youngsters at Reliance Settlement. It was where I first learned to swim, and I bathed here frequently, almost every Saturday. The punts loaded with freshly cut sugarcane passed through here to Rose Hall factory. It was normal for us to pull a piece of cane off the punts then to peel off the hardy skin with our teeth and suck on the sweet cane juices. A few of our friends were already swimming there when we jumped into the canal with our clothes on to wash the stench off.

"Let's go back tomorrow," Laxie suggested again as he squeezed on his pants to dry out the muddy water.

"Nah, dem mangoes no good," I replied shrugging off the idea.

"Maybe we can go pick some guavas," I suggested.

"I hear Dookie yard got some at the back," I continued.

Laxie did not respond. He did not have to. We knew instinctively that we would be scouting that area soon for an opportunity to get into the Dookie's yard and the ripe guavas.

It was almost sunset when I nervously inched my way toward home. I was nervous and hesitant because I knew what would happen to me as soon as I walked into the bottom house. My clothes were dry now, and I tried to look much more presentable. We swam for quite a while and washed off the dirt without taking our clothes off. Later we sat on one of the concrete graves at the edge of the burial ground to dry out in the hot afternoon sun and sucked on sugarcane to quench our thirst.

"Who buried here?" Laxie pointed at the white tomb that had a fence around it, squinting his eyes to read the long name on the head of the tomb.

"You better na point at it," I said.

"Wa go happen." He pulled back to hide his hand behind his back with that numb expression that always beckoned my reassurance.

"Dem old people say dat *jumbie* or ghost go follow you," I warned him. "When you go home, you better throw some salt over your shoulders to stop dem jumbie from following you," I assured him.

"You see wa happen to Premo? A jumbie hold him, dat why he behaving so crazy."

Premo was much older and lived on the backstreet from us. He talked loudly by himself, making funny motions with his hands. We always avoided him by crossing to the other side of the street when we saw him coming. If you want to know what happened to Premo, everyone will say, "*Jumbie* hold him."

Laxie got off the grave instantly, and he was visibly frightened. We stared at the long name carved in the stone.

"I don' know who dis is. It's some *coolie* man," I remarked with my hands behind my back so that I would not point at the grave.

"How com no black people na bury here," Laxie observed.

"I don' know. They got their own burial ground at St. Patrick's churchyard. I guess."

I wondered about that for a while. I knew that only Indian people of Hindu and Muslim religions were buried at Reliance cemetery. I never understood the reason.

"Well, me nah frighten when me bin to that burial ground," Laxie started waving his hands and strutting to show that he was not afraid.

"Me too," I agreed with him.

"Black man can't turn into jumbie," I remarked.

"That's why me na afraid when me bin at St. Patrick's." Laxie seemed pleased with himself.

"Yeah, only coolie man does turn into jumbie."

I nodded in agreement.

Later we moved to rest in the shade of a *goobie* tree by one of the concrete tombs. We rehearsed a story together. If we were questioned about

The burial ground at Reliance Settlement. The tombs of my mother, father, and two elder brothers are on the entrance to the right.

our whereabouts, we would say that we were shooting birds with our slingshots by the Bachan tamarind tree and were searching for *monkey apples* and *banga* in the paddock area. This was a good cover story as we were known to frequent this area a lot. We would deny everything about stealing mangoes. One look at me and my mother would know right away that I was bathing at the canal. This was forbidden also. I would deny that with all my breath, but I knew I was not fooling her. Roland, my elder brother, had already given up the technique of detection. The skin becomes dry and whitish from the muddy brown water of the canal, and the hair looks flat and limp. Rubbing coconut oil all over the skin and a dab of Vaseline on the hair is the best way to hide the fact, but much care was necessary. Every square inch of skin must be covered, and we had no time to do so. Any spot showing is a clear indication of guilt. We did not have coconut oil or Vaseline in any case to erase the evidence.

Looking from the street, I could see my mother in the hammock and my father sitting on the wooden bench alongside. My two elder brothers and sister had gathered around, talking also, and it was almost dinner time. I lingered by the gate for a while, waiting for angry words or the wrath of an explosion of temper from my parents. In case they decided to pass some licks, I would make a dash back to the streets and off to a quick escape. Laxie had already gone home. He lived with his elder brother since both of his parents passed away sometime ago. No one questioned him as I passed by his house. We were very good friends as far back as I could remember, and he practically lived at my house. My mother was kind to him except when she gets mad at something, and both of us would get some scolding. She would always offer him food or share *mauby* and a piece of *red roll* cake or anything that she was sharing with us. No one missed him as he went home, and his brother never asked him anything as he entered the house.

Now it was my turn.

"Navin," my mother was first to call out. "You gonna water dem plants today, boy?" she questioned.

"Right away," I said and inched my way toward the bottom house to get one of our galvanized buckets.

"Where the hell you been all day?" my father intervened.

"Knock about, what else," my mother exclaimed.

From the tone of their voices, I sensed that they knew nothing of the mango tree incident. In some ways, I was relieved and moved through the gauntlet of my family members to get the bucket by the steps. Guilt sidestepped my hunger for now, and dinner would have to wait a while longer, whatever curry and rice were left in the pots on the fireside. I did not want to cast any more suspicions on my whereabouts, and it was better to let sleeping dogs lie. It would take more than two hours to fetch buckets of water from the well on the street to soak the roots of the many rows of plants in the backyard garden. The rows seem endless of bora and ochro and cassava. I had much time to think and reflect, but it came down to more lazy daydreaming.

There were many times when I looked back on those days and marveled at the way I grew up. At age ten, I would be gone for most of the day without any supervision. Sometimes I wondered why my parents never bothered to inquire about my whereabouts or question where I had been all day. They never asked if I was hungry or had anything to eat or whether I was all right.

It seemed that things were fine as long as I showed up in the afternoon and was in one piece. The routine of getting my chores done was all that mattered. I am sure they cared much more than I could imagine, but I never knew of it. Counting and waiting for the long school days to end, I could hardly wait until the end of the school week.

It was a couple of weeks later, and Saturday morning had finally come. Laxie was waiting for me by the culvert at the end of the street. We engaged in idle conversation, played sponge ball cricket on the street, and planned our next move. My little brother Amos had followed me out to the culvert. He kept following me every time I was about to leave the yard and just hang around nearby. Amos would let out a loud cry if I did not take him along with me. Sometimes, I would give him an effortless slap on the back of his head, push him back into the yard, and lock the gate behind him. He would then bawl out so loudly that my mother would come out and give me a good tongue-lashing for not taking him to play by the culvert.

"Wa you na let the boy play with you?" she questioned.

"All right," I said and gave Amos a fierce look to discourage him.

This morning was no exception, and we were anxious to get rid of him. He was holding up our agenda. Laxie and I started to throw a sponge ball in the air back and forth and catching it. All the while, we were intentionally ignoring Amos as he watched us for a little while. Amos got bored, and after lingering for a while, he wound his way back to our house. Unnoticed, we immediately took off in a sprint to the rum shop.

Everyone knew Walter Rum Shop. Katic Cake Shop stood next door, and St. Patrick's Anglican School and the Anglican Church were directly across from the road. Situated along the Canje road, Walter Rum Shop was only a short distance from the Rose Hall Sugar Estate pay office. Every Friday was payday, and the sugar workers convened to pick up their hard-earned money in cash. Cane cutters gathered in groups counting and comparing their wages with broad smiles on their dark dusty faces. Some were still in their blackened work clothes with saucepan and cutlass in hand. Field hands, comprising of young men and women, moved through the gates. They passed the vendors collecting money owed to them for refreshment services provided to workers in the fields. Other vendors lined both sides of the road to sell their goods, which comprised ready-made clothes to trinkets and giftware. Over the high bridge, many fish vendors shouted out the best prices and beckoned buyers for their fresh catch of hassar, congo, mullet, gilbaka, banga mary, shrimp, and other local fishes. Others displayed their neat parcels on the ground of okra, bora, tomatoes, and spinach. Almost any fruit could be found at one of the stands, from mangoes and guavas to papayas and bananas. Some vendors travelled as far as from Albion and Port Mourant Sugar Estates on the Corentyne coast to sell their goods at Rose Hall market. Housewives hurried to and fro to get the best buys with basket in hand or on top of their head and armed with the wages their husbands have just handed over. Everyone jostled to get by through the maze of traffic created by bicycles and pedestrians.

Meeting up with my mother at the market on Friday afternoons right after school was dismissed was always a joy for me. I located and followed her quietly through the thick crowd past the fish corner and over the high bridge. I could hardly wait until we passed by the food stands. Then I would tug at her skirt to remind her that I was right behind and all the time begging her for a *gil* (British penny equivalent to two cents). She would rattle the change in her little cloth purse that she kept in her bosom and handed me a *gil*. My choice was very limited considering the variety available. There were salted nuts and fried channa, saltsew, crushed ice, *Gulajamon*, *metai*, and *poolorie*. My choices were always to buy two *barra* for one cent, topped with tamarind chutney, and a *jalabee* for one cent. I never had any patience to stay with my mother after that. She was always trying to make up her mind on what to buy or engaged the fish vendors in their usual gossip. As soon as I had eaten my *barra* and licked my fingers of the sugarcoated *jalabee*, I made some excuses and dashed away toward home.

A market scene at Rose Hall Estate on Fridays. In the background, recently acquired Ferguson tractors replaced the mules in transporting sugarcane punts from the fields to the factory.

On my way home, I passed by Walter Rum Shop. The chattering roar inside with everyone talking at the same time could be heard as I approached.

I would linger for a while and watch some of the men come and go. Some workers had the habit to stop in and take a few drinks before going home. Others would stay longer, and by the time the afternoon had passed, they would be almost drunk and staggered out when they left. Then there were the few who would not leave until the rum shop was closed late into the night. I remembered older folks who could name dozens of men who had spent their entire week's wages getting drunk. Then they would go home and beat their wives and children if they complained about his drinking. An older man came out almost drunk, his eyes upturned and hands waving as he serenaded everyone with his favorite Indian song, "Pyar ka Sagar" ("Love of Ocean").

His partner made an attempt to push him along by the shoulder as they wobbled their way along the road. As I looked on, I had a feeling that I would find empty rum bottles again as usual. I always wondered about what was going on inside. The rum shop was packed, and groups of the men had moved with their bottles of Russian Bear rum or Demerara rum to the outside to drink. Everyone seemed to be talking at the same time and loudly too. They would drink until the bottle of rum was empty. The empty bottles were discarded in the yard, and if I could get them before the owner picked them up the next morning, I could exchange the bottles for hard cash. This was my ticket to the movies.

We were early this Saturday morning at Walter Rum Shop. No one was around, and the gate was partially opened.

"I go check the back," Laxie said, directing our moves.

"Okay," I agreed.

"You check the sides," he commanded.

"Don't make any noise," I warned him and ducked into the opening of the gate. Laxie followed. I was bursting with anticipation as I scuttled toward the side fence. My eyes were scavenging every square inch of grass. Suddenly, there they were. Four empty half bottles lay in the grass close by the urinal, and one large bottle was leaning behind a mound of rubbish near the fence. My face lit up. *This must be my lucky day*, I thought. Picking up the empty rum bottles, I cradled them in my arms as I pouted to close my nostrils. The smell of pee from the urinals filled the air. Another quick look around and seeing no other bottles, I headed quickly out of the yard. Laxie was already by the gate, waiting with four big bottles, two in each hand. A huge grin showed off his large spadelike front teeth as we trotted off to wait by the bridge over the drainage canal near Dookie's shop. The owner was probably still sleeping from the late closing on Friday nights, and we were lucky that no one saw us. The rum shop would not be opened for another two hours.

"Only four bottles you found?" I asked.

"Yeah, no more around," Laxie responded, still grinning.

"I thought we would find more. The rum shop was full yesterday," I exclaimed.

"Oh well. Okay, let's go before Walter see us," I urged him on.

Later, when the rum shop was opened for business, we exchanged the bottles for cash. Laxie got eight cents for his efforts, and I got six cents. Apparently, Walter paid only one cent each for the half bottles.

I thought I should have received two cents each for the half bottles. There was no need to argue. We were happy though, and once again, we earned our matinee bill. I still needed a *gil* or two cents more to make up my matinee fare. The price of tickets for children under sixteen years or schoolboys was eight cents, and no exceptions were allowed. Adult tickets were fourteen cents. The wheels of thought started to roll on how I would get the other two cents. With money safely in our pockets, we made our way to Rajmahal Cinema to look at the posters one more time. We hung around Rajmahal Cinema quite a lot, and we were up to date with all the latest pictures shown. For the past two weeks, the posters were boldly displayed for the matinee show on Saturday afternoon. I did not want to miss these pictures for anything in the world.

Texas Bad Man and *The Desperadoes* were being advertised as two of the best Westerns ever to be shown at this cinema. We kept asking everyone about them. My brother Roland and some of the older guys had seen the trailers earlier in the week, and they told us that they looked like action-packed pictures. These were just the kind of pictures I liked to see. Randolph Scott, who starred in *The Desperadoes*, was my hero of all time. He was the fastest gun in the West, and we knew we would be in for a lot of action. None of the other bad guys and crooks could stand up to Randolph Scott. That afternoon, when I asked my mother for a gil, I got the usual reply immediately.

"Boy, don't bother me," she snapped back.

A few minutes passed, and I was at it again.

"Ma, can you give me a gil?"

In the meantime, I did my chores to appease her and made sure that she noticed. I tried not to get her upset in the process. I cleaned the fowl pen and put out the zinc to dry. I stayed close by and watched as she cleaned the dozen hassar she had purchased from the market earlier. With her hands occupied cleaning fishes, I had to wait. I knew she kept her money in her bosom, sometimes in a handkerchief with the coins tied into a knot in one corner. My pestering paid off when, relaxing in her hammock later, she handed me a gil. I was happy and skipped off to get ready for the matinee.

Laxie and I sat with the rest of the *gang* (boys of the same age group from the area) in the front bench of the cinema. We did not want our view blocked by taller guys sitting in front of us. Known as the pit section, it consisted of long rows of wooden benches, all on the same level. Beyond the partition toward the middle of the cinema were the *house* and *balcony* sections. The seats were individual chairs that sloped upward to an unobstructed view of the screen. These were the more expensive seats.

The pit was packed today, and only a handful of people scattered in the house and balcony sections. We stared out at the huge Cinema-scope screen in front of us. Excitement built up to the start of the pictures. Randolph Scott was riding tall in the saddle toward a Texas town with two guns on his hips. At least for today, I was inside the cinema and settled down to enjoy the action. I was hoping that there would be no interruptions to the pictures. Many times, the movie would come to a complete halt and everyone stared into a blank screen. I don't think it was the fault of the owner or manager. There were cuts or gaps on the film for being an old film version or a technician's error when the reels were being changed. However, this always brought out the worst behavior of the cinema patrons. I heard every curse word from every corner directed to the owner, who they named Scratchies because he always scratched his crotch area. It's a shame too when all the curses, and every conceivable one at that, were directed at his wife and children. I must admit that I cursed also, repeating every word I heard and enjoyed it. However, there was instant silence when the pictures resumed a moment later.

I remembered the many times when I was not so lucky and no rum bottles were found. It was not easy to reconcile the turmoil of my emotions that followed, especially when a hot picture was playing. There was only one avenue left, and I resorted to it with cunningness and skill. I saw the picture from the outside of the cinema. By the start of the second feature, night would prevail, and it would be dark. The jealousy windows lining the side of the cinema would be opened to allow for some fresh air. Standing on the exit ramps, we peeped in through these windows. There were frequent interruptions though as we were chased away by the cinema's watchman as he made his rounds. We would run away only to return immediately afterward when he was gone. Sometimes he left us alone. In those days, a matinee at Rajmahal Cinema was our only entertainment. It was the only outlet from the daily rigors of village life and the monotonous chores that followed with every step and activity. It gave us a cheap escape from reality. Western movies were my favorite. I was sure that I had seen most of them over the years and some of them more than once. For the few that have become classics, I always relished the thrill of the lone, heroic cowboy who stood tall to fight injustice with all the odds stacked against him. Such were the movies of an era gone by that still stand its time, and I remembered them as if it was only yesterday at Rajmahal Cinema.

The following were my picks for the best Western movies of all time.

Shane (1953)	starring Alan Ladd
Man Without a Star (1955)	starring Kirk Douglas
Last Train from Gun Hill (1959)	starring Anthony Quinn
Gunfight at the OK Corral (1957)	starring Burt Lancaster
Ride Beyond Vengeance (1966)	starring Chuck Connors
Rio Bravo (1959)	starring John Wayne
The Man Who Shot Liberty Valance (1962)	starring James Stewart
High Noon (1952)	starring Gary Cooper

Rajmahal Cinema at Reliance Settlement.

There were times when I wished that circumstances would have been better or just a little more favorable to my daily life. Not even the simplest of luxuries were at my disposal, such as my toothbrush, a pair of shoes, a new slate and pencil, or a reading book to mention a few. I never owned more than two short pants and two shirts at any one time. It was not surprising that when we got together as youngsters the conversations were always about the things we wished we had. Most of the time, it was idle talk, idle daydreaming, and an incessant envy of anyone and every one of our peers that appeared to have an edge over our meager disposition. We shared the same emotions of anger and loneliness and despair that were common grounds for close bondage and forged friendships. We were a closely knit bunch: Laxie, Leonard, Rudy, and for a brief time, one of Katie's sons, whom we befriended.

I will never forget one incident in particular when we tried to take advantage of one of my friends. I never knew his name, and I had always referred to him as Katie's son. Being of similar age, he was one of the sons of a prominent businessman in the area. His business enterprise or cake shop, as we called it, was directly across from St. Patrick's Church and served as a hangout with my other friends on our way to school. There were occasions when we walked to school together and sometimes played sponge ball cricket in the school yard during recess. With a couple of my buddies, we usually carried out our devious activities and schoolboy pranks on the last school day of the school week. The atmosphere was more relaxed, with teachers in a better mood and less vigilant of their students. Friday was set aside for most sports activities with arts and crafts dominating the afternoon periods. We had our own agenda planned, and I doubted whether we would be missed at all. We were bursting in anticipation on how we were going to make out on this particular Friday.

The previous afternoon, as soon as classes were dismissed, we made a rendezvous to plan the last detail. We met behind the church to make the list. Laxie said that he was getting the pepper, the can opener, and a can of condensed milk. Leonard was getting the salted fish and rice and a large butter container that his mother had thrown away. We would use it as a cooking pot. Katic's son promised to get two large cans of sardines with two large loafs of plaited bread. He also assured us that he would bring four bottles of ICEE drinks and some black-eyed pea cake that he would snatch from his parents' shop. We knew that he could afford a lot of good stuff to eat, and we encouraged him to bring anything that he could lay his hands on since his parents owned the cake shop and grocery store. My list consisted of salt, an onion, a box of matches, and four cigarettes that I planned to steal from my father's pack when he fell asleep. He always left his cigarettes and matches on the table. No one touched them for he was the only smoker in the family at that time. These were the Lighthouse brand of cigarettes with no filters, and they were the most popular brand of the time. We had no money to buy the cheaper brand of Texas 99 that sold for one cent each.

I was a little late when I arrived at Katic Cake Shop and Beer Parlor. Laxie and Leonard were already there.

"You got your stuff?" Laxie inquired.

"Yes, I got everything," I answered. I clapped my pockets lightly to signal that everything was there.

"How about you guys?" I asked.

"Everything all set," Leonard intervened, showing off the large paper bag in his hand.

"We got to wait a little," Leonard remarked, looking toward the back of the shop.

"His mother is balling him out at the back," Laxie cut in.

We could hear her voice and those familiar words that could describe any of us: lazy, good-for-nothing.

"Well, dat's not anything new," I said, and we all giggled a little. We knew the score, and I had been there so many times before.

"After today, he don't have to worry about dat anymore," Laxie pointed out.

"That's for sure," I said, shaking my head and agreeing with him.

Leonard nodded in agreement, and we waited on Katie's son to get away from his mother.

Shortly after, Katie's son appeared over the counter and motioned for us to start walking to meet at the back of the church. He raised one finger to indicate that he would be there in a minute. We understood the signal and moved briskly across the road and toward the back of the church.

Katie's son joined us shortly afterward. He had two large paper bags in his hands. We were all excited and rushed over to take a peek in the bags and examine what he had brought. I felt good when I saw the two large cans of Marshall's Sardines in Tomato Sauce. These were the best brand of sardines available and very expensive. My thoughts wandered to a gluttonous feasting treat later in the day. The aroma of the fresh plaited bread and black eye cakes were mouth-watering nonetheless. It was not long now. Running away from home seemed like a very good idea so far.

The bell rang out at St. Patrick's Anglican School at 9:00 a.m. All the pupils began to assemble at arm's length apart in straight rows in the playground. Within minutes, all the pupils and teachers had marched gracefully into their respective classes, and silence prevailed throughout the school compound. Only the hissing sound of steam escaping from the turbine engines of the sugar factory was heard. The shouts and screams from boys arguing about their marble games or girls skipping rope ceased. All sponge ball cricket and rounders came to an abrupt halt. It was time to make our move. Huddling through the dense bushes and weeds that had overgrown the graves and concrete tombstones, we followed the narrow cow path that meandered its way toward the cross canal. Following the canal was a straight walk passing Ramotar's shop and the cluster of the post office, the police station, and the courthouse, heading toward the burial ground and then to Canje Creek. No one spoke a word for a while as we were tense and nervous. We kept looking in all directions to make sure no one we knew had seen us, and we were constantly looking over our shoulders to make sure we were not being followed. No one would miss us anyway, at least not until the late afternoon. I doubted whether the teachers would notice. The worst scenario was that our names would be marked as absent on roll call for that day. Considering the frequency that I had played truant from school, this was not such a big deal for me anyway. By way of the empty punts stationed by the sluice, we crossed over the canal, and then it was a straight half mile trek toward Canje Creek. It was a long walk, interrupted with small talk and frequent attempts at stone skipping. We were in the clear to living freely and on our own.

The post office, police station, and courthouse (from left to right).

I don't know how the idea came up, but I agreed with Katic's son right away when he suggested to us that he was running away from home.

Laxie and Leonard said they would run away too, but they were agreeable to any suggestions. Idling in the cake shop, we had listened to Katie's son complaining and coaxed him along on every step. He was angry at his parents, and his voice was breaking almost to the point of sobbing.

"I am sick of living," Katie's son started to fuss.

"So what happened?" I asked.

"Same old stuff, every day and night," he continued.

"I do all the work, and I can't take the beating anymore." He sighed.

"And I don't want to go back to school anymore." He glanced toward the school from the cake shop window.

"I know what you mean," I pondered and tried to agree with him in any way I could.

"I am going away, and they won't see me anymore." He was serious now and seemed determined.

"Well, I will run away from home too," I stated in a serious tone.

"Yeah, let's all run away," Laxie intervened.

"How about tomorrow?" Katie's son suggested. His face lit up. His forehead crinkled.

"Okay, but we got to take some food to eat," Leonard interrupted.

"Why don't you get some stuff from the shop?" Laxie suggested.

"I can get anything I want," Katie's son responded, puffing his chest out and strutting his steps as he snapped back. He seemed confident now. We were pleased to hear that.

"Hey, get two cans of sardines," I pleaded. Then we continued to call out aloud the things we needed. At the back of our minds, we had a faint idea of what we're about to embark on, and for me, it was more like an adventure I could not pass up. Where this was taking us seemed like the likely solution to our insignificant lives. We knew what we were doing. We were running away from home, running away from the daily chores, running away from the verbal abuse, running away from the schoolwork we all hated, and running away from the beatings of our teachers. We wanted free time and to rid ourselves from the cloud of meaningless activities hanging over our heads. In the case of Katic's son, we could see that he could take it no more, and we were sympathetic to his plight. I supposed that we were at the edge of boredom and frustration, and running away from home would bring it to an end.

My thoughts raced to my never-ending chores: watering the plants every afternoon when it did not rain, fetching cow dung from the stables early every Friday morning, cleaning the fowl pen on Saturdays, cutting the grass for the cow each day, chopping firewood to be dried in the hot sun, bathing the dog in the drainage canal, filling the barrel with water drawn from the well on the street, and more, much more.

We had reached the creek now. We sat close to the edge and watched the muddy brown water flowing swiftly on. Small clumps of grass and weeds and logs floated with the tide.

The drainage canal from Reliance settlement empties its waters into the Canje Creek. At this junction, I skulked from school many times.

"I wonder if any alligator in dem clumps of grass," Laxie asked.

"Sometimes," I said. Then we stared at every clump of grass that went by in hopes of seeing an alligator. We had no luck.

"Hey, look over here," Katie's son shouted in excitement as he pointed to the mudflats. The tide of the creek was low, and much of the sides were exposed to a soft brown sifting mud. A number of small creatures skittered across the mud, and in the split of a second, they disappeared under the mud.

"Those are four-eyed fishes," I said and pointed in the direction that they swam.

"Boy, they are really fast," Katie's son commented gleefully. He was amused.

"Even my brother Roland can't catch them," I boasted, "and everybody know how good a fisherman he is. As soon as you make a move, they disappear." I continued to relate some previous experiences I had with these four-eyed fishes. I never did find out if these species of fish actually had four eyes as the name suggested. However, two large bulging eyes on top of the head were very pronounced that gave it a menacing appearance. They fed on the silt and mud that settled on the mudflats or sides of the creek. Our efforts to hit one with rocks or anything else we could find were futile. The speed in which they eluded danger was amazing to watch.

By now, the midday sun was sharp, and beads of perspiration settled on our lips. We rested under a clump of bushes, flattening the soft grass underneath to make ourselves comfortable and to shelter us from humidity and tropical heat. Katie's son was first to talk about the teachers of St. Patrick's Anglican School, and soon all our conversations steered in that direction.

"I hate Ramgolam," I remarked, referring to my current third standard teacher. "I don't know why he can't get rid of all dem pimples," frowning in disgust. "I can't wait to pass on to fourth standard. I am glad that Suckdeo don't beat as much." I was feeling better, knowing that I could go to school without fear of the whips when I reach fourth standard. "At least not like Ramgolam." Everyone knew what I meant.

"How about Ten-pound Lips and Five-pound Backside," Laxie exclaimed, and we all burst out in laughter. All of us had nicknames for our teachers, and Mr. Robinson was no exception. He was the music teacher. All we ever saw him do was play the piano as we marched in step like soldiers into our classes at the beginning of each school day. I can't remember ever seeing him teach Arithmetic or English to any of the classes.

"Man, how he become a teacher me na know," Leonard said. We all shook our heads in agreement, wondering.

"Wait till you get to sixth standard," I said, cutting Leonard short and pointing at Katic's son.

"You see how Waldron does beat dem school-leaving boys," I said sternly.

"Well, I am gonna leave school before I reach Waldron's class," Katic's son snapped back. He was visually upset and got up instantly. He seemed to get angry every time his thoughts fixated on school.

"I get enough licks from Scarder now." His voice was still bitter as he fiddled to break off some branches from the underbrush. I could see that he was embarrassed for we had often seen him get lashes for getting words spelled incorrectly on his dictation tests or errors in mental arithmetic. We knew about it and avoided bringing the matter up so as not to embarrass him any further. He was not particularly bright, but he was in the select few in the scholarship class overlooked by H. C. Scarder, the headmaster. A special cane was on his desk at all times, which he used for flogging pupils who did not meet the standard of academic excellence he expected of them. The echo of the lashes from on top of the stage permeated the school frequently.

Thinking about it, I was happy that I was not bright enough to be in the scholarship class. I doubted whether I could have endured such treatment. The humiliation of being flogged on the stage while the entire upper-floor classes watched on was more than demeaning. The feeling of worthlessness was even worse considering that pupils who get flogged were usually considered as dunces. For me, it was the ultimate reason for hating everything about school.

"I liked One-eyed Archer," Leonard concluded in the end, and we all agreed. My impression of him was that he was a kind and understanding teacher by any standard with a keen interest in his pupils.

The estate's steam whistle sounded off at noon, and our conversations suddenly turned to the food we brought.

"I am hungry," Laxie said and started peering through the paper bags.

St. Patrick's Anglican School at Rose Hall Estate during my years in primary school. Unused and in disrepair, this wooden building collapsed from decay over the years.

St. Patrick's Anglican School.

St. Patrick's Anglican Church, where I skulked among the tall bushes, which had overgrown the grave markers and tombstones.

"Let's start the cook up now," Leonard suggested.

"No, man, dat will take too long. We can eat the sardines and bread now and then cook later," I said in objection. The aroma of the fresh bread was too tempting to wait any longer, and I craved to satisfy the burning hunger that overcame me.

"Yeah, dat's a good idea," Laxie and Leonard agreed.

We proceeded to lay out the items on the grass. We had no plates, but that was never a problem. In no time, Leonard had cut some *mucka mucka* leaves nearby with the penknife he always carried around with him in his hip pocket. Katie's son wrestled to open the cans of sardines, and Laxie wasted no time in mixing it up with cut onions, an extremely hot ball-of-fire pepper, and some salt. There was a gleam on each face and an eagerness to taste the delicacies in front of us. Splitting the loaves of bread in half, we apportioned the sardines and stuffed our share into the prepared opening of our bread. This was the largest piece of bread that I had ever possessed as my own to devour. What followed was an eating frenzy similar to a pack of wolves feasting on a freshly killed carcass. My eyes and hands and all my awareness focused exclusively on this tasty morsel. For a while, there were only sounds of slurps from the warm ICEE soda rushing down the throat and soft groans and moans of delight from the sardine and bread combination reaching the taste buds. A few hissing sounds escaped our lips to relieve the bitterness of the pepper. Not a scrap of bread fell to the ground.

"Aaah, dis is de life," I bellowed. My belly puffed out now with a great degree of satisfaction. It was as if I had achieved my only goal in life, and if only for a little while, it seemed as if all was well with my life. I resigned myself to lie lazily on the grass and watch the cumulous clouds gathering in the sky. I looked for familiar shapes and outlines of animals that the clouds sometimes can imitate in their ever-changing drift in the sky. Later, we smoked the Lighthouse brand cigarettes I had brought. We pretended to act like the movie stars in the way Humphrey Bogart sucked in the smoke in his chest. We puffed away, blowing smoke like the Rose Hall Estate chimney and all the while coughing and fanning the smoke from getting in our watering eyes. None of us had learned how to inhale the smoke and let it out of our nostrils in the way the older boys did. As a small boy, I was always amazed at this feature and admired those who possessed this exceptional talent. I saw too how they enjoyed themselves when immersed in sucking smoke deeply into the lungs from a cigarette. It was only a matter of time before I had to try it. We were big shots for the moment until the cigarettes burnt out at the tip and the last puff of smoke was extracted. Very little was said for a while, and we lost ourselves to daydreams and thoughts of fantasy. We watched the tides rise and the brown creek water inching up to hide the mudflats. Finally we devoured the black eye cakes to smother the cigarette odor and washed our hands and mouths in the creek water so that it would not be detected when we got home.

Idle conversations turned to jokes about our unusual moments as we poked fun at some of the borderline characters in the neighborhood. There was Naman who walked along the road and sang loudly all the time. These were songs no one had ever heard. My favorite was Bull-poop who cursed nonstop at anyone who called him Bull-poop. Of course, we shouted Bull-poop every time we saw him and then ran for cover down the streets as his curses faded in the wind. Then we laughed hysterically when we talked about Laban. He lived at the backstreet behind our house and had the largest hernia in the world. Everyone called him Laban *Go-Dee*. It was almost the size of a large watermelon and reaching almost to the ground. I thought he should have been in the *Guinness Book of World Records* for this peculiarity. In spite of his handicap, I was always amazed at his skill to ride a bicycle. He would carefully lift and balance his hernia on the bar of the bicycle to keep it in place before he rode off slowly. We were told by the older boys that if we burnt a chicken feather, his Go-Dee would roll off the bicycle bar and he would fall. Of course, we rushed to find a feather and burnt it whenever we saw him going down the road. I never saw him fall. Although Laxie claimed that he did once. I did not believe him.

There were the countless others we had hardly mentioned. I remembered Cockroach, who had the ability to recall a name or face of anyone even after two decades or more. No one could forget Madman Isaac who hacked his wife's head off one afternoon after chopping wood in the backyard. He served a few years in jail and was then paroled. It was a surprise to most of us when he was given the job as the watchman at Rajmahal Cinema, a mystery by all means. He never spoke a word to anyone as far I could tell. We dared not to hang around when he was making his rounds. What surprised me was that he was related to our family from my grandmother's side. There was Pagla, who walked up and down the main road, suffering a mental breakdown after he was jilted by the woman he was supposed to have married. At least that was how the story was told to us. To my surprise, the tall, lanky woman was my next-door neighbor. He often defecated on himself and did not belong on the streets. Then there was Stupid, so nicknamed for his odd behavior. It was usual for many to be called by nicknames for their peculiarity. Everywhere there was always someone being called fat man, broke hand, black boy, three seed (because he had three testicles), and with a Hindi language connotation, there were *langra* (limp), *canwa* (blind), and *bhaira* (deaf).

Reality confronted me when the quarter-to-four steam whistle sounded off and stirred us into action again. It announced the change of shifts at the sugar factory. I knew too well what was in store for me from then on. I had to get a bag of grass cut and take it to the cow pen at Reliance Abandon. The cow had to be tied in the pen and ready for milking.

Ivan, my eldest brother, normally arrived late in the afternoon at the cow pen to take care of milking the cow. He always went crazy if things were not according to his liking, and a few lashes would easily find me when he needed to vent his frustration. It would be worse if he found out I *skulked* (played truant) from school.

"I got to go," I said and got up as the shrill of the steam whistle died down. "I got to go cut grass and pen the cow," I reminded everyone and started walking toward home. Laxie and Leonard followed lazily behind. Soon I was walking briskly, and all my thoughts were focused on the tasks ahead of me. The original idea of running away from home was literally lost to the wind. I paid no heed to it. I was late for my chores. Katic's son trailed behind in utter disgust. He did not say much. There was a sadness in his face, and he hung his head for the most part as we walked back toward home. I never saw much of Katic's son after that. He had stopped talking to us, and later we found out that he was attending a private school in New Amsterdam. I never knew how serious he was about running away from home, and I was certain he felt trapped and exploited by us. I could only imagine the scolding he got from his mother when he went home that afternoon and the pain he had to go through afterward. As for me, I knew from the very start that a treat of sardines and bread was a good enough reason to cut classes. As for the many other times I cut classes, there was no excuse other than the fact that I hated school.

That afternoon, I did cut the grass, and I did pen the cow without incident. It was a pleasure to watch her feast on the freshly cut bamboo grass I had brought. Janie was our only milking cow, and we took especially good care of her. She grazed freely in the cow pasture at the back of Reliance Abandon during the day. Every afternoon, when I arrived at the pen, I called out to her from the top of the cow pen.

"Janie, Janie. Aaah, boy, aaaah."

Hearing the voice of my call in the distance, she would lift her head and make a brisk trot into the cow pen to the freshly cut cane grass or sour grass that I had brought. Every day after school, I canvassed the sidelines and the drains and the edges of the cane fields nearby for the best grasses for Janie. I loved to pat her on her head and around the horns after tying her down for the night. Every day, my eldest brother came to milk her, and she normally gave up six pints of milk before we let her calf suckle the rest.

The milk was sold to our neighbors at fourteen cents per pint. It was a lot of money for my mother in those days. It would be past sunset when I would walk back home with the calf alongside to be tied up in our backyard until the next day. She was a beautiful calf with soft auburn and off-white hair. As I passed through the streets with her, some of the neighborhood children would come up to pet her on the forehead and run their hands along the soft baby hair on her back. I had not come up with a name for the calf as yet, but she was part of our family. We had milked Janie for about four months, and then the calf was set free to mature with her mother in the pasture.

One day, less than two months later, and after a frantic search throughout the pasture area for almost a whole day, we found the calf in a shallow ditch with her hind legs and most of her inner organs missing. I was very sad for a while, and the experience of the loss had a strong effect on my understanding of the true nature of animals. Like any mother missing her child, Janie was heartbroken and stopped grazing. She never touched any of the freshly cut cane grass I brought each day. For many days, she hardly moved, staying close to the pen, looking, expecting to see me bring her calf to suckle. The tears that flowed traced a permanent black mark from her eyes to the underside of her face on both sides. She became weak, and her ribs and hip bones showed prominently. I watched her helplessly each day until my father sold her to a cow miner at Nineteen Village, never to be seen again.

I never found out what became of Janie, but every time I passed by Nineteen Village, I instinctively looked out over the pasture area hoping to see her there. Many years later, I had heard that the cow miner, to whom my father had sold her, raised cattle primarily for slaughter to be sold at the town market. Although growing up as a youngster amid these circumstances was not ideal for me, I must confess that I have had no regrets. As a matter of fact, I have often relived those days in my mind and recounted them more times than my children cared to listen. The comparison seemed light-years apart to their experiences growing up in Canada and the United States.

The thrill of picking a Buxton Spice mango from a tree in our yard at Reliance Settlement more than twenty-five years later. I no longer had to resort to stealing mangoes.

CHAPTER 2

The Early Years

He is not poor that has little, but he who desires much.
—A proverb

Rose Hall Estate was considered the largest of the sugar plantations in the county of Berbice, one of the three counties that made up what was then British Guiana. Situated only a few miles inland from the bustling town of New Amsterdam, Rose Hall Estate nestled on the right bank of the Canje Creek, a tributary of the Berbice River, which empties its waters in the Atlantic Ocean. Originally settled by the Dutch, sugar was manufactured there from the early part of the sixteenth century. From its modest beginnings as small individual operations of a few acres of sugarcane fields, Rose Hall Estate evolved to a modern and elaborate manufacturing facility that encompassed thousands of acres of sugarcane fields. By the time of the country's independence from Britain in 1966, its sugar production in terms of tonnage was comparable to sugar plantations elsewhere in Guyana and certainly rivaled sugar production facilities throughout the other West Indies territories such as Trinidad and Jamaica. Much of the growth and modernization owed its origin to the British, who made a concentrated attempt to exploit the lucrative trade in sugar and to meet the growing demands for it in Europe during the period 1850 to 1960.

It was the lure of gold and the search for the legendary city of *El Dorado* that first brought the European nations to explore the interior regions of South America and especially the Orinoco river basin and the Guianas. It was Juan Martinez, a Spanish sailor, who claimed that he was held captive by a tribe of Indians in the forest and later released. He told the tale of this golden city that he saw with its paved streets, its golden temples, its soldiers clothed in golden armor and bearing golden shields, and its emperor, El Dorado, whose body was sprinkled with gold dust when he appeared before his people. News from the early explorers of the New World and of a city adorned with gold had radiated throughout Europe. We now know that there was never a golden city, but for a hundred years between 1530 and 1630, one expedition after another from different European nations raced to explore Guiana in the hope of finding El Dorado. Even the famous British explorer Sir Walter Raleigh failed to find it after several attempts. He would write in his accounts that "Whatsoever prince shall possess Guiana, that prince shall be Lord of more gold and more beautiful empires and of more cities than either the King of Spain or the Great Turk." As a result, Spain, Holland, Portugal, and England rushed to conquer new lands and exploit the riches. Gold was one of the bases for power and national strength. Hence, the nation that controlled the flow of gold to their treasury afforded large fleets of ships and thus dominance of the seas. For two hundred years after Raleigh's explorations, England, France, and Holland, all claimed at different times to be lord of the rich land of Guiana.

The Dutch were the first to establish storage houses or fortified forts far up the rivers to avoid piracy, such as at Kykoverall up the Essequibo River and at Kwakwani up the Berbice River. At first, the Dutch were merely traders with the natives, the Arawak and Carib Indians, who lived in the forest and grassy savannahs. They engaged in trading of European manufactured goods such as knives, beads, and balls of cloth for tobacco, cotton, gold, dye, and other local products with the original inhabitants. By 1624, the Dutch had permanent settlements up the Essequibo, Demerara, and Berbice rivers.

Although little gold was discovered in the colonies at that time, the coastline fronting the Atlantic Ocean was level and the soil fertile for cultivation of cash crops. Sugarcane was introduced as a dominant cash crop. As the demand for more sugar increased in Europe, the Dutch invited settlers from Holland to come and settle in the colonies to grow sugar for the European market. Later, the Dutch invited colonists from all European nations to come and take up free land on the rivers for sugar cultivation. Many English and Scot planters with their Negro slaves came from other West Indian islands at this invitation.

Most of the coastal plain was below sea level, with flooding being commonplace from the high tides and heavy rains. The Dutch developed an elaborate system of drainage and irrigation. Their ingenuity in land reclamation and irrigation projects is still evident in many areas. *Sluice gates* or *kokers* (locks) were built to regulate the water levels where the canals meet the creek or rivers within the sugar plantations. At low tide, the gates were raised mostly by a single person to allow the accumulated water from the land to flow out to the sea. In the seventeenth century, the rivalry for power and wealth among the European nations of France, Spain, England, and Holland to colonize land in the West Indies and South America was without precedent, with some land changing hands many times. In 1814, the British had seized all the settlements from the Dutch, and by 1831, they had consolidated the three counties of Essequibo, Demerara, and Berbice into a crown colony of British Guiana. Berbice, which was formerly part of Suriname, was seceded to the British by treaty. British Guiana became the only British colony on the mainland of South America until 1966, when it became the independent Republic of Guyana. It still holds the distinction of being the only English-speaking country in South America. The Dutch held on to Suriname, also called Dutch Guiana, and the French to French Guiana. The conquistadors of Spain concentrated from Mexico through Central America, Venezuela, Colombia, and Ecuador to Peru and Argentina while Portugal settled what is now Brazil.

Locks called sluice gates or kokers regulate water levels where the canals meet the creek or river. This canal at Reliance Settlement flows into the Canje River. Sugarcane fields in the background replaced my favorite hunting grounds for wild fruits and birds.

After 1815, the British maintained some of the basic systems of political and legal institutions that were in place by the local Dutch and continued to operate the country in the same manner. In the county of Demerara, Georgetown remained the capital city and seat of government. Executive authority was vested in the local crown representative, the governor, who was appointed by the king or queen of England. Thus, British Guiana became a member of the expanding British Empire and was subjected to various forms of its protectorate and tariff laws.

The British continued to use the Dutch monetary system that was in place. The guilder or Dutch gulden was the currency of British Guiana until 1839, and for many years after that, the Dutch coins in circulation were readily accepted as payment for goods and services. Pronounced by the British as *gil'dor*, the guilder was initially subdivided into *stivers*, with twenty stivers represented the equivalent of one guilder. One stiver and half stiver coins were minted by the Dutch especially for the colonies of Essequebo and Demerary. When the British took over the colonies, the exchange rate was also fixed to the pound with one guilder equal to twenty pence. This was later reduced to sixteen pence in 1836. Special one guilder, half guilder, and quarter guilder coins were minted by the Dutch with the inscription Colonies of Essequebo and Demerary. No coins were minted for the colony of Berbice since at the time the Dutch considered Berbice as part of Suriname or Dutch Guiana. The Dutch stiver and the British copper penny were of similar size and weight and used interchangeably. As the guilder and stiver were phased out from circulation, the British penny commonly referred to as a gil (short for guilder) became the widely accepted means of payment. Because of the low wage rate, workers were paid in pennies. After the British took over the colonies, the guilder coins in denominations of one-eight, quarter, half, and one guilder bore the inscription of British Guiana. In 1839, the dollar was introduced. It was equivalent to four shillings and two pence. In addition, the regular British coins came into use, such as the three pence (6¢), four pence (8¢ or bit) six pence (12¢), shilling (24¢), two shillings (48¢), half crown (60¢) and crown (120¢). With the many changes taking place, in time, even the spelling of the names of the colonies had changed to Essequibo and Demerara.

All financial matters and the way the colony was being controlled remained in the hands of the plantation owners, who were left with their own authority to elect officials to represent them. The plantation owners exercised firm control over all activities within the plantations. They had unlimited authority, and soon this power and authority extended throughout the country. Over two hundred small sugar plantations existed throughout the three counties during the British colonial years. Emancipation of slavery, creating a shortage of labor, and the high cost of water control and irrigation to grow sugarcane drove most of the plantations out of business. In 1969, only nineteen sugar plantations remained. Fifteen of these plantations were owned by Bookers Brothers, McConnell and Company, a conglomerate with its headquarters in England. Known locally as Bookers, it had dominated every facet of life within the confines of the plantations. Bookers was the heart of the country and always kept a watch on the pulse of the economic and political future of the country. It was not unusual for some to refer to the country as *Booker's Guiana*.

Throughout these turbulent years in its history, Rose Hall Estate stood its ground in all its majesty and prospered to reflect the glory of British colonialism. Its more than two hundred feet tall shimmering white double chimneys tower over the horizon and can be seen from miles around. The sweet scent of sugarcane juice filled the air when production was in full swing. The constant humming of the turbine engines ground the sugarcane nonstop and, every so often, was broken by the sounding of the steam whistle announcing the start of the next shifts. Flanked by Blairmont Estate across the Berbice River and Albion and Port Pourant Estates on the Corentyne Coast, it owned and occupied all the land of the surrounding areas. It bordered Sheet Anchor on the north, about a mile from New Amsterdam to New Forest further down the Canje Creek and extends to New Dam and the outskirts of Albion Estate on the east.

All life revolved around the activities of the sugar plantation. No one born on its soil could escape its presence. It dominated every character and inherent behavior of its subjects. It shaped and permeated all aspects of daily life. Plantation life to all that earned their livelihood from its borders was quite apparent to any onlooker. You could easily tell apart a Guyanese who grew up in the plantations from a Guyanese or *town man* who grew up in the big cities such as Georgetown or New Amsterdam. Most of the residents of Canje, from Cumberland to Canefield and Reliance to Adelphi and Betsy Ground, work for the plantation in one form or the other. Many

Entrance to Rose Hall Estate administrative office.
The factory and tall chimneys are immediately behind.

have witnessed their parents and grandparents working for the plantation, and for some, the tradition reached back many generations before them. In our family, the roots reached back four generations.

I was born at Rose Hall Estate in an area everyone knew as Nigger Yard or Bound Coolie Yard. A remnant of the days of slavery, this small area stood immediately adjacent to the sugar factory and was corralled by the main Canje road on one side and a drainage canal that empties into the Canje River on the other side. Several ranges or rows of zinc-top houses, called *logies*, and small huts lined this small area. The range was a series of one-room compartments divided by thin walls. They were semi-private since the wall did not reach all the way to the ceiling. Several families occupied each range with the entire family cramped into the one room allotted to them. By the time of my birth, our six-member family was now the new occupant of one of these units in this hell-hole that served as my home for

View of lifter and factory from the main Canje road.
Empty punts await transfer to the fields for the next harvested sugarcane.

the first six years of my life. There was no doubt that many African slaves once shared these very living quarters, and their spirits still haunt these walls. A wooden door served as an entrance to each compartment. The roofs were fashioned with zinc panels and leaked where the nails had rusted out. The outside walls were made from the branches of *wattle* and other locally grown hardwood trees. The spaces in between were plastered with mud as reinforcement and to prevent water from seeping in when it rained. The floor was dirt and smoothened out with white mud and cow dung to give it a clean livable appearance. A high barbed wire fence separated the patrons of Nigger Yard from the plantation's hospital that traversed the main Canje road. The hospital was only a show piece for the plantation and offered no more than a token medical care for anyone who got sick or wounded. Across the road stood St. Patrick's Anglican School. It was a large two-story building made of hardwoods where the children of the plantation workers received

This area adjacent to the factory was known as Nigger Yard or Bound Coolie Yard.
Row houses or logies once lined this area beyond the fence, where I was born.

free education from elementary to primary school level. Adjacent to the school stood the Anglican church and cemetery. Gomes Rum Shop was next to the pay office near the high bridge where my father and other patrons of the plantation did most of their rum drinking. Further inside was Charlie Low Cake Shop and a local grocery store that served the inhabitants.

The managers' quarters or *Manja Yard* was directly across the factory with its secured fence and manicured grounds. The neatly painted concrete block and wooden-frame houses in white with red zinc top roofs were home to the managers and overseers who came from England to run the affairs of the plantation. Standing majestically among them was the administrative manager's house, a thirty-two room mansion of decadent splendor with its lush sprawling gardens, swimming pool, and tennis courts. All the homes of the *Manja Yard* were furnished with the most up-to-date amenities of electricity, refrigeration, and inside plumbing. The overseers and managers

A view of Nigger Yard from across the canal near our house at Reliance Settlement.

traveled around the dirt roads by jeep or motorcycle furnished by the plantation. When the rains arrived, horses were the mainstay to get around in the mud dams to the sugarcane fields. These were two completely different worlds side by side: one for the workers of shanty towns, of mud and disease and deplorable living conditions, and one for the managers or overseers of opulence and class. The distinction between the two was clear and ruled primarily by fear. A laborer could easily be dismissed from his or her job, and there was nothing that could be done except to beg for forgiveness. The overseers were answered to by "Yes, sa" or "No, sa" ("Yes, sir" or "No, sir"). The two worlds never clashed because of the power of the managers and overseers. Reprisals and punishment for disobedience followed swiftly. The loss of employment meant a livelihood of hard times for the entire family, and that kept the working poor subjugated to the dictation of the plantation activities. No one questioned this authority. We accepted it as our destiny and strived to survive from day to day.

The manager's quarters or Manja Yard houses the overseers from England who manage the affairs of the plantation.

As the first few years of my life passed on unnoticed in this little enclave, there had already begun the slow transformation of living conditions within the plantation compounds. Long gone were the days when Africans, imported as slaves from the Gold Coasts of Africa such as Sierra Leone and Ghana, were housed at Nigger Yard to carry out all the labor-intensive work of the plantation. They cultivated the fields and worked the factories to produce the increasing demand for sugar in England and Europe. Gone were the days when the slaves were harshly treated and confined to squalor conditions with poor sanitation and housing. Their plight for more humane living conditions, coupled with their quest for freedom and the abolitionist movement of the early eighteenth century led to many revolts in the plantations. In 1763, a slave rebellion led by a slave named Cuffy started up at the Berbice River and quickly spread to the other plantations within the county. It was the result of the degrading conditions and maltreatment of the very people who produce the sugar to fatten the pockets of the white plantation owners. The inhumane treatment of the slave workers was reprehensible to say the least. Though the slave rebellion was put down, it had fueled a growing concern within the Dutch plantations and throughout the British Empire itself. Coupled with similar situations in America and throughout the West Indies, it led to more protests and the growing abolitionist movements in Europe.

The British government abolished slavery in British Guiana and all of its Caribbean territories on August 1, 1834. However, the plantation owners continued to extract free labor from slaves until 1838, when all the slaves were eventually freed. Some had initially established themselves as peasant farmers but were largely unsuccessful at farming. As a result, most of the free slaves moved to populate the towns and other villages away from the confines of the sugar plantations. They were highly influenced by the European culture and took full advantage of the available educational and skilled labor opportunities. Many moved into professions in the civil service, teaching, manufacturing trades, and trade unionism. Christianity became the religion of choice as influenced by the early missionaries in the plantations. Forced to adapt to their new surroundings and way of life in the plantations, almost all their indigenous African arts and culture were practically lost. They emulated the English in style, mannerism, and dress. In an attempt to assimilate the King's English, a distinctive Creole language developed. Although it is English and perfectly understandable if spoken slowly and with care, most of the words were condensed or cut short and pronounced without the roll of the tongue. As an example, *come here* became *com hey* and *I don't know* became *me na know*. It must be remembered that it was a long road in the development of this Creole language. Removed forcefully from their native tribal cultures in Africa, the slaves had to deal with the Dutch, the French, and then the English in their efforts to communicate. The Creole language that developed continued to undergo change.

With the loss of the free African slave labor, the plantation owners began to look for new sources of cheap labor. They managed to recruit small groups of Portuguese from the islands of Madera, the Azores, and Chinese from as far as mainland China. The Chinese and Portuguese who replaced the Africans as sugar workers were unsuitable for the demands of plantation work and soon became hawkers and vendors in the retail trade. The Portuguese openly traded in the markets and shops in the cities while the Chinese became shop owners and offered their services as cooks and launderers. Limited numbers of laborers were also obtained from West Africa, Europe, and other West Indian islands, but this was seen as a replacement of the slave trade and the British government put an end to it. The planters then turned their attention to importing workers from India after there were successes seen in places like the Mauritius, where the British maintained plantations also. With the help of the British and Indian governments, the planters were very successful in importing laborers from India to take the place of the slave labor, and the sugar plantations prospered. The Indians, or *coolies* as they were called, were brought over "as indentured servants" or paid laborers for a contract period of five years. Though many were enslaved to the land by indebtedness and poverty, they had to work many years after that to earn their freedom. Life was extremely hard for the stream of newly arrived coolies, of which my first grandparents to this new world were part of the flow.

According to the official record, the first group of indentured Indian immigrants arrived in Georgetown, British Guiana, on May 5, 1838, on the British ship named the *Whitby*. Of the 267 persons that disembarked, 250 were men, seven were women, and there were ten children. In the same year, a second ship named the *Hesperus* arrived with 170 persons, of whom 155 were men, five were women, and ten were children. During the voyage from Calcutta, from where the first groups were recruited, fourteen died on board the *Hesperus*, and four died on board the *Whitby*. Those that arrived were distributed to sugar plantations in Vreed en Hoop, Anna Regina, Bellevue, Waterloo, Highbury, and Vriedestein. Later arrivals were dispatched to places like Bush Lot on the west bank of the Berbice River and as far as Whim Village on the Corentyne coast.

Many accounts have been documented regarding the Indian indentured immigration to British Guiana, but they all seem to tell the same story. Initially, the first batch of immigrants was recruited near the coastal villages in the state of Bihar, near Calcutta. Poverty caused by occasional famine and floods from the monsoon rains created constant hardships among its inhabitants. It was easy to recruit laborers from these areas with promises of high wages and easy working conditions. Most were illiterate and had no concept of distance since many had not traveled no more than a few miles from their villages. They were misled to believe that they were going to work for short periods of time and that the new place where they were being taken was not far away. During this time, the wage promised was about 8¢ to 24¢ per day with free housing and a guaranteed return passage to India. Many of the first laborers were poor city dwellers and were unable to perform work in the fields. Upon return, they reported on the harsh conditions in the sugar plantations. This made recruiting new laborers much more difficult. Thus, the planters turned to other means such as kidnapping. There were even stories of arrangements for convicts to be sent. It also prompted recruiting from other states such as Uttar Pradesh, Tamil Nadu, Kerala, and certain areas that is now Pakistan. A commission of enquiry in 1839 by the governor of British Guiana reported on the condition of the coolies. Some sentences in the report said it all.

- The coolies were locked up in the sick houses and flogged.
- The sick houses were wretchedly filthy.
- The poor sufferers had no mats nor mattresses to lie on.
- Seven persons were confined to one room, all lying on the floor.

- In the beggars' chamber, of the five confined there, two were dead.
- I never saw such a dreadful scene of misery.

In 1841, the British government stopped the immigration of Indian laborers because it began to look too much like the old African slave trade. However, by 1945, the planters succeeded in reversing the decision.

With the British government financing some of the costs of immigration, the flow of immigrants increased dramatically after 1851. The immigrants were contracted for a period of five years and, upon completion, were guaranteed a return passage back to India. During the period 1838-1917, over 240,000 Indians were introduced to British Guiana as indentured workers. Over 75,000 returned to India in the same period. Indian immigration to British Guiana came to an end in 1917 after the India Congress Party, with Mahatma Gandhi fiercely objected to its continuation. The immigration records that do exist with the British and Indian governments documented the policies and movements of Indians to British Guiana. This alone did not tell the whole story. For hard facts and the true nature of the events, the reliance is more authenticated from the many stories that abound from the generations of my grandmother. Their only records were their memories and those of their parents and the many diverse stories of those that came before them. The true records were their own lives, as they witnessed them firsthand. They passed these on to each successive generation by word of mouth.

It was interesting to learn from my grandmother about the stories handed down by my parents that there was more turmoil in the manner Indians came to British Guiana than the record showed. Of course, there were legitimate transfers of workers as indentured servants according to the immigration laws, but there were many who were shanghaied or stolen. One popular story retold by my grandparents referred to their voyage as the *Jahan*, so named after the boat that brought them to British Guiana. That boat was normally anchored close to the coastal villages of recruiting provinces. A dhoti-clad Indian with a funnel or loudspeaker went around the streets announcing that free food was being served on the boat for everyone. As crowds gathered, only selected individuals were allowed to enter the boat. Usually, it was the strong young men and women or those that were suited by possessing some quality that made them a valuable asset to work in the plantations. They were warmly greeted, taken into the hull, and fed and enticed with liquor and music. Unannounced to them, the hull would be closed when the target number was reached, and the boat would set sail across the ocean. Miles out into the open ocean, they were told of their plight and were offered indentured ships to the plantations. Some jumped overboard in an attempt to swim back and drowned while many had no choice but to stay on. They ended up in the plantations and worked the five years to complete their terms in hopes of returning to their loved ones. To say the least, the Indians suffered great hardships.

For the most part, the immigrants were herded into a confined location in the logies or barracks (slave quarters) with very little sanitation facilities. They were prevented from leaving the plantation, and if they did, stiff penalties were imposed including fines, flogging, and imprisonment. Time lost from work was added to the indenture period. The manager had complete control of the indentured Indians and could make life difficult in many ways, including expulsion from the plantation. Progress and technical innovations were slow to evolve, but circumstances did allow for changes over the years. Plantation life changed with it, and so were the social and economic fortunes of the Indians.

It is not known to any degree of certainty what became of the great-grandparents of my mother or father. One thing was certain, my grandmother from my mother's side inherited a house and five acres of land adjacent to the railway tracts in Bush Lot Village, West Coast Berbice. Here she lived for many years, and it was also the birthplace of my mother.

There was strong evidence that the land was the reward for their parents' indentured service. Bush Lot was purchased by the government, and plots of land were given to Indians in lieu of their return passage to India. The cost of repatriation had become an expensive proposition for the government and the plantation owners. With no proof or written record of ownership to the land, as was customary in transactions in those days, the land was reclaimed for development by the plantation owners in the 1950s in the name of progress. Forced out of the land that they may have earned from their sweat and blood, my grandparents came to live with my parents at Reliance Settlement at Rose Hall Estate in 1951. Obviously, it appeared that my great-grandparents did not return to India but chose the rights to a piece of land in lieu of the return passage that was guaranteed them under the indentured contract. The plight of approximately seventy-five thousand Indians, who eventually returned to India, was never documented.

Like my parents and grandparents before them and the countless others who came from India one way or the other, they had formed the bulk of population in the plantations. Their strong religious beliefs and cultural traditions made them less assimilated into the European culture. A very small percentage became Christians. Though there were many that returned to India when their indentured period was complete, many chose to settle near the coastal villages near the sugar estate as workers and peasant farmers. Their weddings, funerals, religious ceremonies, child rearing, and family relationships still followed in the traditions of the motherland. In spite of the harsh working and living standards within the plantations, the East Indians raised large families. It was common for a family to consist of ten or twelve members. However, with each successive generation, most had adapted to the changing social and economic climate. Some of the religious customs became modified from that of our Indian counterparts in India, and with the interactions and influence of the British culture, our original Hindu language was lost in the process. The Indians adapted to the local

Creole language consisting of a kind of broken-down English and slang, which became unique to East Indians of British Guiana. During my days as a youth, there was already an intricate system of education for children of workers in the plantations. Patterned after the British schools, we were educated in English, only with little emphasis to learn Hindi. My parents spoke Hindi to some extent, although Creole English was the common everyday language. In time, the only Hindi I could muster were a few words that were commonly spoken at home and a few words that were picked up from the Hindi movies I frequently saw at the local cinema. The one phenomenon that I could never understand was the fact that I was able to sing songs from Indian movies in Hindi with the exact pronunciation and yet not understand the meaning.

My father (April 3, 1917-June 9, 1981) was already a third generation from his family of East Indian heritage to be spending his entire life on a plantation. He had moved to Rose Hall from Everton, East Bank Berbice, where he grew up. I knew very little of my grandparents from my father's side. Not very much was known about them except that my father was a very young boy when his father died in an accident while pulling a cart (similar to a donkey cart), which was the way he earned his livelihood. His mother remarried and had three other children before passing away some time later. Being the eldest, my father was left with the heavy burden of raising his two brothers and two sisters. My father never spoke much about his parents. Except for their names, Balgovind and Adermani, appearing on his birth certificate, there were practically no record of them. We learned, however, from stories handed down over the years that his grandparents came over with a boat from northeastern India. A close approximation by virtue of succeeding generations, it is estimated that they arrived around the 1860s to work in the plantations as indentured servants.

The names of my father and grandfather (Ramsaroop and Balgovind) were common in areas that suggested the northeastern provinces of either

Bihar or Utter Pradesh in India as the original place of ancestry. These were areas of high unemployment, and workers were readily available although some may have come from as far south as Madras. The name *Ramsaroop* in Hindi means the *beautiful god* and suggested that they were from a fairly educational class of agricultural or artisan workers. Little efforts had been made on my part to trace my roots in India due to the financial burden involved. In addition, the political climate in Guyana had become so harsh that my efforts were met with many stumbling blocks and proved fruitless in the end. In fact, it was reported that most of the immigration records had been destroyed in a fire that had consumed some of the government buildings in Georgetown in the 1950s. This coincided with the new movements in British Guiana for independence and the investigations that were prompted to deal with the plight of the east Indians in the sugar plantations. I am resigned for now to let it remain at that and must read between the lines of other historical information available on the subject. However, from the facts available on the subject from other authors whom I hereby acknowledge, it is my attempt to keep the memory of their lives current for the next generations.

My mother (September 19, 1920-August13, 2003), on the other hand, originated from Bush Lot, West Coast Berbice. My grandparents from my mother's side owned the house and land at Bush Lot. My mother was only thirteen years old when she married my father who was then sixteen. It was an arranged marriage as was customary at the time. She was the only child to Samuel Budhram and Sukhrajia. My grandfather Samuel Budhram died in 1952 of throat cancer when I was just a little boy. I remembered him just lying there on a bed by the window in the living room at our newly built house at Reliance Settlement. He was always moaning and in pain. I don't know much about the life my grandfather except that he was a rice farmer in later years after working mostly as a laborer in the sugarcane fields. The facts about him are sketchy, and only my mother kept his memory alive with stories of his life and passion. He was baptized a Christian of the Catholic faith and was named Samuel as appeared on the birth certificate of my mother. From my mother, I learned that he was over six feet tall, a big man in stature by Indian standards, husky in appearance, and very strong. My mother used to say that he could lift a paddy bag of rice weighing one hundred and twenty pounds with his teeth. Today, none of his great-grandchildren have showed any resemblance to him in physical attributes.

It was said that he practiced black magic and invoked the spirits of the dead. Years after his death, my mother continued the yearly ritual of setting a dinner table every Christmas eve for these three Dutchmen who served my grandfather. The dinner table was complete with her best dinnerware and cutlery. The bone china plates, the silver cutlery of knives, forks, spoons, and candelabra were only used on this occasion and were quickly packed away the next morning. Though my mother had never been inside a restaurant and at a time when we still ate our food using our fingers and using enamel cups and plates, I am still mystified at the table setting and English-style dinner that was laid out for these three ghostly men. The tender cuts of venison, ham, baked bread, peeled apples, dates, walnuts, cheese, and shots of white rum were among the lavish dinner items. The myth that circulated in bits and pieces was that he commanded three Dutchmen or spirits who carried out any of his devious wishes. These Dutchmen followed him everywhere like guardians, and he could unleash them to cause bodily harm to anyone upon his command. Even their names, Anderson, Litchfield, and Fuch and Dime were well known to all of us. My mother had tried to pass on the secrets to Ivan, my eldest brother, who was her favorite son. However, he refused to participate in any way. He refused to hear anything about it out of fear. Perhaps he did not believe in the hocus pocus or felt that it was outright hypocrisy. So the rituals discontinued. From all the ghostly stories and my mother's incessant involvement with jumbies and obeah and the like, I kept my distance for the most part, not wanting to get involved. I was slow to believe any of it, but the fear was there nevertheless. The fear persists, and somewhere in my recessed thoughts, there is a feeling that the Dutchmen are still at large after my mother passed away. I don't know why.

As for my grandmother (1898 to 1976), she worked in the fields as a weeder in the girl gangs. Affectionately called Granny Jones by everyone, she lived a full life. She smoked hand-rolled cigars and indulged in drinking hard liquor with her close friends on special holidays and celebrations. I was in Canada when she died of natural causes in 1976 at the age of seventy-seven years. I always remembered my last visit to her in 1974 and found her full of energy and in bright spirits. Her generosity to me still remained unmatched in all my years since leaving the country to study abroad. The day before leaving the country, I had gone to say good-bye to everyone in the extended family, my brothers, sisters, and close relatives. When I told Granny Jones that I was going abroad to study, she wished me well and said she was sorry she had no money to offer me. Then she took off a gold ring from her finger and gave it to me as a token of good luck. It was her wedding band, and I am sure she had treasured it all her life. I only accepted it because it was rude not to do so. She still remained the only person who had ever given me something of value. No one else even offered me a penny or a promise of help. It was no mystery though that both of my grandparents etched out a living from plantation work, and they were no more than field laborers. I supposed that my grandparents were no different from anyone else trying to make a better life for themselves and their children. One thing was certain: they were poor with little or no formal education.

Among the varied jobs, my father had worked for many years as a stable hand cleaning out the stables. The estate maintained a large number of mules to pull the punts or pontoons loaded with sugarcane from the fields to the factory. This was the only means of transporting the sugarcane through a network of canals that surrounded the fields. In the very early times, the African slaves were used to pull the punts using a rope and brute

My grandmother (Granny Jones) is on the left with other family members (1974).

strength, but this gave way to mules and buffalos and to tractors in more recent years. There were also horses and cattle maintained by the estate. Later, my father moved up the ranks, and for a time, his job was to bathe one of the horses, saddle it, and walk it to the steps of an overseer's house in the manager's compound. My father could not ride the horse. He usually stayed with the horse near the steps so that the overseer, coming down the steps, would mount the horse without his boots touching the ground. This was his work routine every workday, getting up at 4:30 a.m. and being punctual at the steps by 7:00 a.m. Eight cents per day or four *gils* were considered a good rate of pay at this time for the ten to twelve hours he labored. For his dedication and loyalty to the white overseers, he was later moved up the ranks to become a driver, a sort of field foreman in charge of the planting gang.

I remember watching him meticulously sharpening his lead pencil with a razor blade and spending hours each night making entries in his little black pocketbook to keep an account of the time and pay rate of those who worked for him. The old bicycle that the estate loaned him without charge to get around in the back dams was a sure sign of his trustworthiness to the overseers. His dedication had earned him a limited stature within the estate community. He was hardworking, never taking time off work. When there was no work in the estate, he planted rice or was involved in his backyard garden to put food on the table. I have never heard anyone say anything unkind about Sunny Ramsaroop. In his comments to us or in his conversations with us, he always spoke in parables or would emphasize his point with a little story. When my mother would be quarreling with him, he would just shake his head and walk away to tend his backyard garden to avoid the confrontation. He was not a man of many words, but whatever comments he made, his remarks or advice always showed some degree of experience and often with a proverbial insight. Once, he was almost drunk or *sweet* as my mother used to say when she scolded him for his drinking habits when I heard him say, "When goat shit ready to roll, it does only wait for breeze to blow." Then he passed out on the floor to escape her verbal wrath. Amazingly enough, there were some of his proverbs that always lingered in my thoughts:

"A slow cent is always better than the fast dollar."

"One brick at a time does build a dam."

"When you leave cutlass and run for iguana, you would lose both."

"Don't wait until you want to pee before you start to make a toilet."

"Never mind how much you bathe a pig; you can't make it turn into a cow."

"You can take the horse to the water, but you can't make him drink it."

"Don't count your chickens before the eggs are hatched."

"All good things come to those who wait."

"An empty barrel does make the most noise."

"Beware when people say nice things about you; you never know what they are after."

"When your hand is in the lion's mouth, you have to pat his head."

It would be many years later that I fully understood what he meant by those proverbs he so often used. I appreciated the insight he had about life experiences. They sounded very crude at the time, but they were the naked truths about life no matter which way I looked at them. I would eventually pay much heed to these proverbial sayings later in life as their meanings became clear to me. Sometimes they were comforting when the outcome of events was not always so clear. Now I spared no time in making the same comments in similar situations with my wife and daughters. I assumed that they got the messages. With the insight of proverbs, I had also become a man of a few words. I found it amusing.

My mother never worked in the plantation. She was too overwhelmed with the daily overload of housework, preparing the day's meals at 4:00 a.m. in the morning and then again in the afternoon to feed a household of kids and elders. The day never ended with so much to do on her own: washing the clothes by hand, cleaning the house and yard, and stretching her meager pennies to prepare the best food. Her struggles to keep her family were remarkable. She married at the tender age of thirteen to my father, who was then fifteen. It was customary for marriages to be arranged by the parents. I remember the times when we would gather and reminisce about *old times*. She had come home from school one Friday afternoon only to be told by her parents that she was getting married on Sunday, two days later. She had not laid eyes on my father. Although she was married, she always claimed that she did not understand what had taken place. She had to quit school and would do most of the housework and cooking at my father's house. At night, she returned to stay with her own parents. This continued for two years until her father convinced her to stay with my father. It meant a life sentence to housework and child rearing. With so little education and barely able to read and write, she would have her first child at sixteen years of age and the last when she was forty-three years old. She would eventually raise eleven children of her own and also the four siblings of my father. She was always so proud to have raised my father's siblings to adulthood and into successful marriages of their own. I was particularly saddened when in her later years in life they showed a lack of respect and honor she so rightly deserved. Some of her own children were no better. In spite of these odds and the so many hard times over the years, I can't remember a single day that we did not have food to eat or clean clothes to wear. She was always proud to say that all her children grew up well mannered, healthy, and successful with families of their own. At eighty-three years of age, she lived comfortably and tended to all her needs without any assistance. I was always amazed that she rarely went to a doctor and was able to thread a needle with ease. She had no need for eyeglasses. With the small pension she received from the Canadian government, she made a pilgrimage to Guyana each year to escape the harsh winter and loneliness. She preferred to live out her last days in the house my father had built for her at Reliance Settlement in spite of the comforts of the home of her children in the United States and Canada. It remained her sanctuary. She attributed her longevity to working hard every day, getting up before the sun rises and eating mostly fresh cooked vegetables.

Not being of perfect disposition, having a few shots of rum each day had become a pervasive and chronic addiction in her old age. Yet I had never seen her sick or requested medical attention at any time. She passed away suddenly in her sleep on August 13, 2003, in her home in Guyana. It was her wish, and it brought an era to an end.

My eldest brother, Ivan (1936 to 1992), worked for Rose Hall sugar estate. He started out as a sugar boiler and later became a shift manager and finally a production manager. We were very proud of his accomplishments. He was the first to be given an opportunity for an education and was sent to Trinidad to be trained as a sugar boiler. It was two decades later. Guyana had become an independent nation. The sugar industry was nationalized, and most of the white management of Rose Hall Estate was replaced with Guyanese nationals. I was especially delighted when Ivan told me that he was offered to live for free in one of the houses in the manager's compound. It meant an end to an era and an end to colonialism in the plantations. He did not take up the offer though and preferred to build his own house at Canefield Settlement. I always thought that it was a mistake on his part because living in the manager's compound would have afforded him and his family a few economic advantages and a better stature within the sugar estate community.

My other brothers also worked for Rose Hall Estate. Roland (1940 to 1999) was a cane cutter. In his heyday, he was one of the best in terms of tons of cane cut each day. He could cut and load a punt of cane weighing over five tons all by himself and finished soon in the day to indulge in some rum drinking. He started out as a mule boy, leading the mules that pulled the punts of sugarcane from the fields to the factory. Everyone knew him well, and he was skilled at catching fish with a cast net.

My brother Khilashwar Persaud, also nicknamed Inch, worked as a pest control field hand. He inserted rat poison in bamboo shells to kill the rats in the fields. He later worked his way as a clerk in the local accounts office before moving to Ottawa, Canada, to study agriculture at Kemptville College. They were followed by Amos and Prem, who also worked as clerks at the local accounts office at Rose Hall Estate. One of my three sisters worked as a nurse but for Skeldon sugar estate in the Corentyne. Shirley got married early, and Kamal, Datto, and William were too young to seek work.

It seemed only natural then that I would follow in line with the rest of my brothers in the family to end up working for Rose Hall Estate. By some twist of fate, this did not happen. My karma took a different turn, and I ended up as a school teacher to the amazement of everyone, including myself. In the early days, I showed no promise as a youngster and was on the wild side, rude and obstinate, growing up fast and streetwise, and I could do almost anything well. I can't remember being afraid of anything or anyone. I could climb any tree, swim in the creek, or kill a bird with my slingshot at thirty yards or more. I could cut grass, milk the cow, work in the rice fields, and catch fish with my bare hands in the abandoned sugarcane fields. I could make a three-feet board kite from scratch and play cricket very well. Getting into fistfights got my mother angry all the time to the point that I was almost despised. I had the looks of a hardy youngster, a mean-looking face with piercing eyes. I made fun of the other kids who were soft, and I was a bully in the playgrounds. Everything had to go my way, and I had a following of a few good friends. We hung out together as a gang. My mother used to say, "Dis boy chummar [strong]" or "Dis boy ah play one manish man [rascal]."

Although I lived for about seven years only at Nigger Yard, they were hard times. They were the first years of my life, and I had no say in the matter to be born there. It is said that the first three or four years of a child's life determines the personality and character and shape of the future to come. If this is true, then I was in for a rude awakening. My name Yuvraj means an *heir* or *prince*. Ramsaroop means *the beautiful god*, and so I was a prince of the beautiful god. Why British Guiana then? It's my karma, I was frequently told, and my destiny was written in the books. So said the local pundits when my planet or horoscope was read in the Hindu scriptures they kept. I always got this feeling that in my past life, I was a king of some sort or the other. I must have been a bad or good-for-nothing king. To face my punishment, I was sent to British Guiana to see all my deeds and to face life over from scratch. Thus, I began working my way upward again, and I knew for sure that in my next life I would be a king again. It is believed that a person's personality is molded by the life experiences of their early years, and for me, it certainly did. Just to overcome and get through day by day posed a challenge in itself. This kind of experience built stamina to persevere and strength for resilience and knowledge to conquer. It's a far cry from the conveniences of the modern era of my children, but for now, this was the way it was meant to be. I was fifth in line with my elder brothers and sister to share this one-room cottage house that was home to countless African slaves before us. Like generations before me, plantation life was all I became accustomed to learning.

Our fire side for the daily cooking activities at our house at Reliance Settlement.

Living with other families in the row houses at bound Coolie Yard was certainly difficult. Every activity was very basic. Every task required some basic knowledge because in almost every case, it meant survival. Everyone in the family performed specific functions, and so I learned my chores at a very early age. As for chores, there were many. We had no electricity and cooked on a wood stove called a fireside, fashioned from mud and burning wood for fuel. Cutting wood and keeping an adequate supply dried and ready for burning was a daily routine. We had no refrigerator and bought ice occasionally at a penny per pound from a donkey cart vendor whenever he passed on the main road. The ice was kept in *boosie*, ground-up rice shells or sawdust, and wrapped in jute bags to prevent it from melting. With no electric lights, we used kerosene hand lamps or candles to get around in the dark at nights. We had no running water and fetched drinking water in galvanized buckets from an artesian well situated a long distance away on the main road. All the families at Nigger Yard shared four latrines built on stilts over the side canal that empties into the Canje River. The zinc of these public latrines was painted in red and were semi-private with a wall between each stall. All waste fell into the water below with a splash and a frenzy of feeding ensued. Large fishes called the Quoras (an oversized catfish in appearance) scrambled to devour the waste deposits. It was a thrill to see this scene as a small boy. As soon as the latrine doors were closed, the Quoras assembled immediately under and circled like sharks as if they detected someone's presence by sound or had a sixth sense.

A jute bag laid out on the dirt floor was a bed for most of us. The covers were fashioned from flour bags discarded by the shop owners that were hand sewn together by my mother and then washed several times until soft to the touch. Mattresses and pillows were stuffed with *jaru* grass that grew only at the Indian burial ground. This grass remained soft when dry and could last a long time. Food was simple and plentiful. Vegetables were grown in the backyard, and fishes were caught in the trenches and abandoned fields among the vast stretches of canals surrounding the cane fields. A soup of yellow split peas called *dal* and parboiled rice was the staple diet with anything added for flavor from coconut chutney to *alloo choka* (mashed potatoes mixed with salt, pepper, and onions). We ate our food using our fingers and washed the enamel cups and plates in a bucket of water by the side of the house. We also bathed by the side of the house using a bucket of water. Here I washed and wiped my feet before going to bed. Then, it was an art form to wrap myself like a mummy, leaving no part of the body exposed. Only the tip of the nose was uncovered to allow breathing. Several times I woke up with the skin on the heels on my feet nibbled away by rats. Imagine the discomfort in walking on the red-brick road to school in this state. Then there were the cockroaches everywhere. I could swear that I had seen some get up and fly. Some were so hardy that stepping on them with all my weight could not kill them. When the rainy seasons came, we had the mosquitoes to ward off by burning the husks of coconut shells or a mixture of dried and green grasses to create a lot of smoke.

A shortcut through a hole in the fence and under the hospital to cross the main brick road and I would reach St. Patrick's Anglican School. As a primary school, it served the children of all the sugar estate workers from Canefield and Reliance to Reliance Abandon and Adelphi Village. Cumberland and Betsy Ground had schools of their own. I was a late starter in school and was over six years old when my father registered me in "lil' big infant class" or pre-kindergarten because he thought I was now big enough to go to school. I was sick as a child and suffered from an infected left ear. It leaked pus constantly, and was I deeply embarrassed by this curse. I would tend to sit at the end of the bench with no one on my left, tilting my head to keep the puss from leaking down to my shoulders. Although I could have used cotton wool stuck in my ear to prevent the leaking, I did not want anyone to know of the infection and went to great lengths to keep it a secret for many years from friends and classmates. One day, I noticed that the infection had stopped suddenly. By then I was in sixth standard, and I had become completely deaf in the left ear.

The younger children occupied the first floor at St. Patrick's Anglican School. There was big infant, first, and second standard classes. The older pupils from third to sixth standards occupied the upper level. All the classes were side by side in neat rows of wooden benches. A slate and slate pencil were all that I needed. When notation was completed, a quick wipe with the fingers moistened with spit would clean the slate, and I was ready for the next subject of dictation or arithmetic. If the slate was broken, I did my schoolwork on the largest piece remaining. Passing on to third standard, I was introduced to writing on exercise books and using ink pens. Carrying a pot of ink with nib pens and blotting paper was common. We had wooden benches also but with the additional comfort of wooden desks. The *Caribbean Readers* were the standard textbooks written by educators from England.

I cannot remember ever thinking about what I wanted to be when I grew up. Events occurred, and it seemed that all that came to pass was only natural. I went along with the flow of things, without question, without reason. No one ever asked me what I was thinking about or at least "what about school." To put it mildly, school and education was not really important in our family. Learning to read and write was a plus. Learning a trade and earning a living was more the norm of the times. Ivan was a house painter with an opportunity to train as a sugar boiler in Trinidad. Shirley was learning sewing in order to make a good housewife. Young men would not marry a girl if she did not know sewing and cooking. Roland was a mule boy, and KP had no opportunity to go to high school. I was considered a dunce. With all the chores that required my attention, school was the last thing to take up my time. I hated school. It was not so much that I was not capable of learning. Going to school was a frightening experience for me. My only fun was during recess or lunchtime when we bounced marbles for buttons under the school or played sponge ball cricket in the school yard. I mostly feared the whip of the teachers. Corporal punishment in the schools in British Guyana was standard and legal. It was a remnant of the British Empire and was the norm at St. Patrick's Anglican School.

Every teacher had whips from the *lil' infant teacher* or prekindergarten to the sixth standard teacher. Some would send pupils out to get black sage bush whips before the start of classes. Waldron and Scarder had *wild canes*, a sophisticated flogging equipment. It lent stature to those who carried them and inflicted a menacing sting. They lasted longer because its strength prevented splintering. I got my taste of the whip from an early age.

My *big infant* teacher or kindergarten teacher was a mean-looking, hard-faced black woman. She dressed neatly and always wore bright red lipstick. She walked briskly in small steps that her tight-hobbled skirt allowed while making a musical clip-clop on the wooden floor with her high heel shoes. Everyone knew and respected Mrs. Ferrell very well. I had a password to alert my friends when she was making her rounds since we were not allowed to talk while in class. I used to call her Ferrell compound, which was the name of a cough medication commonly used. Coughing a few times served as the alert. Notation was always her first subject, followed by dictation and reading for the morning session. Notation was a subject by itself even for six-year-olds. We drew two columns on our slate to separate tenths and units. She would call out a number (for example, 28), and we had to write it down on our slates. I remembered writing 20 for the twenty, but I was confused about where to put the 8. In my first effort, I put the 8 next to the 0, and so I had written 208 instead of 28. She walked up and down between the rows of wooden benches peering into our slates from behind our shoulders. My answer was wrong, and in an instant and without warning, two or three lashes from her black sage whip penetrated across my back and shoulder area. The sting of the whip rang out through my body, and I squirmed in my seat. Girls got their lashes on outstretched hands, right on the palms. It was common for pupils to go home with marks on the hands or back. Older boys in the upper classes got their lashes on their backside, stretched over a desk or bending over to touch their toes. Stories abound of some boys who wore two pants or put exercise books under their pants to lessen the sting of the whip. Some bawled and screamed while others took the beatings quietly and cried silently. Sometimes, the lips trembled and the embarrassment hurt, but complaints were few from pupils and their parents. It was normal in the schools and fully sanctioned. I can't remember a single teacher at St. Patrick's Anglican School who did not whip his or her pupils. I knew them all.

To my despair, no explanation or instructions were given to me when I wrote the number wrong the first time. There was no coaching from the teacher, and I supposed she had no time to spare to give me any personal attention. In my little mind, I thought that I was fairly smart. I was not retarded or anything like that. So when the teacher called out the next number 54, I made a very smart move to get it right this time. I wrote down 50 for the fifty. I decided to put the 4 in front of the 5 this time. Thus I wrote 450. In an instant, two more lashes followed on my back. Whining in pain and grossly embarrassed, my eyes watered, and I tried to hold my composure and prevent the tears from streaming down my face, barely able to concentrate on whatever she said anymore. At the back of my mind, I knew my friends were watching as the scene unfolded. It was difficult to learn in these circumstances for only fear prevailed. My only wish was to be somewhere else, anywhere. I would eventually learn to write all numbers like 28 and 54 correctly, but it was not until I became a teacher that I understood the concepts of hundredths, tenths, and units. It was no wonder that I looked for any opportunity to skulk and was truant for most days in the school year.

The whips continued through the classes as I advanced to sixth standard after being given a rapid promotion by Mr. Sukdeo from fourth standard. I never understood the reason behind it except that I was in good company with Shun Persaud. He was a bright pupil, and we were just friends that did some favors for Mr. Sukdeo. Behold and to my surprise, I found myself in the hands of Mr. Waldron, who prepared pupils for the school-leaving exam. He was a terror to most pupils who passed through his hands. His beatings were merciless. Many opted out to go to high schools in New Amsterdam rather than face the wrath of his wild cane. Others just quit school to work in the sugar estate or the rice fields. In many ways, I admired him. He dressed immaculately and spoke with great command of the English language. He did not tolerate any lateness or any form of rowdiness and misbehavior in his class. His instructions were stern, well-understood, and to the point. Not particularly bright by any means, I found myself in the dunce section of his class, and I was in good company with my friends Harry Boy, Salipenter, and Lilly, sitting in the back bench. We were obscured from Mr. Waldron's view for most of the day. There we carried out our carefree adolescent pranks and misbehaving.

Mr. Waldron did not pay much attention to us in the dunce section and came around only to peek down at the school yard below. He would assign work for us on the blackboard and then surrounded himself with the clever pupils at his desk. These he handpicked because they excelled in the subjects of English, Arithmetic, and Nature Studies.

They had a better chance of passing the school-leaving exam or primary school certificate and thus received more personalized instructions. I did not care much for the schooling anyway, although I realized that I was more afraid of the teachers. How I could have withstood the constant grilling and the overburdening homework assignments were puzzling. However, I felt sorry for some of the girls. They were very pretty and neatly dressed each day in their maroon and white uniforms. They wore shoes and carried several pens and a stack of books. They were the schools' most popular pupils and from upper-class families. It was a pity to see them getting lashes on the hands. Teenage girls crying was a sad scene for me.

It was a miracle that I never got any whipping from Mr. Waldron, and I wondered about this many times. I could never explain it scientifically, but there must have been some sudden jolt of my brain cells. My memory was good, and I was able to do complex arithmetic calculations mentally. I could look at a word once in a dictionary, and I never forgot how to spell it. It was as if the word was copied in my brain's memory bank. Tests each day on mental arithmetic and dictation were routine, and I excelled in both. I convinced myself that this resurgence of energy coincided with the sudden stop of the infection in my left ear due to my going deaf as a result. Visits to the hospital did not help, and we resorted to bush medicine. Hydrogen peroxide was poured in. Juice extracts from the leaves of the mangrile tree and a host of concoction was poured in. None worked. It is said that when energy is lost to one part of the body, this energy vibrates to other parts of the body. At least this is what I believed. All I knew was that there was a sudden change in my academic outlook. I remembered getting better marks and more questions answered correctly each day in our mental arithmetic and dictation exercises than most in the select group of pupils. Mr. Waldron had taken notice and had requested that I joined the pupils to whom he gave extra lessons on his own spare time. The first Saturday that I attended for lessons will never be forgotten for the crude and unmannerly way in which I conducted myself.

He was explaining the techniques of doing long division in arithmetic. Pupils were called up to perform calculations on the blackboard while the others followed the next steps closely. Sitting at the back bench, I did my best to hide from being called upon. It was my unlucky day when Mr. Waldron called my name. He asked that I complete the long division problem on the blackboard. Shivers went through my spine instantly as he threw the chalk to me and took up his place sitting at his desk. Catching the chalk with one hand, I stepped up to the blackboard. Much to my dismay, I had solved the problem correctly, and Mr. Waldron was quick to praise my accomplishment. Then I did one of the most stupid things ever. I threw the chalk back to Mr. Waldron. Unaware that I was throwing the chalk back to him, it hit him on the forehead. I must admit that it was a crude response on my part and totally lacking in manners. All I heard after that was laughter from the rest of the pupils as Mr. Waldron began to fume. I can still hear the comments as I made a hurried exit: "Get out of here," "Unmannerly fellow," "Don't come back," and some other expletives. This was one more reason for my phobia of sitting in a classroom. The humiliation still haunts me, and I always opted for the back row.

In September 1960, the results of the school-leaving exam or primary school certificate was posted in the newspapers. My name was among the two dozen or so pupils who had passed from the class of over a hundred pupils. Most of those who were given special attention had failed, much to my satisfaction. Considering the little teaching I received and my own obstinate reluctance to schooling, it remained a mystery that I had learned enough to pass this exam. Whatever little I had learned, it was more so from my own curiosity. I wanted to know about the world around me and was eager to pick up information on any subject. With little guidance and almost no spare time, I was saddened that I hardly read many books. The standard *Caribbean Reader* and *The Student's Companion* were my only sources. The only novel I read was *The Mutiny on the Bounty*, and that was required for the school-leaving exam. I had become fascinated with the character of Fletcher Christian in his independent and strong vision of life. It certainly implanted a burning craving in my dreams to go live in the Tahiti islands someday. For the PTA exam, I had to read *Great Expectations* by Charles Dickens. Later I read *The Adventures of Tom Sawyer*, which became one of my favorite books. With a flair for adventure and mischief, I saw myself in Tom Sawyer's shoes on many occasions although Huck Finn represented more of who I was. One thing was becoming increasingly clear to me. I had to rely on my own initiative and intuition to learn and to understand. This would become my trademark in later years, being self-taught and self-reliant in every way.

I am reminded of this every time I listen to the Mighty Sparrow, the Caribbean's most versatile calypso king from Trinidad, who said it best in one of his famous calypso songs:

According to the education you get when you small
You will grow up with true ambition and respect from one and
all.
But in my days in school
They teach me like a fool.
The things they teach me I should be a block headed mule.

How I happened to get some education my friends,
Me'n know
All they teach me is about Brer Rabbit and Rumpelstillskino
They wanted to keep me down indeed
They tried their best but didn't succeed
You see, me head was duncy and up to now I can't read.

Who cares about Peter
Peter was pumpkin eater
Some lil lil people tie Gulliver
When I was sick and lay a bed
I had two pillow on my head
The goose laid the golden egg
They teach me like dog to know what is school
If me head been bright, I would a be a damn fool

CHAPTER 3

No Future in Sight

Efforts and courage are not enough without purpose and direction.

—John F. Kennedy

There was nothing significant that affected my life in the year 1960, but I remembered some of the events very well. In the fall, after turning fourteen years of age, and for some unknown reason, I began to notice a few little things around me that made up my monotonous days. I wondered why I had not yet owned a pair of shoes or wore shoes of any kind for that matter. A couple pairs of khaki short pants and a few worn-out poplin short-sleeved shirts were my only wardrobe. I cannot say with any conviction that I really understood the social and economic forces that undermined the circumstances for my underprivileged condition, but harboring any remorse for it was never on my mind. My parents did their best to provide the basic comforts of food, housing, and clothing for our growing family. However, I was sure I strayed a bit and acted out in a few rebellious ways for this was common in escaping the harsh realities of the times. It was simply the way things were in those days. However, events that were once routine for me had begun to change slowly, and I moved right along with them. In my world, I could say that I was growing up and did so just as fast as time permitted.

Arriving late for school one Monday morning at the start of the school year was the turning point of some of my most precious moments. From a distance, I could hear the screams and sighs from pupils of my class who had gathered in the school yard around one of our teachers. He was reading out aloud from the morning newspapers the names of those pupils in my class who had passed the primary school certificate examination. This was commonly known as the school-leaving exam. My name was not mentioned, and that was not surprising. I resigned to the fact that I had failed. Only twenty-six of the over one hundred pupils who wrote the exam from our school had passed. I took comfort realizing that most of the pupils who had failed were much more brilliant than me and more poised to succeed.

One of the names among the list of pupils who had passed puzzled all the teachers. No one knew the name *Guvari*. The mystery was resolved a few weeks later when our headmaster verified with the Ministry of Education that Guvari was the misspelled name of student number 4726. That was my assigned number for the exam (Yuvraj no. 4726). Learning that I had passed the school-leaving exam was wonderful news for me, but by then the novelty had passed. No one said "congratulations" or "that's good, boy" or "best of luck" or any of those phrases that lifts the spirit in these moments. There was no fanfare and no suggestions or advice from anyone on what to do next. Life just rolled on for me to the next stop as usual with no future in sight.

As the name suggested, the school-leaving exam was a milestone marker and the end of primary school education for the majority of pupils. Some moved on to private secondary schools in New Amsterdam. Berbice High School and Berbice Educational Institute were among the elite high schools that prepared students for the College of Preceptors (CP), the Junior Cambridge, and the General Certificate of Education (GCE) examinations. I was not aware of the significance of these exams. In time it had become apparent to me that every high school student's dream was to obtain passes in five subjects at the GCE exams at the ordinary level with English and mathematics among them. This standard was the equivalent of grade 12 in the United States although I always felt that the GCE certificates represented a higher standard of education than in the United States or Canada. It must be noted that this was the same exam that high school students attempted in England and most British Commonwealth countries. This achievement was the stepping-stone to career jobs with the government's civil service, a career in the teaching profession, or entrance to universities and colleges. The syllabus or curriculum, testing, and grading of the exams were conducted exclusively by the University of London in England. All appointed dates, times, and places of the exams were supervised closely by the Ministry of Education in Guyana. One nail-biting feature of the procedure was that each individual student must wait approximately eight to ten weeks for the grade results, which were sent out directly through the mail from England.

Those pupils who were not so fortunate to attend high school went on to work for the sugar estate or helping at home or in the rice fields. A few who were lucky to pass an entrance exam got admitted to the sugar industry's training school in Port Mourant to apprentice as engineers, electricians, and fitter machinists. I continued to languish at St. Patrick's Anglican School and attempted the pupil teacher's appointment exam (PTA). This was the standardized local exam administered by the Ministry of Education. High school was never an option for me and very much beyond the meager economic situation of our family. I was sure that my parents could not have afforded the $25 to $30 per term for the tuition fees plus the additional expenses of school supplies and transportation. Since no one in our family had ever gone to a high school before me, there was no expectation on my part. Only Amos, a younger brother, attended high school a few years later when our financial posture had improved.

I went on to sit for the pupil teacher's appointment exam in 1961 and failed in my first attempt. Controlled and supervised by the Ministry of Education in British Guiana, the PTA was a passport to a teaching career in the primary school system. It allowed for paid employment as a teacher and an apprentice-style training over four years as an understudy under the supervision of the headmaster or senior master of the primary school. After successful completion, the same status and salary scales were achieved, comparable to teachers with the GCE certificate and five passes at the ordinary level. With a faint realization and without any strong motivation, I was crawling in this direction. In 1962, I attempted the PTA exam for a second time.

By this time, I was no longer involved in helping out in the rice fields and no longer had to tend to any cattle. The sugar estate had discontinued renting out land for rice cultivation to sugar workers, and my father had sold the last three steers that we owned. This was inevitable and due largely to the tremendous changes that had begun long before in the decade of the 1950s. Life was affected on all fronts in the sugar estates as a result. Most of the changes followed the ideas and political consciousness of the new leaders of British Guiana. A new spirit among these leaders of the country was rising. There were constant food shortages, and the disruptions from shipping of imported foodstuffs created hardships. Falling prices for sugar had meant longer periods of unemployment for workers in the sugar estates, and this fueled more discontent throughout the country. Among the political leaders, there was the urgency for the country to become more self-reliant. The trade unions in the sugar industry became more vocal and bargained aggressively for better working conditions and higher wages. British Guiana was still a British colony, and all its affairs were controlled from England, including the profits from the sugar and bauxite industries, which flowed overseas.

A nationalist movement for an independent British Guiana gave birth to the formation of the People's Progressive Party with Dr. Cheddi Jagan, an Indian dentist, and L. F. S. Burnham, a Negro lawyer, as the leaders. Their main idea and framework for representing the people were to effect social changes. They wanted to lift the standards of living from the decades of repressive British rule. There was an overwhelmingly strong opposition to continued colonialism with the goal of obtaining independence from British rule. The success of India in obtaining independence gave impetus to this movement. It was a driving force in other colonies in the Caribbean area with Jamaica, Trinidad, and Barbados among them.

In 1953, the People's Progressive Party had won a commanding victory in the national elections and, with a majority of seats in the Parliament, was able to form a government with Dr. Cheddi Jagan as the prime minister. There were deep dissentions and divisions within the party based primarily on ethnic grounds. Their demands for immediate parliamentary changes led the British government to suspend the constitution. Many of the party members were jailed, and the British dispatched troops to keep the peace. It was the beginning of the many dramatic changes that the citizens of country would endure for the next decade. The rivalry between Dr. Cheddi Jagan and L. F. S. Burnham intensified, and in 1955, Burnham split with the People's Progressive Party to form his own People's National Congress Party. Now the country was divided solely under racial lines, with Jagan and his PPP wholly supported by the majority of East Indians (45 percent) while Burnham and his PNC commanded the support of the Africans (40 percent.) The hatred between the Indians and Africans would last for years beyond that and continue to this day.

Although I did not fully understand the issues of politics and government at this time, I became increasingly receptive to the ideas and speeches of both Jagan and Burnham during the election campaigns. The People's Progressive Party (PPP) came into power with Dr. Jagan as premier in 1957 and again in 1961. The economy of the country was experiencing a higher level of economic growth with government intervention in all aspects of daily life. One of the actions of the PPP government in 1961 was to take over all the church-denominated schools in the country. These were schools that were controlled and operated by the churches but were built with public funds. Fifty-one such schools were affected, and there was much opposition from the churches. It was seen as too much government intervention with the fear that the action was on the fringe of socialism. As a result, the teachers were paid by the government although the school property remained on land owned by the churches. One such school was the Reliance Sanatani Hindu School that came into existence at Reliance Settlement near my home, just a short distance from St. Patrick's Anglican School. Various new multilateral schools were built in populated areas throughout the country, and education became more accessible at the primary school level to all. Health care was improved with the implementation of free health centers that were set up in strategic areas for pre-natal and post-natal care.

The new St. Patrick's Anglican Primary School at Rose Hall Estate.

In many other areas the progress was more noticeable with new bridges and roads being built. The opening of the Tapacuma, Abary, and Black Bush Polder rice developments schemes were a tremendous boost for the agricultural industry. Locally, the sugar factory at Rose Hall Estate was being modernized with more surrounding land cleared for cultivation of sugarcane. New land was also being cleared for housing for the sugar workers with paved streets, drainage facilities, and running water among the amenities. Reliance Settlement, Canefield Settlement, Reliance Abandon, and Adelphi Settlement were among the first areas of development.

The small area known as Nigger Yard was bulldozed to the ground and remained so to this day. Only Dookie Shop, Katic Shop, Walter Rum Shop, and a couple of houses lined the main road. At the very back, a modern garage housed the estate's welding and mechanical workshops. The main Canje road was paved for the first time, and a new school was built adjacent to the old St. Patrick's School with spacious individual classrooms and some upscale facilities. A dispensary replaced the hospital with a full-time medical staff for the benefit of the sugar workers and their families. It served the community well with basic care such as dressing of wounds and medication for aches and pains. It was normal to receive a few pills or a green chalky-tasting liquid that the dispenser handed out to each patient who registered. I remembered my infrequent visits to the dispensary for different ailments. Regardless of the ailments, I did receive the same oversized white pills and the green chalky-tasting medicine for it. For more serious ailments, including surgery, everyone still would seek treatment at the New Amsterdam Public Hospital. All medical services here were free of charge, and to a certain degree, the services were very good. Most of the doctors were recruited from other countries. There were few Guyanese nationals who returned to practice in British Guiana. Those who came back usually set up their own private practice. Specialized services were available at the Georgetown Public Hospital, where there were more adequate facilities and equipments.

In 1953, we had moved to our newly built house at 42 West Reliance Settlement just across the canal from *Nigger Yard*. My father was granted a house lot on a land lease basis and paid three dollars a year to the sugar estate. Only sugar workers with seniority and with regular work history qualified for these lots. My father wasted no time in building a house by using the hard-earned cash from the profits of his rice farming coupled with the savings my mother had managed from his wages. It was a simple two-bedroom framed house built on nine-feet-high greenheart wood stilts and red painted zinc roof. A whitewashed picket fence surrounded the yard and lined in the front with a hedge of hibiscus flowers and rose bushes. In the backyard, a variety of fruit trees lined the perimeter, with sweet cherries by the fowl pen and a gooseberry tree with its roots deep into the outhouse. I always wondered why this particular gooseberry tasted so much better, almost sweet to the taste, than gooseberry grown elsewhere. The rest of the yard was ploughed with a hand fork into neat rows for garden vegetables such as ochro, cassava, bora, seime, eggplant, and spinach.

A very large heavy iron container stood beside the kitchen area to catch the rainwater from the gutters. With the absence of any machinery to move it at the time, it had remained in this very spot for more than fifty-five years when our house was built around it. It was many decades later that its significance came to light to me. In 1998, while touring a museum in Louisiana depicting the early days of a sugar plantation, I observed an identical iron container on display. A few years later, I visited two other sugar plantation ruins in New Smyrna Beach and South Daytona Beach in Florida where similar containers are on display. These were known as coppers and were used to boil the sugarcane juices. Scum rose to the surface and was the byproduct in fermenting rum. The remaining mass reached a thick syruplike stage or molasses, which was then cooled and dried repeatedly into crystals of sugar. My imagination raced to the activities, sounds, and smell of sugar and rum surrounding the copper near our house. I wondered about the hundreds of slaves who toiled on this copper, what fate it held for their lives and their masters, and how many hours I had spent as a young man sitting, contemplating on this copper. What secrets lie beneath the soil where our house still stood! With the exception of some minor repairs and remodeling, the house still stands in its original form today. The copper still keeps a watchful eye, beckoning.

A remnant of sugar production at this location from earlier times, this iron container still stands at the back of our house at Reliance Settlement.

The clean environment of the new settlement represented a tremendous improvement in our living standards and boosted our morale and self-esteem. I had no quarrel with all the developments, but some of the basic necessities would not reach the Ramsaroop's household until decades later. We still had no electricity, no running water, no refrigeration, and no inside plumbing. I continued to sleep on a rice bag and on the floor for many

An iron container at a sugar plantation museum in Louisiana, USA.

An iron container at a sugar plantation ruins in New Smyrna Beach, Florida, USA.

Our House at Lot 42 West, Reliance Settlement, East Canje, Berbice.

The culvert at the end of the street and view of our house.

years and took baths with a bucket of water in a zinc enclosed bathroom in the backyard. I spent all my days here until immigrating to Canada in 1969. All my youthful memories are entrenched here and of the personality that was molded. I am sure that it embodied the foundations of the person I had become.

The latrine in the backyard was troubling for me. I had nightmares for years about it, and to make matters worse, I had to use it every day. It all started when my father and my uncle Daddas began to dig a six-feet-deep hole to construct a latrine over it. This was right after we had moved into our new house. As a youngster, I always liked to hang around and watch the elders working. Sometimes I became helpful in doing small chores. However, it was more to observe and learn. I think it was instrumental in the skills I picked up in carpentry, arts, and crafts. About five feet down, they had dug up some bones and were quite puzzled about what to do next. After some discussion, they finally dismissed it with a shrug of the shoulders. My father said, "Aah, it's just a latrine." I watched intently as they just left the bones there, and in no time, a latrine was constructed above the deep pit. As a youngster, I was puzzled about the bones there. Why were there so many bones in one place? Soon after, what became a nightly occurrence still remained a mystery to me. Every night, I would get this dream and wake up screaming. It was the same scenario each time.

In my dreams, there were three black men. One of them was completely bald and had no clothes from the waist up. He was a big man in stature with cold eyes and a blank stare. He always looked directly into my eyes. He appeared to have completed a formidable task in the tropical heat as beads of perspiration streamed down his sun-baked body. The other two men stood motionless closely behind but with the same bone-chilling stare. I was not being chased or harmed in any way, but it appeared that they beckoned my presence. The black men would walk slowly toward me, and I could see their faces magnifying as they approached closer. Soon their faces were so close that I could feel a cold wind across my face with every blink of the eye. The bald man reached out his hand as if to take me with him. Scared out of my wits, I screamed continuously but was unable to run or move away. Sometimes my screams were loud and sometimes muffled in low audible moans, but it penetrated the night each time. A quick push or jolt by my mother, and it was soon over.

Somehow I could not escape the harrowing thought of these three black men. Why only me and what they were trying to say puzzled me. My fear was real. Using the toilet during the day posed no problem, but at night and before the sun rose was a different situation. I heard drops of water falling, one drop at a time. No one else ever heard these falling drops of water when they visited the toilet. It could have been my imagination from all the ghostly stories and jumbie stories that were so prevalent. I avoided using the toilet at nights out of sheer fear. It was not until I immigrated to Canada that the dreams and nightmares stopped and immediately at that. In my imagination, I still see the faces of these three black men beckoning me. Many years later, I learned that this area, now known as Reliance Settlement, was used as a burial ground for the African slaves who worked on the sugar plantation. At some point, this area also served as a small venture for sugar manufacture evidenced by the copper container left there. I am tempted to think that the bones my father had dug up for the latrine were the remains of these slaves who were buried there, and we had disturbed their resting place. The area was just across the canal from Nigger Yard. They may have been trying to reach out to me to incarnate their spirits in me or just to convey a message in me. Suffering silently in fear of using the toilet, I would never let it be known to anyone, but I often wondered about the whole affair. Was this a brush with the underworld or the shadows of black magic showing its face? Were these men similar to the spirits my grandfather had once evoked and commanded? Were they trying to get my attention? All that I can discern from the experience was that their presence in my dreams was strong, and I would later develop a deep respect for the circumstances surrounding death, the afterlife, and the many folklore around the spiritual beliefs.

An outhouse in the back yard . . . a standard feature of our home at Reliance Settlement. Toilet paper was a luxury item that never reached the Ramsaroop's residence.

Bottom house activities involve anything from preparing daily meals to relaxing in a hammock and idle gossip. My mother is on the right with other family members.

All the daily activities were played out in the *bottom house*. Open-air and spacious, there were two handmade wooden benches and a hammock tied to the house posts. We gathered here for eating, relaxing, and the ongoing gossip mongering. The floor was dirt but level and smooth. In order to give it a clean appearance, it would get a *dab* every Friday. It was a ritual for my mother and sisters to hand-mix cow dung and water to smooth out the surface area. Of course, the cow dung smells, but it does dry out to allow for a hard walking surface. It was a normal household activity throughout the sugar estates. I had become so accustomed to the smell that after a while, it became unnoticed and second nature. Getting the cow dung was one of my chores. Every Friday morning, I was awakened around five o'clock, which was usually about the same time my mother gets up to start the day's cooking. With a large galvanized bucket, I headed for the sugar estate's stables. There were always other neighborhood youngsters like myself who also headed for the stables, and there was much competition for the cow dung.

I remembered many times when the cow dung became scarce with fewer bulls in the stables, and some housewives paid twenty-five cents per bucket for the gold.

Often, there were eight to ten of us scurrying sleepily toward the stable. Very few words were spoken, and we approached with the same ritual. There was a frenzy to cross over to the stable yard. Double rows of punts packed with sugarcane that lined the canal made for easy access to the stable yard. No one was allowed in the stable yard, and there was always a watchman present at nights to keep out intruders. Steers, horses, and mules were left in the yard when there were not enough stalls in the stables for them. Every morning, the yard was dotted with dung from the steers, horses, or mules. The differences were easily recognizable to a trained eye, and I had no trouble to identify cow dung at a glance. The watchman never tried to prevent us from taking the cow dung, and every Friday morning the rush was on for it.

Punts of sugarcane from the fields lined the canal awaiting processing.

I would cross hurriedly over the punts, and if the punts were empty, I walked on the flat corner *gonnals* or planks and always toward the steers or bulls. In a swift motion, I scooped up the cow dung by hand into the bucket and then quickly to the next mound nearby or within sight. Like all other items, cow dung takes a different form and texture. Cow dung stays in one solid mass and shaped like a plate or an oversized Frisbee. Horse and mule dung on the other hand breaks up into coarse round bits similar to tennis balls.

When the choices were there, I took only the compact, hardy type of cow dung. It stayed well in the bucket without spilling over the sides on my way home since I carried the bucket on my head. On other occasions when my luck was not there, I had no choice but to take the watery cow dung that often spilled over to my shoulder and hair. A quick jump in the canal, a dab of coconut oil over the body, and some Vaseline on my hair was all that was needed in preparation for school later.

Smoothing out the bottom house with a dab of cow dung.

I only attended school because it was compulsory. Although I did try to learn and to keep up academically with the other pupils of my class, there was a more carefree attitude in which I approached my days at St. Patrick's Anglican School. I always sat at the back bench of the class with a few of my friends with whom I shared a common bond in truancy and the constant misbehavior. I tried mostly to hide from the teacher's view and not to be noticed. I was terrified to be called upon by the teacher, and this inferiority complex ruled my school days. As a result, playing hooky was commonplace for me on many days, and my interests were more occupied in completing my chores at home rather than the necessities of reading and writing and arithmetic. My wickedness followed me like a shadow, and I opted out for its sickliness at every opportunity, always trying to get one step ahead of my friends and teachers. It opted into mischief most times.

Every day we were recessed to obtain a ration of milk and biscuits. The teachers, at an appointed time, served all pupils with a cup of milk prepared from a concentrated powder and water stirred in a bucket, with two high-protein biscuits and a cod-liver oil tablet. We had to swallow the cod-liver oil tablet in front of the teacher. Many times I was able to keep it under my tongue and spit it out later when I left the line. I hated the taste. This was one of the programs in the schools to combat poverty and malnutrition that was instituted by the United Nations under UNESCO, with the cooperation of most third world countries. Before classes resumed later, a few of us would dash off into the bushes beyond the cemetery for the rest of the day. Sitting in the bushes, I would write my tables and put a big check mark on the slate with a piece of chalk as if the teacher had marked my work.

"Look, Ma, I get everything right today," I used to say as I showed my mother my slate.

"That's good, boy."

A quick glance and she would continue her food preparation for dinner.

Health care was high on the agenda of the World Health Organization, and some of the benefits did trickle down to the schools in the sugar plantations. Men in overalls and gas masks, as if they had just landed from Mars, sprayed the toxic chemical DDT in the drains and any place they could find with stagnant water. There was a bold attempt to eradicate disease-spreading mosquitoes, ringworm, and other waterborne bacteria. With this increasing awareness for cleanliness of the environment and personal health, it was a relief to me personally when dozens of carrion crows, these doomsday vultures, no longer descended on the Rose Hall Estate market area after it was closed late in the afternoon. It was normal for the fish vendors and fruit vendors to discard their unwanted wastes of decaying fish and rotten fruits by the roadside. At dusk each day, a flock of carrion crows descended like clockwork for the cleanup. Sometimes Laxie and I competed with the scavengers for the best discarded mangoes.

The dispensary at Rose Hall Estate, the only medical care facility existing to serve all sugar workers and their families. All services were free.

One of the most dreadful scenes for me was the sight of the dental vans parked in the school yard for the annual checkup of every pupil's teeth. The vans conducted their visit to each primary school and was another benefit to school-age children on behalf of the World Health Organization. The distinctive smell emanating from the vans and the eerie sound of drills penetrating the quiet air was chilling in itself, not to mention the horror stories circulating among us that the dentists used pliers to pull the tooth clear out of the gums. All that stood out in my mind was an image of swollen jaws and bloody balls of lint in the mouth and, of course, excruciating pain. Unable to circumvent my fear of the dental vans, I resorted to a cunningness that I can now only laugh impishly in hindsight.

When it had become time for our fourth standard class to be examined, we were sent down to the van in batches of fours and in alphabetical order of our registered names. One of my very best friends named Dhanraj had returned to report that the dentists had found two decayed molars in his lower jaw, and both were scheduled for extraction that afternoon. With my name being Yuvraj, I was among the last batch to be examined by the dentists. Entering the van, I noticed that the dentist was busy looking at his charts and filling out forms.

"Your name?" he asked.

He did not look up at me and continued to scribble on his charts.

"Dhanraj," I said softly.

I eyeballed the menacing reclining chair in one corner. An elongated light fixture hung over the chair, and alongside there was laid out an array of stainless steel dental instruments.

"Okay, Dhanraj, let's take a look."

"Open wide," he commanded.

I did not make a sound but stared at the dental instruments from the corner of my eye. Everything seemed cold.

"Well, you have two bad ones," he concluded and scribbled a note on his chart.

"Send in the next," he requested as he let me out.

I did not utter a word, and I dashed away in a hurry to escape that peculiar smell. I knew I had two teeth to be extracted and that laid heavily on my mind.

That afternoon, pupils were again sent down to the dental van in alphabetical order. I watched nervously as Dhanraj came back writhing in pain. He had both hands on his mouth as if to contain the pain from the two molars that were yanked out of his mouth. It was not long afterward when our teacher called on Dhanraj to go back down again. Apparently, it was my chart that was being examined. Two more of his probably good teeth were also yanked out, and he came back almost in tears. Both sides of his jaws were now swollen, and large balls of lint filled his mouth to contain the bleeding. Not saying a word to anyone, I could not contain my relief on my way home that afternoon, knowing that my cunningness prevailed to avoid the dental vans. Like the tide, dental decay waits for no man, and I eventually paid a high price, in much more pain in later years, when as an adult I had to have a couple of teeth extracted. It was the same feverish cringe all over my body as I made myself comfortable in the dentist's chair.

The rains in spring signaled the start of the rice-planting season, and there was no escape for me from the hard, arduous labor that ensued. Rice farming was the mainstay and a valuable cash crop of the East Indians in many of the rural areas surrounding the sugar plantations. Vast tracks of land were brought into cultivation at Mahaicony and Abary in Demerara county, the Pomeroons in Essequibo county, and Black Bush Polder in Berbice county. At Rose Hall Estate, thousands of acres of irrigated rice fields were made available to sugar workers at New Dam and Hicken Savannah on the fringes of Albion Estate. Each sugar worker in good standing qualified to receive three quarters of an acre or of prime rice land for cultivation during the off season. My father and brother Roland usually qualified, and each year we embarked on rice cultivation on an acre and a half at New Dam. Growing older every year, I got involved more regularly into every aspect and details of rice production. In the end, the rewards always outweighed the hard work and intensive labor involving the entire family. We had rice to eat for the entire year, and the cash obtained provided for the purchase of furniture and other household items. It kept the family together, and we survived the years without much hardship when wages were cut off from frequent stoppages in the sugar estate. There was a steady change from year to year that affected each member of our family. We progressed economically, and life was more tolerable. We were happy. Family values were maintained and kept at an unforeseen high level. We did not have to rob, borrow, or steal. In time every member of our family lived responsible lives of their own.

None of the things I did later in life compared to the work I did in the rice fields. None even came close to it. The rice fields at New Dam were at least three to four miles from our house. Getting up at about four thirty in the morning, I walked briskly to get there. The burden of carrying the equipments such as a hoe, a rope, or a bucket added to the long journey and made it more difficult when the mud dams become slippery from the daily rain showers. In preparation for the planting season, I was always up to my knees in mud and water. The sharp edges of bamboo grass, sticks buried in the mud, and the always present snails in the mud were natural hazards for small cuts and bruises to my bare feet. Many times, the cuts went unnoticed, and when the bleeding persisted, a plaster of mud around the wound was the only remedy to stop it. There was little and no time for first aid, and the work continued without interruption. The numerous scars on my feet are a constant reminder and bear ample witness of those days.

At midday, the sun beats down on my shoulders and baked the land below. To quench my thirst, a few handfuls of water were gulped down from the nearby trench or a clearing of the rainwater that covered the rice fields. I was always full of anticipation when my mother would arrive late in the morning with food. A couple scoops of boiled rice with eggplant curry sufficed for the day. It amazes me to this day how this food was so tasty and delicious when eaten at the rice fields. It never tasted the same when I had it in abundance at home. I have never complained. There was no need. The work went one from one stage of rice production to the next. My father and elder brother Ivan did the ploughing. Ivan was able to keep the steers in line as he ploughed by himself. My father had some difficulty in controlling the steers. This is where I filled in, leading the steers by the reins while my father concentrated on the plough as it made deep cuts of dirt in the ankle-deep water. I kept pace with the steers and felt the enormous power of their steps bearing down behind me. I prayed that I would never stumble and fall and then have the steers run over me. Resting was occasional and only when my father stopped the steers for their own sake. At the end of day, the steers were let loose to graze in a separate paddock nearby. Tired and worn down, I made the three to four miles trek back home. Hunger propelled me to walk briskly for a hot dinner awaiting. By the next morning, the routine started all over again.

Simultaneously, there was the ongoing effort to prepare the *beyari* or nursery for the seedlings. Here a small patch is cleared of weeds and all water kept out by building a mound with mud around it. The nursery must be maintained dry in the early stages as the seedlings germinate. There were always sudden thunder-showers that flooded the nursery. I dreaded it. The water had to be bailed out by buckets, and it meant a few thousand buckets of water. Each day the task was left to Roland, KP, and myself. Bending and lifting buckets of water in the thousands was backbreaking work, but we understood the importance of getting it done. Without the seedlings, there would be no crop, and the entire season will be lost. Allowed to grow for about six weeks, the seedlings or *beeya* were pulled by the roots and tied into small bundles for transplanting into the prepared rice field beds. The day of planting was special and a family affair, with all hands available helping. Two or three stalks of beeya are planted about a foot apart with the roots firmly into the soft mud. It was always a great satisfaction when the planting was completed.

It took about ninety days for the rice stalks to grow to about three feet high with ears of golden paddy hanging effortlessly toward the now soft, dry ground below. I never forgot my first sight of it, a field of gold of a thousand or more acres of rice stalks swaying in the gentle wind. The time for harvesting had come. In a fortnight's time, the paddy was being shipped to the rice mills for the milling process that strips the paddy of its golden shell to release the coveted rice grains. We camped out in the rice fields, sleeping in the open, as the rice stalks were painstakingly cut by hand with a grass knife similar to a miniature sickle. Dragged in bundles to a prepared patch of ground or *karian*, the rice stalks are spread out on the ground around a center post. Here the steers are tied together at the collar to walk over it in a circle. The weight of their hoofs trashed the ears from the stalks, which were then discarded and more replaced. It was my job to keep the steers walking in a steady pace, and I walked right along in repeated circles. The aches and pains and the strains to endure the many discomforts went right along too. I never raised an objection. It was not necessary. It all vanished in pure satisfaction when the last bags of paddy are unloaded at the rice mill later on. A grin on all faces said it all. The monetary reward was especially sweet. My father usually kept enough rice for the family to consume for the rest of the year while the balance was sold to the British Guiana Rice Marketing Board for about sixteen dollars per bag of twenty-two gallons. Six to eight hundred dollars for the crop was considered a good year. To put this in perspective, our house was built at a cost of eighteen hundred dollars. I was proud to have helped in every activity along the way. Although not a thank-you or a penny for my efforts came in my direction, I have had no regrets. It was expected of me, and I have always revered the experiences. It was like no other.

Like most stages in life, all things usually come to an end. Sometimes it is in bitterness and sometimes it is in sweetness. The year 1959 was the last season we cultivated rice at New Dam. We had a meager crop, plagued by droughts and low water levels in the canals that irrigated the fields. Furthermore, with the expansion of the sugar estate, more land was brought into cultivation of sugarcane, and New Dam was a prime source. The residents of New Dam were resettled in a place called Gangaram in upper Canje, and the Hicken savannahs were no longer available for us to keep the cattle grazing in the after season. That summer was also the last for my formidable task in taking care of our remaining two steers, Blackboy and Whiteboy. We had to keep them tied up in our backyard at Reliance Settlement, and their upkeep became my responsibility. Each day after school was dismissed, I took them out to graze by the drainage canal near our house. The cattle found unattended around the settlements were usually impounded at the police station, and so I kept a close vigilance over them, not letting them out of my sight. An impounded cattle was a costly affair to us, and at any sign of the cow catchers, I had to quickly drive them back home and off the streets.

One incident in particular with regard to my favorite steer Etano would never fade from my mind. We never found out the circumstances surrounding his impoundment at Albion Police Station, but it was sixteen days later before my father was notified. With both my father and brother Roland not wanting to lose a day at work, I was dispatched to Albion Police Station to get the steer out of the pound. Armed with sixteen dollars of impound fee and twenty-eight cents exactly for the return bus fare to Albion, I set out with the memorized instructions on what to do that was drilled into me by everyone the night before. Paying the fee and with the help of one of the policeman, I managed to get my rope I had brought around his horns. It was with some difficulty. With little to eat in the pound, Etano was restless and paced back and forth to get out. I always loved the menacing look of this steer with huge shoulders and wide horns as far as my outstretched hands. His black hair had become dusty from the mud and dung in the pound, and his ribs and hip bones showed prominently from being starved. I was sure he had recognized me as I prodded him out of the pound. I had named him after a movie I had seen years before, about a story of a boy and his steer named Etano.

Immediately after he was let out of the pound, Etano broke into a trot and headed straight down the dam beside the police station leading toward his home base at Hicken Savannah. He seemed to know exactly where he was going, and I tried desperately to keep pace with him while holding on to the long rope that trailed behind him from his horns. It was an hour or so later and a few miles from Albion before he crossed over a canal and to his home at Hicken Savanah. I swam across the canal frantically also to keep pace, but suddenly the journey was over. Etano stopped and started to graze peacefully, knowing he was home. Relieved and exhausted, I was in familiar territory when I looked around to see New Dam in the distance.

Now I had another dilemma. Getting the tightly drawn, water-soaked rope from around his horns proved more of a challenge as Etano would not let me near him to get it off. I was afraid of him, and I knew he was eager to gourd me if I came too close. I was angry and did let out a few curses. Hiding behind the trunk of a tall coconut tree, I enticed him with some fresh juicy *para* grass I had pulled by hand from the nearby canal. After some gentle patting on the head as he lost focus of me, I was able to pry the rope loose from his horns. Looking back as I walked away and coiling the rope around my shoulder, he had the look of one majestic specimen. It would be the last time I saw Etano.

I made the decision to walk home. Rubbing the coins in my pockets, I did not want to part with it. It was too painful for me to give up the fourteen cents as bus fare. I was prepared to lie if I was asked about it. In it my mind dazzled at a matinee at Rajmahal Cinema and a treat of a refreshing *mauby* drink with salted fish cake on a roll at Charlie Lows Cake Shop. It was a long walk home.

"You got the steer out of de pound boy?" my father called out.

It was late in the afternoon, almost past dinnertime as I entered the bottom house.

"Yeah, everything all right," I responded promptly as I warily hung the rope to its customary place on the corner post. A few of my brothers and sisters had gathered after dinner. I hesitated for a while to give an account about the condition of the steer and the events of the day, but there were no more questions. There was no need for details. I supposed that it was expected of me to get the job done. I was thankful that everything went well that day without incident. I wondered what would have happened if I had failed to get the steer out of the pound. Only my friend Laxie wanted to know what happened that day when we gathered by the culvert later in the evening. Teasing, I made up some stories of how I saw a jaguar in the trees and how a huge alligator was in the canal as I crossed over. It was intended to impress him that I was brave and without fear to be alone in the savannahs. Apparently, I never told anyone that I was gripping in fear. This eventually developed as a hallmark of my style in everything I did later in life. I never showed my fear.

There was not a day that went by that I did not have reflections of Etano. My father had sold him in order to pay the expenses of my eldest brother's opportunity to train as a sugar boiler in Trinidad. Now, I was contended to watch over Blackboy and Whiteboy. Every afternoon, I took up my position perched on top Dookie's bridge as the steers grazed along the drainage canal. Many thoughts crossed my mind. A fire burned inside me for the many things I longed for but were beyond my immediate reach. Many had to wait for many years later. I watched in envy as students came off the bus as they returned home from their high school classes in New Amsterdam. Some rode by on their bicycles. There was something that I found unique about the sight of high school students. Looking studious, they always impressed me by the many books they carried in their school bags or under their arms with rows of pens lining the breast pockets. Boys wore khaki pants with white shirts and a tie and, of course, shoes. Girls wore navy blue, crimson red, or hunter green uniforms of their respective high schools. The pep in their hurried steps and their bright smiles were a haunting image for me. I was embarrassed to compare their clean-cut image with the mud crusting on my bare feet, with my old khaki short pants and shirt.

Of all the things I missed in my life, not attending a high school topped the list. I hesitated to think that it may have made a difference in what I had become in later years. Maybe so, but I would never know. However, I often wondered if attending high school would have changed my fortunes. I always thought that I was not cut out academically for high school or for the rigors and the demands of an academic career. I knew it would have had an impact in some narrow area. For years I wished I had attended Berbice High School in New Amsterdam. My goal was to play in the cricket tournaments to compete with the high schools and colleges from Georgetown. I was a good cricketer by many standards of my time, a medium-pace bowler and an opening batsman. I was better at the game than most of the players that made up the team at Berbice High School. In one of the matches between Berbice High School and St. Stanislaus College of Georgetown, I had seen Steven Commache representing his college. He went on to play for the West Indies Test team, the pinnacle of cricketing excellence. Berbice High School would have afforded me the chance I desperately needed at the time. Instead I played a notch down in caliber for the Rose Hall Estate Junior Team in the inter-estates cricket competition. Cricket was my premier passion, and I played at every opportunity. I emulated the batting of Guiana's favorite cricketer Rohan Kanhai and the likes of Ken Barrington of England and Neil Harvey of Australia. In time, my father had to sell our last two steers, and it brought an era to an end. These were changing times, and I drifted to other endeavors.

A view from Dookie's bridge as the steers grazed along the edges of the canal. The public latrines have long disappeared on the right side.

Practicing my batting skills at Rose Hall Estate cricket ground.

Years later, I continued to play cricket in the Garden State Cricket League in New Jersey.

High school students at Berbice Educational Institute, New Amsterdam, Berbice. Minwatti Tulsi is in the first row on the left.

CHAPTER 4

School Teacher at Sixteen

It is a miracle that curiosity survives formal education.
—Albert Einstein

Euphoria, ecstasy, sublime bliss, or walking on cloud nine were not enough words to describe the way I felt that Saturday afternoon. There were only two other times that I came close to feeling this way in my many years of struggles to succeed in life. It was a brief moment in time, but it changed the course of my life forever. I sat on top of the stairs and stared blankly across the street toward the drainage canal. The usual games of little girls skipping rope and little boys playing marbles or sponge ball cricket on the streets had come to an end as everyone found shelter in the cool shade of the bottom house from the hot afternoon sun. Many of the housewives had gone to the market for their daily purchases of fresh fish and vegetables for their special Saturday dinner. There was not a stir from anyone, and not a sound could be heard from anywhere around. Even the birds stopped chirping and the echo calls of the kiskadee halted for a while as the tropical heat roasted the earth below into a haze in the distance.

My thoughts were far away, dancing in wonderland, thoughts of glory, fame, opportunity, and wealth. They were idle thoughts that melted somewhere in my subconsciousness. I was completely oblivious to my surroundings. Every now and then, I would glance at the newspaper spread out on my lap to the glow of my name in fine print. Although misspelled, there was no doubt about it in my mind that it was mine. The names of all the students in the country who passed the pupil teacher's appointment exam (PTA) in 1962 were listed on the Saturday's newspaper, the *Daily Chronicle*. There it was, halfway between all the names under the county of Berbice-Yufraj, St. Patrick's Anglican School. It was a sight to behold. Only two other students had passed from the entire school district of Canje. Suddenly, my world had been transformed.

How I could have missed my name in the newspaper earlier that morning puzzled me for a while. I knew I looked at every name as I scanned each column. I was certain my name was not on the list. Maybe it was the excitement and anxiety that had built from the previous day, or maybe it was the darkness that still lingered in the predawn hours. Maybe the print was blurred or there was not enough light under the lamppost as I gazed hurriedly through the long list of names. What a disappointment I had when I did not see my name. My heart sank very low. The bubble of anticipation that had built up since the day before burst open at the seams, and a heavy weight descended in my stomach. The notion that I had failed for a second time was beyond belief. The day before, there was a three-line statement in the *Daily Chronicle* that the results of the PTA exams would be published on Saturday's edition. No individual results were usually given by the Ministry of Education. All students found out their exam results by the names submitted by the Ministry of Education and published in the newspapers of those who had passed. That night before, I could hardly sleep. I awoke practically each hour after midnight, only to glance at the little hand-winded clock on the table and doze off again. The time neared when I finally woke up to roosters crowing in short intervals to announce the dawn of a new day. I made off to New Amsterdam with my father's bicycle. The estate had loaned him a bicycle as a reward for his position as driver or foreman to make his rounds in the back dams. It was a good three-mile ride, and the old bicycle made a lot of noise. The chain kept slipping off the sprocket with every other turn of the pedal, much to my annoyance and everyone else nearby. Newspapers were not available in the Canje area until noon, and I could not stand the suspense until then to know if I passed the PTA exam. The roadway was desolate, and because it was Saturday, there were no cane cutters hurrying to catch the trucks to the fields. Only a couple of stray dogs barked furiously and chased my bicycle as I passed by Dookie Shop. They must have been awakened as the pedal cranked into a grinding noise with each repetition. I had to speed up while shouting and kicking to get away from this utter nuisance. Although the dogs never bite, their barking stopped as soon as I had passed the house. The same wrath awaited the next passing cyclist.

Not finding a paperboy by the Globe Cinema on Main Street, I raced down the long wooden ramp to the Berbice Ferry Station. As usual it was crowded with the bustle of early commuters boarding the Torani, which ferries vehicles as well as passengers across the Berbice River to Rosignol. At the stand near the entrance, I quickly paid four cents for a paper and hurried under the light of the lamppost to check out the names. My eyes scanned the columns up and down. I did not see my name, and a heavy weight filled my chest. Resigned to fact that I failed again, I slowly returned home. I had failed the PTA exam in my first attempt in 1961. Failure a second time was disaster. In my heart I knew it was a death sentence of years of hard manual labor in the fields.

No one asked me about my whereabouts that morning, and I never mentioned the results of the PTA exam either. I had not expected to pass anyway. I always thought that the other five students in the class were much brighter and had a better chance of success. They were always in a studious mode, reading and making notes, while I did a lot of just goofing off and idle daydreaming on the pretence I was studying. There was not a whole lot of formal instruction received either. Our class was merely two benches and desks in the second story hallway in front of Mr. Lampkin's office, the

The Torani crossing the Berbice River ferrying passengers and vehicles between New Amsterdam and Rosignol.

headmaster. He left us to study by ourselves for the most part while he was mostly engrossed in his administrative duties. We clowned around a lot, and when he was absent we were gone also. On many days a few of us would ride to New Forest to pick mangoes and to engage in more idling and clowning around. They were times of fun, and sitting for the PTA exam at the end of the school year brought to a close my primary school education at St. Patrick's Anglican School. While awaiting the results of the PTA exam through the summer, I made a half-hearted attempt to attend a new high school that was getting started by Mr. Gopaul at Adelphi Village. All classes were being held at a vacant grocery store building with mostly second-rate teachers who were not fully qualified in getting teaching positions in the government primary school system. It was a bold attempt by Mr. Gapaul, and his high school started out on a solid footing with more than a hundred students.

"We guarantee that your son will pass the CP exam," he said to my parents as he tried to convince them to enroll me.

"Let's give this boy a chance," he continued convincingly.

It was agreed that the tuition of $30 for the first term was not payable until the end of the term. I decided to attend since there was nothing else for me to do that summer. It came to an end about two months later when the PTA exam results were published.

Earlier in the day, Laxie and I had gone toward the creek flat. We did our usual Saturday routine of hunting for wild fruits and shooting birds. We crossed the punts to the well-known Baichan tamarind tree. The story passed on was that a man named Baichan hung himself on this tree, and his ghost still roamed the area. It was an eerie feeling to be under the tree, and not many of us went there alone. It was a hideout for many. Some workers rested there, and others made cookouts under the tree. Far beyond, a semi-jungle area stretched out toward Canje creek, dotted with clusters of low bushes, tall grass, ponds, and swamps. We walked through the known, beaten footpaths to look for wild fruits. *Monkey-apples, banga, see-me-too, bulbulee and popo* were common. We always carried our handmade slingshot in our back pockets together with rounded selected slugs of granite stones picked up from the corner of the road. Considered very good with the slingshot, I hunted local birds relentlessly. Very often I stalked and shot down the varied species of red-neck robin, dye neck, blue sacki, kiskadee, and including the illusive hummingbird we called Dr. Sui. Any bird killed was later feathered and roasted over some twigs. A pocketknife in my pocket and a box of lighthouse matches were regular items that I carried with me at all times. Sometimes I stole a cigarette or two from my father's pack when he was not looking and smoked them in the bushes. The day was complete with swimming in the canal and sucking on sugarcane with the rest of the neighborhood gang. It was a common activity for us, and I relished the adventures.

On my way home that Saturday afternoon, I had passed Cyril Dabydeen and Hassan Ali, two teachers from St. Patrick's Anglican School, riding along on their bicycles on the main road.

,   ,   ,,   ,

"Congratulations," I heard one of them remark.

"Wa dem teacher say?" inquired Laxie.

"I don' know," I replied, but I was startled at what he had said.

"Dey not talking to me," I reiterated shrugging my shoulders as we continued toward home. We raised our hands when we made eye contact with the teachers as this was a sign of respect when passing any teacher. For friends and acquaintances, a nod of the head was sufficient.

"Well, dey bin looking at you," Laxie prodded and squinted his eyes as if to tease me. "You in big trouble, boy," he remarked with an impish grin on his face. "You betta watch out at school on Monday."

I did not understand what he meant and paid no further heed to his teasing. My mother had gone to the market now, and my father was asleep on the rocking chair. With nothing else to do, I decided to scan through the names again and settled down with the newspaper on the top of the steps. I just wanted to see if I could recognize any of the names of those who had passed the exam. All names were listed by counties Essequibo, Demerara, and Berbice. Going down the list under Berbice, my heart must have missed a beat when my eyes stopped at Yufraj, St. Patrick's Anglican School.

"I passed," I blurted out loudly and jumped up in jubilation.

Looking at my name again, I was up on my feet in a hurry.

"Look, Pa, I passed," as I rushed in to dangle the opened page of the newspaper in front of his face.

"Dat good, boy," and he continued to doze off, head resting on his shoulder in the rocking chair. I did not want to disturb him any further.

"I passed, I passed," I said softly in whispers to myself time and time again.

I settled back down on top of the stairs, wide-eyed, with a broad smile, and dazed. I had that certain feeling, an indescribable feeling. I was looking but not seeing anything. Everything appeared calm, and all my senses were lost to the surrounding. The heart felt full as if expanded to the limit to fill the chest, but there was no heartbeat. Only a blank stare rests on the face and the eyes transfixed on an object in the distance.

It took a while, but reality began to sink in. I was beginning to realize what this had meant and what the future held for me. Becoming a school teacher at the tender age of fifteen years and ten months meant instant recognition for being a brilliant student and a high degree of respectability from young and old alike. A teacher anywhere in the country was a pillar in the community. The elderly folks referred to you as teach, and the younger ones called you Sir, or Mr. or Miss, or Mrs. Then came the attraction from the opposite sex and the unequaled popularity all around. There were the financial rewards and a sense of professionalism that permeated the character of a teacher. A teacher was versed in the academic subjects and social studies and kept abreast in world affairs by the mere fact of the reading habits that constitute everyday activities. Teachers were role models, and on their shoulders rested the challenges that molded and shaped the future of the next generations of children. A teacher read the faces of children and harbored their fears and propelled their motives to succeed in life. A teacher represented such a driving force that no one ever forgets their teachers in their lifetime. I certainly remembered all my teachers, though not with the reverence I should, but their value and teachings contributed to my education regardless of how little or subtle that might be. Now I was up to the same challenge. A teacher was a stepping-stone to success in life.

Close to sunset, I dressed in my very best attire—short khaki pants and a blue poplin shirt. I took particular care to press the seams with our flatiron that I heated on the iron grate on the *fireside*. My feet and body was well-anointed with coconut oil. A dab of extra Vaseline kept every hair in place and combed back in the Elvis Presley style that I liked. I had no shoes, but I was walking on thin air as I headed for the local hangout at the culvert in front of Rajmahal Cinema. By now it was apparent that everyone knew I had passed the PTA exam, and I was the talk on the road. Some fellows that I never knew before came up and said congrats. Others shook my hands briskly. Surrounded by friends, the conversations steered in all directions. I sensed that the tone was different, and when I spoke up, there was silence and everyone listened attentively. We joked about how I may not hangout with them anymore now that I was heading in a different circle. I felt good, and I wondered why the others did not pass. They were all much more prepared than me. Did I pass by accident or sheer luck? Whatever the circumstances, I began to look to the road ahead and the future. One thing was for sure, I was breaking away from the traditional trend that had bound life to the plantations. I was spinning off into another direction and into another dimension. Unlike the generations of Ramsaroops before me, I would escape from not working a single day at Rose Hall Estate. It was the start of a radical departure for me from the years of plantation life as I had come to know it

"So we got to call you teach now, eh?" Laxie remarked. There was a foolish grin on his face.

"Yep," I replied, shaking my head in modesty.

"No, you got to call him sir," Leonard intervened, giving Laxie a playful slap behind the head.

"Hey, I like the sound of dat," I agreed as I pointed a finger at Laxie, and we laughed at the silliness of it all.

I savored the moment, but deep inside, my thoughts lingered to an imaginable future of uncertainty. As if I had suddenly emerged from a winding trail in the dense woods to the junction of the main roads, the direction pointed to several but clearly defined pathways ahead. I knew that I must confront the challenges that presented themselves in any and which way I could. Without visibly showing it, the nervousness was deep within.

It would not be long after that the novelty of it all had worn out, and I settled on the realization that everything I attempted to do from here on would be of my own making. Only my own efforts would get me to the bright lights in the distance, and only my own strengths and perseverance would prevail. The desirable amenities that make up an enjoyable lifestyle, clothes, food, transportation, and simple comforts danced in my imagination and served as the motivational driving force from within. All is possible with a good education and more. I knew then what I had to do, and I knew that I could do it because it would depend on no one else but me. It was my ticket out of a lower-class, poverty-stricken, dead-end lifestyle.

Growing up as a teenager posed many problems, and growing up fast I surely did. With every new experience came the inevitable roller coaster of emotions, struggling to meet the demands and expectations as they became apparent. There was no escape from the trials and tribulations of facing up to the world, and I certainly had my share of pains, those growing up pains. There was much that I learned in those foolish years, and if one lesson stood out among them all, it was that life imitates the passing of the seasons. Everything changes with time, and after the happiness and laughter always come the disappointments and tears. I had my share of disappointments, more than I can recall.

In the start of the first term in 1963, my career launched as a pupil teacher at Reliance Sanatani Hindi School. Situated only a few hundred yards from St. Patrick's Anglican School and within walking distance from my home, it grew rapidly in enrollment from its initial inception to teach Hindi to the children of the predominantly East Indian population of the area. In the late 1950s, it developed as a church-denominated primary school in similar fashion to that of Catholic and Anglican primary schools in existence. Most of the primary schools throughout the country were founded by the churches and built on church land, and so the church exercised some control in the form of the governing body. In 1961, the government had taken over control of all church-denominated primary schools in the country. The salaries of the teachers were paid by the government, together with other financial assistance in terms of maintenance and supplies. All curricula were standardized and supervised by the Ministry of Education. At Reliance S.H. School, the makeup of the student population were predominantly East Indian children from the settlements at Reliance, Abandon, Adelphi, and Canefield. It was sad that no black pupils ever enrolled here, choosing to remain at St. Patrick's Anglican School, which continued to have a diverse student population. There were no black teachers during my tenure, and for the most part, it never mattered to anyone as far as I could tell. There were no objections raised, and both schools coexisted peacefully and in fierce competition academically as well as in sports without incident. My younger brothers and sisters continued to attend St. Patrick's Anglican School.

Primary school teacher at age sixteen at Reliance S. H. School (1962)

Sometime in mid-October, I learned that I was accepted for a teaching post at Reliance S. H. School. I knew many others were interviewed for the few positions at the school, but I was lucky I guess. At least I was the only one who had passed the PTA exam from the district and a sure shoo-in for the position. More so, the manager of the school's governing body was related to my brother's wife, and the general secretary was the brother to my sister's husband. I suppose it could be said that it was a family thing as was common in small communities. Everyone seemed to know everyone else, either by blood relationships or by close friendly ties. In any case, I was a shoo-in for the teaching position. While waiting outside the school for the interview on a Sunday afternoon, a couple of hours had passed before I was summoned. From the idle conversations with the other candidates interviewed, I found out that they were grilled on their background and experiences. When my turn came up, no one asked me any questions.

"You gonna start next Monday," Mr. Bissessar, the manager, commanded with a broad smile. The others watched on, and it appeared their decisions were already made. I was shy and lost in bewilderment. I left feeling happy and nervously shook the hands of everyone to thank them for their resolve in giving me the opportunity. It was the start of my refinement from the rough edges of my free-spirited days only a month ago. Courtesy and kindness became second nature, and I struggled to control the everyday Creole dialect and balky tone that I was so accustomed to speaking. Naturally, I dropped the harshness and the curses and street slangs that had become the bulk of my repertoire of words.

My first day as a teacher had arrived, and I got up early to get ready. There was a permeable consciousness that everyone would be looking at my every move. I could feel the tension and the butterflies in my stomach and the blood rushing through my body. I was wearing long pants for the second time, and I would be in public view. They were gray felt pants purchased from the Rose Hall market. I was so shy that only Amos saw me in them the first time. Feeling awkward and almost embarrassed to walk to the cinema in long pants, I had Amos tow me with the bicycle through the streets to avoid the obvious comments that usually ensues.

"You turn big man when you wear long pants," everyone used to say.

It was the transition and certainly a big leap from boy to man. No ceremonies were performed and no dances and chants celebrated the event, but the eyes of the young and the old recognized it just the same. It personifies the ascent to adulthood regardless of age and signaled that it was now permissible to drink rum and smoke cigarettes without retribution. It is no different than a Masai boy receiving his first spear to hunt and his initiation into manhood by killing a deer in the wild. It was rare to see a boy wearing long pants in those days except a working few. Those that did were called *forced ripe* (child acting like an adult) and looked upon with suspicion and sometimes ridiculed. I felt uncomfortable as I tucked in my blue short-sleeved poplin shirt and fastened my red clip-on tie. I wore a pair of bumper shoes as they were called with black felt top and thick rubber soles that were bought from Bata Shoe Store in New Amsterdam.

"I got to wear shoes now," I pleaded with my mother.

At least she did not hesitate to give me the cash of $2.95 (Guyana) that it cost for my very first pair of shoes. Countless times I looked in the mirror on the hallway wall, checking and combing my hair and fixing my tie so that everything was in place. I walked down the steps to comments of "eh, eh," "hmmmm," "wow," and everyone stopped to watch. When I stepped onto the street, our next-door neighbor and her little children were on their veranda with smiling faces.

"You look really nice, teach," our next-door neighbor commented.

I nodded and waved to her son who had come down closer to the street to get a better look. My mother and little brothers and sisters were lined up on the stairs also looking on proudly. I walked nervously toward Reliance S. H. School. It was only two streets away across Canje road, but it felt like forever. I must have counted every step, looking down at my shoes and pants folds swaying in the wind, and only glanced up occasionally.

Reliance S. H. School was a short walk from my home at Reliance Settlement.

Reliance S. H. School, East Canje, Berbice.

I spent over seven years here as a primary school teacher.

Greeted warmly by four other new teachers, who were also starting out on this day, we had gathered by the front door. Several young pupils said "Good morning, sir" as they passed. Being called sir was respectful, and I liked the sound of that right away. This was going to be all right, I thought. For a while, the nervousness subsided. I was not alone now. The scrutiny I expected was far from it. There were children everywhere, smiling faces, girls in green and white uniforms and boys in khaki pants and white shirts. Cries of laughter echoed from the school yard on both sides. Smartly dressed male teachers in white shirt and ties and female teachers in skirts and blouses gathered in groups by the entrance.

I was no longer conscious of my long pants, and it all seemed so natural. It was the entrance in a new world to me.

"Morning, Mr. Singh," I said along with the other teachers as we greeted the headmaster upon his arrival.

"Good morning," he replied cheerfully.

There was bright smile on his face. His tall six-foot stature with briefcase in hand and the firm handshake made a lasting impression. With the rest of the rookie teachers, I followed him toward his desk on the stage and to a start of an exciting career in teaching. As the years rolled by, he would become my mentor, confidant, and adviser, together with Mr. Ramphal Singh, the deputy headmaster, and Mr. Richnauth, the senior master. I would end up spending the next seven years under their patronage and guidance at Reliance S. H. School. These were the best years of my life. They were the years of my stunning innocence, falling in love, and growing into adulthood. I basked in glory and experienced the agony of failures and disappointments. They were the years that molded my character and outlook in life. The veins of experiences still run through me today, and all my actions tend to radiate from there. I can say without equivocation that teaching was the stepping-stone to my successes in later years. It made me a more mature individual and promoted an independent thought process from the very start. I was reminded of the many Guyanese doctors, lawyers, and politicians who were once school teachers before gravitating to their professions. Then there were the thousands who immigrated to Canada, England, and the United States who managed to launch successful careers with their beginnings as school teachers. Teaching certainly helped me in more ways than I care to think. As a teacher, I learned to assert myself and overcome the shyness. I took extra care to pronounce words correctly and to speak in full sentences with correct grammar. Courtesy and cordiality to others became commonplace, showing respect and always valuing the wisdom of elders. I became bolder and ventured to explore the secrets and the knowledge to understand the world around me.

As a pupil teacher, my agenda was laid out. I must follow the traditional path of four years as an understudy to the senior teachers. The first, second, third, and fourth year teacher's exams must be passed each year in succession in order to advance to a teacher's third-class status and then to a permanent teaching position. Failure of the same year twice meant the teaching position would be terminated. This was similar to the journeyman or apprenticeship system of the city and guilds that was the product of the long-established British system of education. However, the standards, exams, and syllabus were administered locally by the Ministry of Education. No certificates were handed out, and a teacher's status was updated and registered each year by the headmaster at the Ministry of Education. Salaries increased incrementally with the passing of each year's teacher's exam. My starting salary was $60 (Guyana) per month as a pupil teacher. In 1962, one Guyana dollar was the equivalent of one Canadian or U.S. dollar. First year teachers advance to $65, second year to $78, third year to $92, and fourth year to $108. For the first nine months, I did not receive any salary. I had to wait with the rest of the new teachers. There was a general strike among the government workers, and the disruptions created chaos within the Ministry of Education.

Students who attended the secondary or high schools prepared for the Cambridge School Certificate or the General Certificate of Education (GCE). The GCE was more prestigious, and the exams, syllabuses, and standards were set by the University of London in England. Students in England wrote the same exams and were the mainstay of educational systems in most British Commonwealth countries. A fee was paid to take these exams, and it was open to anyone. Any combination of subjects could be taken at any time, and the exams were held twice per year in July and January. A pass in any five subjects at the ordinary level including English and mathematics was the equivalent of a third-class teacher with a salary of $108 per month. Most students at the high schools aimed for this distinction. Five subjects at the O level and two subjects at the advanced A Level was the equivalent of grade 13 in Canada and grade 12 in the United States. Reliance S. H. School had teachers in varied degrees of qualifications. Only two teachers held third-class positions by virtue of their GCE passes and were graduates of Berbice Educational Institute in New Amsterdam, a privately run high school. None of the teachers had a pass in any subject at the A level. I was at the lowest end on the totem pole with my PTA.

In July 1963, I passed the first year teacher's exam and the College of Preceptors Certificate in seven subjects with several distinctions. Both exam results were announced within the same week.

I felt great, and everyone was taking notice. The adulation poured in from all corners. I began to think I was brilliant. A lot of things were changing in my lifestyle, and my head was swelling too big with all the complements that came my way from Mr. Outarsingh and Mr. Ramphal Singh and others. I decided to skip the teacher's second year exam and signed up to write the third year exam in 1964. A feeling of overconfidence played heavily in the halfhearted efforts that I attended to my studies. I had purchased a brand new Raleigh sports bicycle from Chu Kang Store for $128 on an installment plan paying $10 per month. Most afternoons would find me hanging out by Rajmahal Cinema or riding along Canje road *liming* with others teachers and friends from the neighborhood. Sometimes it was a trip to the movies at Globe Cinema in New Amsterdam. The gallivanting took its toll, and I got distracted from studying.

Then came the drinking. It started gradually as I succumbed to the peer pressures of friendship, wanting to belong and have fun together. It was one Banks beer here and one Banks beer there as I hung out at different cake shops and beer parlors throughout Canje and New Amsterdam. I loved the feeling of getting high and the false self-confidence that prevailed when the alcohol numbed the brain. Saturdays would find me with a bunch of other teachers and friends at the Paradise Bar in New Amsterdam. We would start out with whoever could afford a quarter or half bottle of Russian Bear rum and Coke and then progressed to full bottles complete with roast pork as snacks.

It always seemed to start with none of us claiming to have any money. By the time we got high and in the full swing of our inexcusable exuberance and idiotic behavior, the cash flowed freely from secret pockets inside the pants and the inside of shoes. By late afternoon, I staggered to ride home on my bicycle. I don't think I was an alcoholic although I may have been close to it. I never got into any trouble, found in the gutter or any of those horrific things that become an alcoholic. I just enjoyed the drinking on some weeknights and especially on weekends. There was not much else to do. I no longer played cricket, missing my opportunity to advance to any higher level, after having found myself in a new circle of friends and drinking buddies.

When the results of the third year exam was announced in September 1964, I had failed. It was devastating news. The pit in my stomach sank to its lowest level. The cruelty in which my hallowed world collapsed sobered me to a frightening new reality. All the good times that came with the luster and luck suddenly vanished in thin air. Embarrassed to show myself in the

Children at play in the school yard at Reliance S. H. School.
No amenities existed except a fountain for drinking water.

streets, I stopped hanging out with the crowd and crawled back into my secured shell and loneliness. I heard the remarks and the snickering from some that I was too wild and spent too much time chasing the girls. It shook me up a great deal, and I began to question my ability. Failure of this exam a second time and I would be out of teaching for good. I could not let this happen and face such a prospect and the humiliation. I was a changed person overnight and vowed not to fail another exam again.

I became a loner, keeping to myself most of the time, and exercised self-discipline. The gallivanting stopped when I began to concentrate on my studies, burning the midnight oil into the wee hours of the morning. In the beginning, I was unable to stay awake for more than an hour to study and ended up sleeping at the helm. I discovered that with a little sleep during the day, I could stay awake all night. I read stories about people practicing mind control and self-discipline and spared no pains to experiment on myself with the little information that crossed my path. The ancient sect of the Rosicrucians had a marked effect on me, and I was certainly influenced by the mystical teachings. I lifted weights to develop the pectorals and biceps of my scrawny frame and then moved the muscles individually at will. I was locked on the notion that a healthy mind is a healthy body, thus control of the muscles meant control of the mind.

I practiced deep breathing rhythms to lower the heart rate and then fall asleep at will. The theory involved lying at rest and thinking of nothing. Every thought is blanked out to the point of only darkness. Even the light penetrating the eyelids is blanked out into darkness. At first the time frame ranges from five to ten minutes, but with regular practice, I had narrowed it down to less than a minute. Every day at lunchtime, I would fall asleep at about 11:45 a.m. and wake up at exactly 12:15 p.m. in time to return to my teaching job. After school was dismissed, I slept again from 3:45 p.m. to 5:30 p.m., falling asleep instantly without a hitch. The mind could be set like a clock if the thoughts were planted. I remembered countless times when I was unable to solve an algebra or geometry problem, thinking of the problem before falling asleep and waking up to a clear solution. Sometimes, it was the simplest of things that were overlooked. In July 1965, I passed the third year teachers' exam and regained my self-esteem and a renewed self-confidence. Failure is good sometimes. It is a self-motivating factor, and success is always around the corner as long as the resolve is not abandoned.

Now I awoke to the sights of bigger and better things. I began to hear more and more about GCE exams from the other teachers. A number of new teachers had joined the staff by then, armed with GCE credentials. It bothered me that the new teachers earned more in salary in spite of the fact that I had already taught for three years. This was not working out, and I disregarded the teacher's exams. A fire was burning inside me now. My salary was only $92 per month. I had to stop and regain my composure and looked on in awe when I learned that one of the new teachers on board, Ms.

Minwatti Tulsi, was a third-class teacher making $108 per month. She was impressive, and all the teachers and children loved her. None of the other female teachers matched her academic caliber or came close. I lingered in the background but aspired for equal footing. She was very pretty, and her family owned a grocery store and cake shop at Canefield Settlement. She had the prettiest legs in high heels that I never failed to admire from a distance. I knew I liked her but was afraid to start up a conversation. I did not know what to say. She was way out of my league, but I was certain that I wanted to match her qualifications.

In June 1966, I signed up for five subjects at the GCE O-level. I passed four subjects—Literature, Scriptures, History, and Geography. I got a failing grade in English.

In January 1967, I signed up for five more subjects. I passed all five subjects—English, Mathematics, Economics, Biology, and Human Anatomy/ Physiology and Hygiene. That instantly gave me a third-class teacher status. By this time, passing at nine subjects was more than any other teacher in the Canje district schools. My salary jumped to $166 per month. I realized that everyone was stunned. Mr. Outarsingh glorified my achievements, and Mr. Ramphal Singh thought I was a genius in the making. I basked in the attention I was getting.

In January 1968, I went on to write three subjects—Geography, Economics, and Economic History—at the advanced level. Mr. Ramphal Singh thought that I was crazy to attempt this level so soon. He was concerned that I was taking on too much in three subjects. I paid no heed, and by the time I wrote the exams, I was very versed in the subject matter. I passed geography only at the advanced level and was given an O-level pass in the other two subjects. I knew I answered the questions well because I knew the subject matter but was unable to express the ideas fully.

I explored alternative ways to read and analyze issues beyond the textbooks on economic and related topics, following Dr. Cheddi Jagan's columns in the *Mirror Newspaper* that were published weekly. He was premier of British Guiana in the 1950s and opposition leader after the 1964 elections. I found his articles and ideas on economic theory very stimulating and convincing. The topics he covered were in line with my studies, and I adopted his style of explaining the issues in economics and politics affecting the country. The columns became my most priced source of information, and I gobbled up every word. The correspondence courses I took from Wolsey Hall College in Oxford, England, proved invaluable. Also, the costs of books and materials were a strain on my salary.

In June 1968, I passed Economics and Economic History at the advanced level. At this point, I was the most qualified teacher in any of the schools in Canje, holding ten subjects at the ordinary level and three subjects at the advanced level. Only a handful of other individuals at that time had a pass in one subject at the advanced level in the Canje area. I was at the apex of my game. The method was a simple one. I collected the exam papers on each subject from the past five years from the Ministry of Education in New Amsterdam. I had found out by accident that these old exam papers were kept there and the education officer was more than happy to let me go through the stacks of boxes in the back room to find them. I studied the texts and made notes in point form to answer all the questions in the exams for the last five years on the subject. I was pleased to recognize that more than half of the questions were repeated in each exam, some in each successive year and some in alternate years. If I could answer all the questions then, I was certain to answer the questions that repeated themselves. With all the material covered on the subject, I was in a good position to pass the exams. It worked every time for me and in every subject. My only drawback was trying to grasp the concepts on my own. There was no one with the expertise or background knowledge on the subjects I tackled such as economics and world geography.

The teaching staff at Reliance S. H. School (1968).

Outarsingh (headmaster) back row fifth from left.

Ramphal Singh (deputy headmaster) middle row fifth from left.

Ricknouth (senior master) middle row third from left.

Minwatti Ramsaroop (my wife [pregnant]) first row second from left.

I am second from left in the back row.

After holding back all the odds stacked against me, I knew many of my friends and fellow teachers from the school district were stunned while Mr. Ramphal Singh and Mr. Outarsingh grappled to explain my performance. Mr. Ramphal Singh thought I had natural ability and assured me that I could do well in any field of studies. Mr. Outarsingh once mentioned that I was more cunning and that I always looked for shortcuts to problem solving. He thought that I was disagreeable many times because I challenged his assertions, and that was a good trait for any high-achiever. I was not so sure although I knew I was more self-opinionated and asked the more difficult and embarrassing questions. There was so much that I did not understand. Whatever the case may have been, I held their views and opinions in high regard and always followed their example. Both had read books voraciously and widely at that, and I tapped into this rich source of knowledge at every chance. During recess, Mr. Ramphal Singh would send me to get any volume from the set of encyclopedias from the school's library. The encyclopedia set and another hundred or so children's storybooks were all that made up the library and were donated by Mr. Outarsingh. He had brought the children's storybooks from the United States when he went to Indiana University on a government scholarship to study visual aids in teaching. I used to turn to any page and ask Mr. Ramphal Singh to tell me something about a subject heading. I was always amazed that he had some knowledge about the heading whether it was a place, a person, or other subject matter. With words, he was equally stunning with their usage and meanings. At times it appeared that he may have memorized the entire Oxford dictionary.

I emulated the "browsing" technique as he called it. The idea was not to read everything fully. Looking at the word and then scan for a phrase or sentence that said something about the word was all that was required. Every time that word was seen again, another bit of information would be picked up. If the word was interesting, there was the tendency to read on in more depth. Over time, every concept became wedged into the photographic neurons for quick recall. It became a habit of mine, and in my spare time, I always had one volume of the *World Book Encyclopedia* on my desk, flipping the pages. A person with such broad general knowledge was my idea of an educated person, and I am yet to run into another individual of similar caliber.

Mr. Outarsingh was more philosophical in his approach and always spoke in parables or used a story to explain his point of view. He knew something about anything and everything and always had an opinion. At least that's how I saw it, in his attempts to answer some of my inquisitive questions. My standard-four classroom was next to the stage where he had his desk and a bird's-eye view of all the classes on the lower level. Quite often, we were engaged in conversations about subjects unrelated to teaching, and it provided me the opportunities to pick his brain. It was rare if I did not learn something from his insightful and fluid expressions of opinions, showing a wise fortitude of knowledge. He sparked my interest to go abroad to further my studies after I had passed the GCE ordinary level subjects. His consistent advice to me was that Guiana had no future for me.

"This country is not for you," he used to say. He was the only one that I knew who had a firsthand experience on what it was like to study at a university abroad, and I hungered to listen to the times he spent at Indiana University learning visual aids in teaching. He exercised his stern discipline on all—students, teachers, neighbors, and his family. Some disliked his harsh ways. In spite of this, no one could argue about his dedication to the education of children at Reliance S. H. School. He was instrumental in the growth of enrollment and the high standards of academic achievements. He had transformed Reliance S. H. School into one of the best in the Canje district. His crowning achievement was the enormous effort in raising funds that built two extensions to the school to accommodate the growing enrollment, which had topped over four hundred pupils. He organized raffles, supervised trips for students and teachers to visit an Indian reservation

at Oreala up the Corentyne River, and solicited gifts from merchants in
New Amsterdam to be used as prizes in the raffles. I was more than eager to
participate with the rest of the teachers in these drives. Those were wonderful
times for me as a teacher at Reliance S. H. School.

*Always a lesson to learn from my mentors, Mr. Ramphal Singh and Mr. Ricknauth,
during a recess period a short distance at the back of the school.*

Their influences on me were positive in many respects, and like
everything else, I regretted to say that there was a down side also. I was in their
company too many times and followed in their path of drinking. With other
teachers and friends, we found ourselves hopping from bars and whorehouses
in New Amsterdam to Number Two to Albion and Rose Hall Village and as
far as Skeldon on the Corentyne coast. They were so well-known at the rum
shops everywhere that the owners stayed open all night to accommodate
them, at least when I was among their company. The next morning, the
drinking continued. On some Friday nights, I never bothered to return
home. There were many that had a name for us—*Rum*-phal, *Rum*-naught,
and *Rum*-saroop or dem *Rum*-boogies.

In spite of all my turbulent years at Reliance S. H. School, I can say without equivocation that I was a fairly good teacher. At least I thought so at the time. I tried my best in the circumstances, given how little I knew and how little I was prepared by instructions. I believed firmly that my teaching skills were developed more so from maturing as an individual and from firsthand experiences in the art of observation. I taught the lower classes from first standard to fourth standard and biology in form 1 and form 2 in my final year. I taught fourth standard for most of the years at Reliance S. H. School. It was not until I had studied psychology, sociology, and philosophy at university level that I truly came to realize what teaching was all about. Knowing the subject matter to impart was one thing, but getting the students to understand and assimilate that knowledge was more of the challenge. Knowing the psychological makeup of a child at different ages and the socioeconomic factors that aid in learning lends itself to good teaching skills. I looked back with remorse at my uninformed and unskilled methods to teach children. I was disgusted at myself, thinking that whipping some of the children, which I did, would benefit them in any way to learn. I thought the best teachers were those who have matured in age and have children themselves. A six-unit course in the social sciences such as sociology, psychology, and philosophy should be a must for any teacher in elementary school. In my opinion, every student should not be taught the same thing at the same time. Individual attention is the best policy considering that each child is different in ability and upbringing. I know now that I would be a better teacher at any level if I had to do it all over again.

Preoccupied with a deep urgency to be successful at my own exams, I got buried in my own selfishness to study at every spare moment and neglected to think through the teaching process. There were bright and cheerful pupils. It was a pleasure to watch the eagerness and insatiable appetite they expressed to digest the new knowledge thrust upon their innocent minds. Yet it was not until the final months of my teaching career that I began to realize the many diverse and subdued faces that yearned for that little extra attention and personal guidance. It was my failure to recognize these faces that showed shades of tiredness and hunger and the shyness of those at the rear of the classes who cunningly avoided eye contact because they were afraid of their ability. Then there were the obvious signs that were missed: the sad eyes that pointed to stresses at home, the twitching of the lips that pointed to nervousness, the tattered and soiled clothing that pointed to a lack of close parental supervision, and the haunting motionless look that pointed to an inner desire for simple love and affection. To a few, I may have been successful in imparting knowledge as a teacher should. To others, I may have succeeded in motivating them to aspire to a better future, but I was resigned to sadness for those I failed to set a spark. I knew I should have done better. I may have been a role model to many other young minds. This I will never know. What surprised me most was to find out years later that I was an envy to many of my peers. This I could not fully understand.

In hindsight, I knew that as a teacher I could never use a whip again on any child. I saw no reason for it, and no one would be happier when it becomes illegal in all schools in Guyana and elsewhere. From my own experiences, I knew the fear it created in me and the obvious hindrance to a free expression of thoughts and ideas. It was no wonder that I hardly spoke up in a classroom setting or asked questions even when I did not understand. I am aware that corporal punishment in schools takes on different forms, but I am more concerned with the aspect of whipping, flogging, caning, or paddling. The infliction of physical pain is no more than child abuse and degrading to any child with the consequence of numerous psychological effects such as anxiety and lowered self-esteem. How deeply it had permeated in all schools is alarming. With its roots in the British Isles, it had become common practice throughout the British Commonwealth since colonial times. It is acceptable in places like Indonesia, Saudi Arabia, and South Korea. Most astonishing to me was to find out that even in the

United States of America, corporal punishment still exists in the schools. The USA prides itself in such high ideals of freedom and democracy and all the decency of basic human rights, yet it allows this adherent practice to continue. In 2002, Pennsylvania became the twenty-eighth state to ban the practice and make it illegal.

Apparently, corporal punishment is still legal in twenty-two states. Why? The case is made for its continuation because challenges to its legality have been unsuccessful in the courts. There is very little reprimand to teachers with no liability on their part. Foremost is that the power of corporal punishment often rests with the school boards, and many prefer to keep it as a tool in their favor for control of unruly pupils. There are still many proponents of corporal punishment. They believe that children must be punished for genuine wrongdoing such as lying, cheating, stealing, bullying, and the expressions of unpopular ideas. Corporal punishment sends the message that such behavior is unacceptable.

However, on the other side of the issue, there are many alternative considerations of punishment such as detention, community service, extra schoolwork, and others. Teachers must foster an atmosphere of respect between pupils and themselves and find ways to communicate more effectively. Resorting to the cane is not the answer. It seems that only bad teachers resort to corporal punishment, and how much does it take to know that it is just wrong? In our society today, there are laws against punishment of this sort to animals, prisoners, or military personnel. Yet we do it to school children. It's barbaric. I can only apologize deeply to all my pupils for my horrible mistake and poor judgment.

CHAPTER 5

At the Crossroads

Love is the strongest force the world possesses, and yet it is the humblest imaginable.

—*Mahatma Gandhi*

S ometimes, the simplest of decisions for me were the most difficult to make, especially when choices had to be made that concerned the future. The uncertainty of future events always created an emotional tug-of-war that played out in my mind. This could be painful at times. After a decision was made, it seemed that cognitive dissonance would set in, and an imbalance was created within the thought process. Anything negative about the decision might enhance the imbalance. Only supporting information became crucial to restore the harmony of emotions and to satisfy the feeling that the right choice was made. I have realized that without this harmony, life can be a cruel teacher at times. Only the imaginary world, in a crystal ball, made decisions any easier.

There were many times when I wished I knew more about the choices I had made. I shuddered at the countless other times when the outcome was far from what I expected. Such were the marvels of my life experiences and the lessons that were learned. Usually it was the hard way with many failures. I had my share of uncertain twists and turns and the pains of having made some bad choices. Then there were the educated guesses that diminished the uncertainty and prompted a sense of confidence, but these were only a few. Imagine the broken spirit when the guesses went the other way and all hope collapsed. My only recourse was always that gut feeling in me that served as a premonition to every move and a faint awareness of a sixth sense that catapults a decision from within.

Being at the crossroads, I wanted to do things in a different way, almost to the point of standing out as being unique in some activity. To this end I used my ability to my advantage. Keeping an eye on the future, trying to imagine myself ten years ahead in time where I could see clearly, I carved out a definite course of action. I struggled to ignite and set ablaze a spark to go abroad to study, and the thought of a better lifestyle consumed me. In the meantime, I succumbed to let life roll on and let destiny take its own course. My conscience was my only guide most times.

On August 11, 1968, I got married at age twenty-two to the former Ms. Minwatti Tulsi. It culminated in more than four years of courting since our first meeting one night at a music fair at Rose Hall Welfare Center grounds. She was the only one who had made such a fusible impression on me. I remembered how impressed I was at her successes at the GCE exams and the easy manner in which she carried herself. Her disposition was always dignified, and I supposed that came from an upward upbringing and family background. There was definitely something about her. Soon, we were in love, and our feelings blossomed into an inseparable bond. There was a natural physical attraction between us, and the electricity grew stronger with every passing moment. The relationship started on shaky grounds though, and I always thought that her parents did not find me a suitable match for her. It was only natural when poor boy meets rich girl. Her mother was the daughter of one of the richest merchants in Canje, and her uncle was the first and only doctor from the area. Her father owned a truck and ran a lumber retail business in addition to a cake shop and grocery store. Like all parents, I was sure that they wanted the best for their daughter and discouraged her from any involvement with a shady character like me. For a while, things were on the rocky side. I assumed that it was my successes at the GCE exams that changed her father's behavior toward me. Suddenly, I was welcomed, and her father was proud to tell his friends of how many subjects I had passed at the GCE exams.

Within a few months, an engagement ceremony was arranged between our two families. It was interesting to note that an engagement was not the same as in Western countries. As was customary in those days, the father, accompanied by a handful of friends and relatives, presented gifts to me as a form of dowry. At that point, a ring was also presented to me as a symbol of the bond between myself and his daughter. It was not until the actual marriage ceremony, some months later, that it was my turn to present the bride with a wedding ring. Everyone thought that we were already secretly married from the way were carrying on during the past four years that we courted. We stayed at school until late in the afternoons before I would take her home on my bicycle. On Saturdays I stayed by her home talking all day. In the afternoons we would go for bicycle rides to visit Mr. Outarsingh's house at Sheet Anchor Turn Village. Sometimes we went to the movies at the Globe Cinema in New Amsterdam. These were our only outlet for entertainment and they were happy times.

I was contended and was at peace in mind and heart. The relationship provided a safe haven for my undivided concentration on my studies at night. Though love is a two-sided sword, one side propelled me to achieve higher goals in my relentless quest to be on top of the academic ladder. I was fortunate I did not have to face the other side.

The ceremony was according to Hindu rites and customs with the usual preparations and fanfare months before. It was an elaborate wedding by any standard with almost everyone invited from Reliance and Canefield settlements. I was a king for that day. We had the utmost respect for the institution of marriage and the sanctity of the traditional values of East Indian culture. I think it was more so to please our parents and to hold our heads high. Our wedding was beautiful, with nonstop rituals and ceremonies that went on for a week. Some of them were just frivolous, much to my dislike, although I was sure there was some significance in there somewhere. In spite of it, I never questioned but rather relished the attention and honor that was bestowed.

Friday night was reserved for *matticore*. I was not allowed to leave the house. My body had to be anointed with dye (turmeric) several times by a family member. Then the usual singing and dancing to the rhythm of *tassa* and *drums* followed with the women taking a parade down the street to *dig dirt*, the symbolism of which I have not grasped. The festivities continued on Saturday with the cooking of an enormous quantity of food to feed the guests. The variety of vegetarian foods ranged from rice to pumpkin, *aloo curry* (potatoes), *bagie* (spinach), *dal* (yellow split peas), and the more important cooking of the *puree* (a paper thin flour pita deep fried in oil). During the day, the *puran* leaves (water lily leaves) were gathered from trenches wherever they could be found in abundance. All food was served on these broad leaves, and it was an art form to eat on them using only the fingers. We had hired a jukebox to dish out the latest in dance music, and the merriment went on late in the night. I remembered a fistfight that had broken out in the yard when a couple of guys had a few too many drinks of rum. This was not unusual, and they were quickly escorted out. I could not take part in any of festivities, though I did have a drink of rum with a few friends without anyone noticing. In the meantime, the same sort of activities were taking place at the bride's residence.

Sunday was special for me as all attention was focused toward making me feel like a king for that day. There was not much that I had to do from being given a bath early in the morning to getting dressed in my *jura-jama* costume or *Sherwani* and wearing my *mour* or crown.

Baraat party escorted by my father, being greeted by bride's parents, family, and friends on my wedding day.

I revered the part as I felt like a king. In traditional Hindu culture, the wedding embraces the ideology of uniting two separate beings into one spiritual identity in a relationship for life. The wedding ceremonies began with a procession or *baraat*. My friends and family accompanied me in hired cars to the home of the bride's residence for the marriage ceremony. For some, trailing behind in bicycles or walking the couple of miles distance was all in the fun. There was much merriment with dancing and music on the way. With the performance of *aarti* (blessings), I was greeted warmly and welcomed by the bride's parents. The entire wedding party was ushered under the *mandap* or *maro* (bamboo tent) where the marriage ceremony was solemnized. The Mandap housed the sacred fire which represented the presence of God. Decorated and adorned with flowers and balloons, the Mandap became the temple for the union of the bride and groom.

The pundit called for the bride accompanied by her parents and family to sit next to me. A white shawl or curtain separated us to signify our two separate and distinct lives. The pundit conducted the ceremony, chanting verses from the Vedas (Hindu religious texts) while he directed us to perform religious rituals and take our sacred vows. The pundit performed *Lakshmi pooja* or prayers. Lakshmi is the goddess of wealth, and in a Hindu household, the daughter symbolizes Lakshmi as the prime wealth of the household. In essence, the bride's parents were giving their wealth, their daughter, to the groom. To finalize this gift-giving gesture, the white shroud was removed, and the bride's parents place the hands of the bride into the hands of the groom. The joining of the hands sealed the bond of their consent and to signify that the bride and groom will live together as one body, mind, and soul. The ends of our wedding garments were tied together to symbolize this sacred union.

Prayers with rice and *ghee* (purified butter) were offered to the sacred fire or Agni, which has a purifying influence and serves as the divine witness to us taking our marriage vows. We walked around the fire seven times to solemnize the wedding process. My wife led the first three rounds, and then I led the last four rounds. Each time around the fire, we stopped to step on a *sila* or stone to signify that the marriage would be as strong as the stone. In Hindu philosophy, the seven steps represent the seven virtues that would bring us together for seven lives. Each of the seven steps has special meaning or blessings as the pundit explained:

- to share in the responsibilities of home and children
- to develop physical, mental, and spiritual powers to protect our family
- to live happily and take care of each other
- to acquire knowledge and harmony by love and respect
- to be faithful and raise strong virtuous children

- to cherish each other in sickness and in health and longevity of our love
- to remain lifelong partners by this wedlock and true friends for life

After the final round, my wife moved from the right to my left side to be closer to my heart and to signify the completion of the marriage.

Among some touching moments were placing *Sindoor* (vermillion) on the part of the bride's hair as a form of blessings and for her good fortune. The wedding ring was exchanged, and this became the cornerstone of the marriage for the rest of our lives. In addition, gifts were exchanged, and we received gifts and well wishes from the guests present.

I still remembered one of the things that stayed with me over the years since I hardly paid any attention to what the pundit was preaching in his infinite wisdom. He looked me straight in the eye as I placed the ring in my wife's finger.

"You see how this ring is round? It has no beginning and no ending," he exclaimed. "It's the cycle of all life," he continued to explain. "So like this marriage, let it have no beginning and no end. It is only a gold ring, but let the significance of what this ring represents guide you at all times."

There was no such thing as a honeymoon since it was customary for the bride to return home to her parents on the day after the wedding. I had no reluctance or objections to any of the ceremonies that consummated the marriage until much later in my life when I became skeptical of the whole situation. In spite of our long courtship and constant togetherness until the day we got married, we did not engage in any premarital sexual activities that were common to Western societies. Rather, our love flourished more with a backdrop from the realm of Indian movies. A gentle kiss, the serenade of a love song, the holding of hands, or a simple smile without words that said what was in the heart.

A happy day and a turn of a new leaf on August 11, 1968.

It was not until Nanda was born exactly nine months later on May 31, 1969, that I seriously considered moving out of the country. It was amazing what the scent of a newborn baby held in the arms or a touch of the tender hands and feet did to my concepts of the world. For me it was like a sudden transformation. Everything around me was seen in a different light, and my visions stretched far and wide. My father was right when he said that a man never becomes a man until he sees his first child. Idle thoughts and daydreams gave way to an urgency to boil water or gather food or build a house. I reasoned that it must be the same instincts that propagated our ancestors from early cavemen to provide for the extended clan. In mothers the maternal instinct to protect and feed the offspring also kicks in. Instantly I turned sour on the whole traditional customs that was permeating my life. The elder folks had consulted the local revered Hindu priest or pundit to get a reading about the child's astrological forthcomings.

"The pundit say it's bad luck for you to see the child," the elders said to me.

In order to appease everyone, for the next four days, I had to keep away from mother and child. I was disillusioned but went along anyway, not questioning the elders. Then there were the readings from the Hindu books and scriptures that said that the child must be named in a certain way.

"The pundit read the baby's planet," they pointed out. "You should name this child with a *na* in her name," they suggested, "Or something like that. The name must get the word *na* in it," they insisted.

I took their advisement and listened with contempt, but my mind was already made up contrary to all the names suggested. Since I was not allowed to see my wife or child, I had gone one afternoon to the movies at Rajmahal Cinema. An Indian movie, *Jab Jab Phool Khile*, was showing starring Nanda, one of the most popular actresses of the era in Hindi movies. I was entranced with one of the most enchanting love songs of this movie that I had ever heard. I loved her free-spirited style of charm, independence, and grace, and this I thought was the style I envisioned of my daughter. Before anyone had any more suggestions, I had already registered the name Nanda Devi, meaning majestic and sacred, at the local dispensary. I wanted her to have a short and simple name that is easily pronounced and spelt. I had a feeling that she would not be living in Guyana for the rest of her days, and I did not want her to have the same problems that I was having with my name. In Canada and the USA, people like short names like Tom and Dick and Mary and Linda. At the estate's dispensary, where all births in the district are registered, I made sure that the clerk spelled my name correctly on the birth certificate.

I did not care much for the religious beliefs either and the burdensome rituals they professed at each occasion. I never went to any church or pray at the Hindu temple. Celebrating various Hindu festivals were wonderful times, and I participated fully. In March the festival of Phagwah was celebrated with much fanfare and was a joy for the entire family. Also known commonly as the burning of Holi, it was attributed to the burning of Holika, the female demon who represented evil. According to Hindu mythology, the king of demons had decreed that all residents stop worshipping their gods and start praying to him. His own son, Prahlada, refused to obey the king since he was a devout follower of Lord Vishnu, the protector, as manifested in his divine powers in preserving peace and truth. Being angry with his son over the situation, the king of demons made several attempts to kill his son. He failed each time. Finally the decision was made to have his son sit next to his sister, Holika, and be burned on a pyre. The demoness Holika could not be consumed by the fire because a shawl that she wore over her head protected her. Prahlada readily accepted his father's orders and prayed to Vishnu to keep him safe. As the story unfolded, when the fire was lit, the shawl flew over to cover Prahlada and Holika was burned to death instead. Prahlada was protected by the shawl and remained unharmed. The next day, the people celebrated the destruction of the demoness Holika and the evil she represented. The tradition continued in much of India and wherever Indians settled around the world. In British Guiana it became a national holiday. In my community, the pyre was usually set up near our house, by the canal, with contributions of wood from most residents. As a boy, I remembered searching the neighborhood for scraps of wood and cutting down small branches of trees for the fire. The next day's celebrations comprised throwing water on one another or a dab of mud during the morning session. In the afternoon, it changed to throwing powder or *abeer*, a red liquid, over the body. Men and young boys dressed in white shirts followed in a procession down the streets, chanting and singing to the beat of drums and brass cymbals. My shirt turned red by afternoon, and it took days for the abeer stains to wash off from my skin. Nonetheless, it was one of the best celebrations each year in which I have participated.

In late October, we celebrated Deepavali. Shortened to Diwali, it is best known as the festival of lights and has its roots imbedded in the Hindu scriptures. Written many centuries ago, the Ramayana traces the epic story of Lord Rama, who was exiled for fourteen years in the forest to honor the wish his father had made to his stepmother. When the people of Ayodhya heard that Lord Rama was returning home to take up his rightful place as the succeeding king, they lit small ghee lamps (Deepa) in rows (awali) to light up his path in the darkness and show him the way to the kingdom.

I remembered the preparations my mother made in which all of us in the family took part. The house and steps were washed and the yard cleaned of all debris. White mud was used to fashion small deepas and left to dry in the hot sun. In the evening the deepas were filled with a small amount of ghee or oil and white cotton cloth was twirled into a wick. Lighting the deepas was the fun part. I must confess that Deepavali was always a beautiful evening as I walked the streets to see which house had the most deepas lit up.

I have always felt that the practice of religious festivals and ceremonies comforted the soul and brought peace of mind, having no objections to those who practiced their religion according to their beliefs. I was born a Hindu, and a Hindu I have remained. My parents were very religious and lived according to the long-established traditions that had developed into our culture. They showed their faith with periodic *Jandi* or *Pooja* ceremonies officiated by local pundits and abstained from eating meat or fish on Fridays. I married according to Hindu customs to please them and everyone. My firm beliefs were that they were wonderful, but I have seen the wickedness and the corruption of the pundits that preyed upon the fears of the mostly uneducated Indian population. I didn't think that performing a *Jandi* and making offerings to the gods would bring salvation to anyone. It was more of an opportunity for the pundits to earn a living from the numerous gifts they collected. I never understood why money had to be placed at every turn, only to be collected by the pundits afterward. It was no different in the Christian churches either. There may be some substance in making peace with yourself and an expression of living a righteous life. It's not that I don't believe in God. In fact I have a strong faith in God, more so than the countless who just show up in church on Sundays or did a *Pooja* once a year. I talk to God all the time. It's all in my mind and in my spiritual beliefs. I thought that religion was more of a one-on-one conference with my chosen God and conducted in silent contemplation in a solitary environment. In my many times of crisis and need for guidance, I have called upon Lord Rama, Lord Krishna, Lord Ganesh, Jesus Christ, Gautama Buddha, Mohammad, and Moses among others.

This was one area I decided to leave for my children to make their own decisions based on their own individual upbringing. I wanted them to find their own meaning and listen to their own hearts and their own inner strengths to find god or some form of spirituality. I don't think any child should have God handed down to them as if it was a god-given right of the parents to do so. My firm belief at the time was to let them be of age to reason and then teach them the philosophy of all the religions in the schools system. Then let them make up their own minds. I am sure there would be less hatred around the world today and the endless wars that took so many lives because of it.

In my lifetime I have seen the destruction and loss of life because of religion, and in those years, there have been many needless wars. Since 1947, in India and Pakistan, the Hindus and the Muslims hate one another and have fought several wars with much destruction and loss of lives. They still cannot live in peace with one another, and the hatred continued to spread to communities far beyond their homeland. In British Guiana, it is a miracle that we lived side by side in mutual respect, and there has been almost no incidence of religious conflicts that I could remember. Both of our next-door neighbors were Muslims, and together we celebrated all religious festivities without giving much thought to the difference. I am proud to have grown up in this environment.

Across the Atlantic, in Ireland, the Catholics and the Protestants hate one another and have engaged in terrorist activities against one another for decades. These were Christians killing Christians in the name of slightly different religious beliefs. Even the Pope in all his infinite wisdom and the anointed one chosen to represent Jesus and Christianity failed to quell the violence. The British government did nothing to stop it.

In the Middle East, the Jews in Israel and the Muslims in the neighboring states hate one another. Since the 1948 there have been ongoing hostilities with no end in sight for the near future. Recent incursions of Israel into the Muslim territories of Gaza and the West bank were seen as genocide against the Palestinian people. Nations around the world stood by and did nothing. They continued to take land that did not belong to them in order to build settlements for the influx of Jews from other nations of Europe. It is estimated that 80 percent of these people are known as Khazar Jews, which mean that they have no biblical or historical attachment to Israel. As a result, conflicts flare up constantly as the Palestinians fight back with help from neighboring states for their land. The region has become a breeding ground for religious hatred and unrest. These people carry that hatred everywhere they go, and it has permeated each generation.

In the 1970s in Cambodia, the Khmer Rouge guerrillas and communist revolutionaries seized power, and what followed was a nightmare for its people. All foreigners were expelled from the country, and then began the mass extermination. It was estimated that the Khmer Rouge killed a quarter of the country's population of about ten million in what became known as the killing fields. Religious and ethnic differences were the justification. The world did nothing to stop it.

In the 1980s in Iraq, the Kurds in the northern province were gassed by Saddam Hussein. Entire villages were wiped out while thousands of men, women, and children lay dead in the street and in the homes where they stood. Declassified documents showed that the United States government knew of the atrocities and did nothing to stop it because it was gearing up Iraq for the war with Iran. It all happened because Saddam Hussein disliked the Kurds who were of a different religious faction in the country.

In the 1990s in Bosnia, over two hundred thousand people lost their lives when the breakup of Yugoslavia led to ethnic cleansing of Muslims by the Bosnian Serbs. The media reported extensively on the Siege of Sarajevo, where concentration camps existed with weapons of war and the systematic rape of women. About eight thousand Muslim men and boys were massacred in the town of Srebrenica. Here the conflict was between the Eastern Orthodox Christians as they slaughtered the Muslim Albanians.

In 1994 in Rwanda, the Hutu soldiers of the government massacred their Tutsi countrymen. The United States refused to intervene in the genocide, and the tiny United Nations force was unable to stop the slaughter. Over eight hundred thousand men, women, and children were killed, hacked to death mostly by machetes.

In 2003 in Darfur, the atrocities grew out of a civil war between Sudan's African tribes and the country's Arab-led government. The ethnic cleansing was aimed at eliminating the African tribes of Darfur. It became the first genocide of the twenty-first century, and the world watched the slaughter without intervention. It was estimated that over half of a million people perished.

Most recently, thousands died after the United States invasion of Iraq and the struggles for power there between the Sunni Muslims and Shiite Muslims. They profess to be brothers living side by side, worshipping the same god, yet they strap bombs to their bodies and blow themselves up to kill innocent men, women, and children in a public place. All this madness is done in the name of their religion. Right here in the USA, the white Christians in the Southern Bible states openly express their hatred for Catholics and the blacks and everyone else. The list goes on and on. Yet generations of children from these very people continue to follow sheepishly the religious beliefs and traditions that bind and enslave them to senseless rituals that have no meaning in life. I chose to break away completely from this traditional past of my parents and to set free the next generation in my children to do as they please. The only benchmark I used to justify this was to ask myself if my children were any better or worse. Have they missed something out of life? I can't think of any.

I had visions of moving to the New Amsterdam area and build a concrete house in the suburbs. There would be inside plumbing and electricity and all the conveniences of a modern and higher living standard. I would buy a car to commute to our teaching job. Nanda would attend the private Catholic schools and have the opportunity for an excellent high school education. I would raise ten kids and never have to worry about where their next meal would be coming from. I knew that in time I would be promoted to senior master at the school by the sheer strength of my qualifications and to headmaster someday. I saw the advantages of the combined salary of myself and my wife. We were making comparable wages and, in most cases, more than that of the headmaster or supervisors at the sugar estate or managers at the banks. The future looked good, and I had it all in the palms of my hands. Yet, as fate would have it, it was not meant to be. My thoughts were persuaded elsewhere and by circumstances.

I considered attending the University of Guyana but was not impressed with its slow progress and lack of prestige. It opened in 1963 and began its operations in temporary premises on Queen's College with classes held at nights only. It occupied its permanent site in Turkeyen in 1969 and offered only general degree programmers confined to the arts, natural sciences, and social sciences. Tuition was a nominal one hundred dollars per year. Further, it would mean that I had to seek another teaching job in the Georgetown area or work for the government's civil service. Both of these options were impractical for me at the time. My concept of a university was one with a reputation for academic distinction and world recognition. I envisioned a large campus with a diversified student body. My first choice was London School of Economics in England, which rejected my application and placed me on a waiting list. I understood the competition for a place there.

The city of New Amsterdam at the mouth of the Berbice River

Most Saturdays would find me at the British Consulate office in New Amsterdam perusing the information bulletins and manuals kept on British universities. I applied to most of them and got rejected by every one. I did not have much information with regard to universities in the United States. I had never heard of Harvard or Yale or Princeton universities. I did not know the street addresses of the universities and would just write the name of the town, for example University of Utah, Salt Lake City, Utah, USA. I suspected that many of my requests for application material never got a response. The only one to accept me was Wisconsin State University. I was offered a place in the Pre-medicine program. I quickly ruled this out when I found out that the tuition alone was over $4,000 (U.S.) per year. A unique opportunity was lost to the wind there. I always thought that I had the ability to become a doctor. The importance of available financial support for education would have an indelible mark on my psyche in later years. By now my finances were no more than a few hundred dollars saved. I continued to support my parents financially and, from my salary, was able to set aside savings for my future endeavors.

I had to deal with one very sensitive question that weighed me down for months. My departure from the country would mean the loss of financial support to my parents and would be felt sharply. My father was sick from a stroke and only managed to do some farming. KP had gone the year earlier to further his studies at Kemptville College in Ottawa, Canada, and only Amos was working. My reasoning was a simple one. I supposed that if I was hit by a truck and killed, they would not starve. Life would continue somehow. It takes only four years to earn a degree, but the help afterward that I would be able to provide would be invaluable. With a degree, the opportunities were great in Guyana, and I had plans to return home. What a thrill it would be for me to manage one of the sugar estates especially Rose Hall Estate. Then there were opportunities at the Bank of Guyana and with the offices of the Ministry of Economic Development.

There were high hopes when I applied for a scholarship offered by Booker's sugar estates to qualified children of sugar workers. The scholarship including all expenses was for study in economics in England and a permanent management position in the sugar industry in Guyana. Consumed with enthusiasm and zeal, I attended a prearranged interview with the board of selectors at Booker's headquarters in Georgetown. Only two other candidates were invited for the interview, and I knew my prospects were very good. Comparing notes with the other candidates, we engaged in small talk before the interviews. I definitely had the upper edge with more passes at both the ordinary and advanced level at the GCE exams. The interview went well as I answered politely the questions posed by the four interviewers sitting in a semicircle in front of me. I was pleased when one of the interviewers said that he was impressed with my qualifications.

"What high school did you attend?" he asked further, leaning on his sturdy elbows with knuckles supporting his face.

"I did not attend any high school, sir," I replied.

There was a long pause, and I could see the folds raised on his forehead as he leaned forward.

"How can you pass all these subjects without going to high school?"

I got the feeling that my answer was not convincing. The interview ended abruptly with the usual handshake, and I was showed the door. In a letter received a few days later, my application for a scholarship was politely rejected. I satisfied myself, reasoning that a background education of an elite high school such as Queen's College in Georgetown weighed more prominently on the minds of the interviewers than my self-studies. It was regrettable that they failed to recognize my true potential.

My attention turned to the universities in Canada such as McGill University, University of Toronto, University of Guelph, and McMaster University. My ten subjects at the O level and three subjects at the A level were sufficient for entrance and was the equivalent of grade 13 in Canada (same as grade 12 in the USA).

Only McMaster University in Hamilton, Ontario, accepted me in their BA in Economics program. I was happy to have been admitted, but sadness prevailed in our home circle with the prospects of me leaving the country.

I had everything laid out for a comfortable future in Guyana. Yet I chose to give it all up. All I saw in the distance was Nanda growing up in Canada and attending schools of higher caliber. It bothered me immensely to think that I must send her to a primary school in Guyana where some teacher would want to raise a whip to her. I knew that whoever that teacher was, he or she will definitely find my knuckles embedded in his or her jaws. I had to leave Guyana at any cost.

As I looked back, I had developed a strong belief in education as the only means out of poverty and serfdom. In education, there lies power and the whole world at your feet. It's the only thing that you can have and not have taken away. It matters not where you are and how little you have to start with. Education overcomes the boundaries that separate men by color and breaks down the barriers that separate men by wealth. However, it is not easy to come by. You cannot pick it up from orchards, and you cannot scan the ocean depths for it. Education comes from a wanton need to know what is in front of you because you have already seen what was behind. It takes years of a never-ending effort to succumb to the rigors of hard work, sweat, and tears. In the end it's worth every second that was spent because it was your time and effort. You did not have to depend on anyone or anything, and if there was no money to buy books, there was always the library. You didn't have to be the smartest or possess any exemplary ability. For some it took more time to read and understand than others, but nevertheless, it's the same knowledge that would be gained in the end.

There are no limits and no demarcation for academic subjects either. Education permeates all the trades and hands-on skills in every facet of life. Education takes dedication and persistence. When it is all said and done, the fruits lie in the enjoyment of life and the understanding of the forces that shape the events far and wide. For me the realization was firsthand. No longer did I throw rocks at stray dogs or kill birds with a slingshot. No longer did I get into fistfights or curse because I did not agree with someone else's opinion. As a young man, I had become gentle and kind. Now I understood the world around me and the historical perspective from which they were derived. My quest for a better education and a better life was never ending. My gut feeling was persuasive, and I elected to move on at any cost, knowing that my wife and daughter would follow in due time. On the other hand, there was much fear of the unknown. My limited vision prevailed, and so I pretended I was in the same situation as Christopher Columbus sailing into unchartered territory with only an idea in my mind of what I was looking for. The rest was left to chance, but I had to leave the country.

The final push was my consideration of what the future prospects held for Guyana in the political fronts. As I advanced in my studies, I began to keep a watchful eye on the political pulse of the country.

Television and extensive in-depth news coverage of world events were nonexistent, and the only sources were the local newspapers and magazines. However, I still recalled some of the events that shaped the progress of the country in the 1960s during my tenure as a primary school teacher. The trend was toward social and economic deterioration, loss of individual liberty, and injustice. This alone hastened my efforts to leave the country at all costs.

In the 1961 general election, the People's Progressive Party had won a majority of legislative seats to form the government for the third consecutive time. Dr. Cheddi Jagan, an East Indian dentist educated in the United States, once again became premier with the solid support of the East Indian population, who comprised the majority in the country. In his book *The West on Trial*, Dr. Jagan wrote a detailed account of his fight for Guyana's freedom. One of his main goals was to obtain independence from British rule, and thus began a turbulent period in the country's history. His budget proposals in 1962 that would raise taxes on civil servant salaries and put a tax on some food items created a stir of protests. Riots broke out in the capital city of Georgetown, and the governor had to request British troops from England. A battalion of troops was stationed at the manager's quarters at Rose Hall Estate. It was a rare sight for me to see soldiers for the first time on patrol with riot gear and high-powered guns. The tax proposals were later withdrawn.

Next, the government introduced the Labor Relations Bill in early1963. It was designed to put the ultimate authority for recognition of trade unions into the hands of the Ministry of Labor. Since the Minister of Labor would then make the final decision in cases of arbitration, the bill would in effect put the PPP in a position to control the entire labor movement. There was stiff opposition from the Trade Union Council (TUC), which represented twenty-six unions including the civil service and the Man Power Citizens Association (MPCA), which represented the sugar workers. A general strike was called, and it crippled the country for eighty days from April 18 to July 6, 1963. It affected me severely. With the civil service shut down, my teaching papers were further help up, and I was not able to receive my monthly salary. I eventually had to wait nine months for my first paycheck. The Labor Relations Bill was withdrawn.

In the meantime, the Guyana Agriculture Workers Union (GAWU) was formed to represent the sugar workers and was headed by one of the PPP members. Obviously, the PPP party wanted control of the sugar industry, which would enable it to rule with an iron fist. The government, through the PPP machinery, actively participated toward forcing the sugar workers to withdraw their membership from the recognized MPCA union and join the GAWU union. It failed in its attempt to get enough sugar workers to switch their membership to its roster, for this was the requirement for recognition

Soon afterward, GAWU made a bold move and called for a strike throughout the sugar estates on February 11, 1964, in its determination to get recognition and represent the sugar workers. The enforced work stoppage was disastrous for the entire country. Violence broke out throughout the sugar estates. Hundreds of acres of sugarcane fields were set on fire needlessly. Between March and August of that year, more than 170 people were killed, with buildings burnt and hundreds injured through terrorist activities. The appeal of GAWU was for the East Indians in the sugar estates to break away from the MPCA, reinforcing the racial strife between blacks and Indians. The country was divided along racial grounds. A state of emergency was declared by the governor, which lasted for a few months. I remember the days when a curfew was enforced and we could not congregate in groups in front of the cinema after sundown. Not a day went by without an incident of sabotage or arson and outright murder as strikers and strike breakers clashed.

One incident in particular was close to home. An unusually loud blast woke me up in the early morning hours of April 17, 1964, and I rushed to the source on my bicycle along with others. As it was learned later, Bhagoutie Rambajhan had blown himself up as he attempted to dynamite the strike relief center at Adelphi Village. Apparently, he lit the fuse too early and did not allow himself enough time to scale the wire fence to place the bomb. What I saw was a horrific scene of carnage. His severed head lay in the middle of the road with one leg hanging from a tree across the road, and bits and pieces of body parts that were turning green scattered everywhere. I knew him well as he was a friend of my brother Roland, and they occasionally would go fishing or drink bush rum together. It was suggested that he may have been bribed with a few bottles of rum to place the bomb. This incident and together with the many other incidents of bombing and the use of dynamite suggested strongly that this was the work of sophisticated organizations such as the American CIA and the British Secret Service.

There was no doubt that the British government with cooperation from the United States government played a major role in the affairs of British Guiana. In 1997, secret documents of the United States that recorded the events of the early 1960s were declassified and showed the extraordinary concern of the United States at the prospect of British Guiana becoming another Cuba in the Western Hemisphere. Communications between the United States and the British Foreign Secretary confirmed President Kennedy's worries about Dr. Jagan's and the PPP government's ties to Cuba and the Soviet Union. Dr Jagan, in his writings, speeches, and actions of his party, had given the impression that he was communist oriented. Jagan himself had visited Cuba, and there were Cuban advisers working with the PPP party members. Some of his party members had been to the Soviet Union, and trade opened up with countries like Yugoslavia and Czechoslovakia.

I considered joining the Progressive Youth Organization (PYO), which was the youth arm of the PPP party. I had heard of some teachers and sugar workers who were sent to the training grounds at Success Village on the east coast of Demerara, a collegelike set up for indoctrination into the party's communist ideology. In fact, many were sent off on scholarships to Cuba and Russia. I had explored that possibility but decided against it when I got too involved in passing my own teacher's exams. Later, I would learn that my fourth standard teacher Mr. Sukdeo had gone to Russia to study.

The fear in the United States was that if British Guiana obtained independence from Britain, Jagan would lead British Guiana into a communist, socialist state. This led to the CIA's active involvement in strikes and other measures to bring down the Jagan government (*New York Times*, February 22, 1967, and *Sunday Times*, April 16, 1967).

In the meantime, the Jagan government was engaged in a fierce debate with the British government on the terms and prospect for the independence of British Guiana. At the same time, the violence was escalating as the GAWU strike progressed into months, and this led the British government to take drastic measures. Powers held by the PPP ministers were transferred to the Governor. These were sweeping powers, and on one occasion, it was used to detain PPP activist members and even the deputy premier. The governor now had the power of a dictator and could do almost anything.

The constitution was further eroded when the British foreign secretary handed down his decision to have a general election, held in British Guiana in December1964. This was the prerequisite to independence. However, the election would be held under proportional representation. Under this system, the country would comprise one legislative district. Each party would receive a portion of the fifty-three seats in the legislative assembly, based on the percentage of votes polled. (The foreign secretary increased the legislative seats to fifty-three.) It eliminated the first-past-the-post system under which previous elections were held. Under the first-past-the-post system, the PPP had won twenty of the thirty-five seats in the 1961 elections to form the government. Since voting was along straight racial lines and the Indians accounted for nearly 43 percent of the votes, it was clear that Dr. Jagan and the PPP party was assured of victory in any election because of the arrangement of the election districts. A coalition of the other two parties the PNC and the UF would not have put them in government despite the fact that together they polled a little more than 57 percent of the total votes.

Under proportional representation, none of the parties in existence could poll more than 50 percent of the votes. It meant that two or more parties would have to form a coalition to form the government. It also encouraged smaller parties to spring up, enabling them to get a seat or two in the assembly and become part of the government. This was seen as a way of bringing harmony to the racially divided society and to have a more representative government. Of course, the PPP party was opposed to the new PR system. Others saw it as a means of stealing the election from under Dr. Jagan. When the 1964 election results were announced, the PPP won twenty-four seats; the PNC, twenty seats; and the UF, seven seats. Four other parties contested the election but received relatively few votes. Consequently, the governor called on the PNC to form the government with the firm backing of the UF. The leader of the PNC, Forbes Burnham, became the premier. It was clear that Jagan was cheated, and the country paid a heavy price in the years to follow.

The political situation was changing grounds. After Guyana obtained its independence from Britain in 1966, there was a conscious and deliberate effort by the new Burnham administration to dismantle the institutions that were the backbone of the country. Racial strife was the overriding factor, and the demarcation between blacks and Indians polarized the nation. The constitution underwent various changes as Burnham abolished free elections and consolidated his position as president for life. Guyana was now a dictatorship but friendly to the United States and Britain. That was the way it was desired; one less problem for the superpowers to worry about. As I studied economics and political science for my GCE exams, I kept a wary watch on the changing situations. The sugar and rice industries were nationalized. Top positions in all facets of the government were being manned by a party loyalist to the Burnham administration. There were many with little or no more than an elementary school education that were appointed managers and directors because it was their payback for handing out leaflets during the rigged election campaign. Highly qualified East Indians had to work under their patronage. It was an insult to their education and prestige. The brain drain had started. Doctors and lawyers sought immigration abroad, and this trend was followed by workers in the government civil service. Within the Ministry of Education, school teachers were on the move also. The government was considering that all teachers must complete a period of two years in the national service, a period of military training with the defense force in the interior of the country. I found this repulsive, and it was the final straw in my efforts to move on. I did not see the value of such service to teachers and the disruptive elements in their lives. I had to leave the country.

CHAPTER 6

Ten Years in Canada

The two most powerful warriors are patience and time.
—Leo Tolstoy, War and Peace

W hen my overnight flight from Port of Spain, Trinidad, arrived at Toronto International Airport in Canada, I knew there would be no one there to greet me. I was alone on a journey that would eventually push me to my limits and challenge my innermost strengths and weaknesses. At first, it did not matter to me because I had prepared myself with high expectations. I was full of confidence and exuberance to embark on an exciting career. Little did I know that my faith was marred with twists and turns that tested my skills to adapt and persevere. My troubles had just begun on this twelfth day of September 1969. For the next four years, only my ambition to pursue a university degree and a distant dream of a better lifestyle propelled me to accept the challenges. Instinctively, it became my only goal during those trying years. Once again, I faced the uncertainties of the future, and there were many hurdles in my way. With every passing day, there was a constant struggle to survive in this foreign land.

The immigration officer perused my mandatory travel documents of chest x-ray film, smallpox inoculation card, medical certificate, and student visa. He paid particular attention to my passport with its certification from the Royal Bank of Canada branch office in Guyana showing $852 in Canadian funds available before stamping my passport with the entry date. The automatic sliding doors closed behind me as I stepped out from the customs and immigration department's secured enclosure and into an unfamiliar world. It was a strange sight. Two men in overalls stopped to let me pass and then resumed pushing a mop across the polished marble-tiled floors. Clusters of men and women huddled in conversations while others in business suits hurried in every direction with suitcases dragged behind. It was unusual for me to see for the first time several white men dressed as porters and pushing carts overlaid with luggage toward the taxi stands. It was certainly different from my preconceived and limited impressions of life in Canada. My notions of what I observed began to change immediately, and I kept a keen eye for the little things. From the ramp I could see hundreds of cars in the parking lot, and in the distance thousands more passed every minute on the highways in every direction. The air was fresh and crisp, and the coolness caressed my skin. The oversized digital sign in front the Air Canada Terminal flashed 3:15 p.m. and 72 degrees in alternate succession. My thoughts were transfixed on the changing signs, and for a little while, I was lost in this new world.

Suddenly, there were no more unpainted zinc top houses, no more coconut trees lining the roadside, no more donkey carts blocking traffic, and no more broken-down cars passing intermittently along the dusty roads. The absence of bicycles chugging along the corners of the brick roads to avoid the potholes and little boys and girls in bare feet walking to school was quite noticeable. The air was fresh and dry. No more beads of perspiration settled on my forehead and lips from the absence of humidity and heat. With my small grip (suitcase) laid down at my feet, I looked in every direction, my eyes scanning the numerous billboard signs for instructions and directions to incoming passengers.

I had no idea where to go, and I was pondering on what to do next.

"Anyone for Hamilton?" I heard a taxi driver called out.

"Yes, here," I called out waving and moving briskly toward the taxi stand.

"Get in the back, sir," he said as he took my suitcase and proceeded to load it into the opened trunk. He politely motioned me in with two other passengers, and we took off through what seemed to me like a maze of traffic for the one-hour drive to Hamilton, Ontario. My eyes scanned the scenery of tall buildings and the manicured landscape along the highways as the taxi merged into a sea of vehicles on the Queen Elizabeth Expressway. Only one thought burned into my mind. I wondered if I would be able to drive a car at this high speed on a highway. It seemed so farfetched.

The registrar's office of McMaster University had arranged for someone from the student services to pick me up at the Royal Connaught Hotel, which was the taxi stop-off point. The neon sign on top of the Bank of Commerce building across the street read 6:30 p.m., and no one had come for me as yet. The sun had gone down now, and the sign flashed 9:30 p.m., and still no one came to pick me up. I paced up and down the sidewalk and watched the hustle and bustle on Main Street. Everyone seemed to walk as if they were in a hurry, but I was only getting used to a different scene. Life moved with a much faster pace than in Guyana. I felt lonely and longed for the simple comforts of home. My thoughts flashed back to Nanda's smile as I kissed her good-bye and the teary eyes of my wife and a few family members who had come to see me off at Timehri Airport. I was sad for leaving Nanda at only three months old. I had lost forever the beauty and joy of her first few years of growing up. I kept wondering if she was missing my presence and maybe crying. There was no way to communicate with anyone in Guyana. I hardly knew how to use a phone, and I knew of no one in the home area who had a phone to receive the call. Two weeks would pass before my letter of safe arrival in Canada would reach home by a regular airmail letter through the post office. It was not until around

11:00 p.m. when a student arrived to pick me up for the short ride to the campus, after the hotel clerk was kind enough to follow up with a phone call to the student center on my behalf. I could have walked the distance if I only knew the way. Arriving on campus later, he just let me out and said, "Welcome to Mac," before speeding off.

There was a group of West Indian students at the International Students Center building, which came to be known as the Downstairs John. Apparently, it was the only building that showed signs of human activity, and the numerous floodlights illuminated the evergreens that lined the front entrance. Darkness prevailed on the rest of the campus, and all that could be seen were the silhouettes of numerous buildings that dotted the landscape in every direction. I walked in to the customary welcome.

"Eh, wah happening deh man."

All the dozen or more Guyanese and West Indian students were engaged in a lively conversation about their majors and expectations for the coming year. I stood on one corner listening to their comments and constant laughter. Close to midnight, the group of students began to disperse, and they all scampered out in different directions. With no place to go, I had decided to stay there until the next morning. Then I would start hunting for a room. Two of the students came over. I introduced myself to Hirawan Tihal, a premedical student, and Halvidar Singh, a Guyana scholar working toward his doctorate degree in physics. They would eventually become my best friends throughout my student days at McMaster University. Later that night, after some idle conversation, Halvidar had offered me to stay the night with him until I could find suitable housing the next day. We simply had to wait until his landlord was asleep. It was not until around two o'clock in the morning that we snuck in quietly to his room on the attic level. I would never forget his act of friendship and kindness.

In the next few days, I scrambled to get settled. McMaster University bustled with activities as thousands of students descended upon the campus to complete the registration process. I familiarized myself on the use of the phone for the first time, and from an advertisement in the local newspaper, I soon rented a small room about three miles away from campus and within a short walk to downtown Hamilton. A retired couple was very happy to have me as a tenant. Not so much out of any need for money but like so many others in the surrounding community, they provided a service to the university in opening their homes to needy students. I found everyone trustworthy and with a resolute politeness. It was quickly apparent from the start that I would have financial difficulties. I had paid my full years tuition of $580 and a month's rent in advance at $10 per week. Then there were $128 for the basic textbooks and supplies that I had to have and the $65 in registration fees. I was left with $38 (Canadian) in my pocket from the total funds with which I had upon arrival in Canada. There were no student loans available to foreign students at that time, and I expected to receive no financial help from anyone from home. After the first few days, I was having grave doubts about my ability to succeed and seriously considered returning to my teaching job. Sitting in a class and listening to lectures from professors was a completely new experience for me. From the conversations with the half dozen or so other Guyanese students I had met, I learned that the others were from Queen's College and one of the girls was from St. Roses High School. These were two of the elite high schools in Georgetown, Guyana. All the students had passes on two subjects at the General Certificate of Education, advanced level. When I mentioned that I had not attended any high school, one of the students remarked that I would not be able to cope with the high academic standards at McMaster.

"You fail already, chap," he said with a degree of sarcasm. I never mentioned that I had three subjects at the advanced level. That same student had failed his final exam in economics the first year and had to repeat the course in the summer. This was much to my satisfaction. There were no more than a few dozen foreign students in the student population of over ten thousand. I found them all very friendly and agreeable. The Canadian students were eager to learn about my country and culture. Then there was the matter of studying five subjects with a book list covering twenty-eight books. It was scary, but I had done most of the subjects such as economics and geography before. I had left too much to get here, and I would be the laughing stock if I were to return home to Guyana. It would certainly be shameful. I was determined to succeed by any means.

I settled on a routine of reading ahead by one chapter in all my subjects, spending most of my time at the library between classes. Unable to purchase all the required textbooks, I relied on the copies that were readily available at the library. I ploughed through the subject materials and researched projects with ease since most of my subject matter was a rehash for me in areas of geography, economics, and religion. Passing the first few tests and with high passing grades, I became confident that I would have little difficulty academically. I had much spare time too, and with the last few dollars remaining in my pocket, there was an obsessive urgency to find some kind of part-time work. As a foreign student, I was not eligible to accept employment without approval from the immigration department. This was usually granted at the end of the school year for the summer months. Then it was back to the immigration department to obtain a renewal of my student visa for the forthcoming year. Fear of deportation loomed on my mind constantly, and I always opted to do the right thing.

It may have been my luck to see a Painter Wanted sign at the student employment office on campus. Since it did not involve working for an employer on a full-time basis, it was not necessary for me to obtain a work permit from the immigration department. Bending the truth somewhat, I had convinced the office that I had years of experience painting houses in Guyana. I had whitewashed the picket fence in our yard several times as a small boy, and so I figured painting a house was no different than whitewashing, a piece of cake for me. Nonetheless, I was dispatched to paint two rooms at a doctor's house just a short walk from campus. I tried to be careful and to appear like a professional painter, but I did make a mess of splashing paint around, and it took almost a week to complete the job. Every day before I departed, I scanned every square inch of the floor area and cleaned every drop of paint that fell. All the corners were wiped twice with the painting materials neatly stored away. After some scrutiny, the doctor's wife was quite satisfied. There was a smile on her face as we engaged in a short, pleasant conversation. How surprised I was to learn that her husband was the chief cardiologist at the newly established medical school at McMaster University. Although she paid me $43 in cash for the work, I was very pleased. Much to my delight, she referred me to do some painting for one of her friends nearby, the wife of another doctor. As it turned out, that was a moment that brought me warmth with a smile. Early the next morning, I showed up at the front door of the doctor's house. The doorbell was answered by a cute little blonde. I guessed she was about three or four years old. Her bright eyes looked at me from behind the screen door.

"Hello, can you tell your mommy the painter is here?" I said.

Without any expression, she ran back immediately toward the kitchen area.

"Mommy, a Chinese man is at the door."

When I heard her, I could not help smiling, never encountering a more humorous moment. This was my only other part-time work for the school year, and it took almost two weeks to complete. I had become a bit more skilled at painting by now, and I knew I did a good job because the doctor's wife was very pleased. With the additional $82 earned, I had to stretch every penny to last until the summer. That was not enough to stop my parental instinct when I passed by Kresge's Department Store on my way home one afternoon. I could not resist the impulse to buy a cute little dress for Nanda. Sometime later, my wife sent me a picture of Nanda wearing the dress and showing her pretty smile. I treasured that picture ever since then for it always brought tears to my eyes. It was one more reason I had to succeed. *I will be all right if I could survive until then*, I thought. In the summer months, most students work to pay their tuition and living expenses with employment opportunities available from Hamilton's large base of industrial and steel-producing industries. Stelco, Dofasco, International Harvester, and Westinghouse were among the giant companies employing thousands of students each year. From what I had been told by the student advisor, I was almost certain to find employment. That was a very encouraging prospect for me.

The lessons learned from the painting jobs had become a hallmark of my work attitudes ever since. Every task approached was handled as if it meant a final exam for entrance to Harvard. It reminded me of the experiences of Booker T. Washington that I often retold as a primary school teacher to my pupils. It seemed that life had come full circle to me, and now I must practice what I had preached.

Here is a quote from his autobiography *Up from Slavery* (pages 52-53).

> After some hours had passed, the head teacher said to me: "The adjoining recitation-room needs sweeping. Take the broom and sweep it."
>
> It occurred to me at once that here was my chance. Never did I receive an order with more delight. I knew that I could sweep, for Mrs. Ruffner had thoroughly taught me how to do that when I lived with her.
>
> I swept the recitation room three times. Then I got a dusting cloth and I dusted it four times. All the woodwork around the walls, every bench, table and desk, I went over it four times with my dusting cloth. Besides, every piece of furniture had

been moved and every closet and corner in the room and been thoroughly cleaned. I had the feeling that in a large measure my future depended upon the impression I made upon the teacher in the cleaning of that room. When I was through, I reported to the head teacher. She was a "Yankee" woman who knew just where to look for dirt. She went into the room and inspected the floor and closets, then she took her handkerchief and rubbed it on the woodwork about the walls, and over the table and benches. When she was unable to find one bit of dirt on the floor, or a particle of dust on any of the furniture, she quietly remarked, "I guess you will do to enter this Institution."

I was one of the happiest souls on earth. The sweeping of that room was my college examination, and never did any youth pass an examination for entrance to Harvard or Yale that gave him more satisfaction. I have passed several examinations since then, but I always felt that this was the best one I ever passed.

Within a month, I moved to a cheaper room at 447 Main Street, paying $7.00 per week and no rent in some weeks in return for occasionally keeping an eye on my landlord's two small kids while he was out on errands. This worked out well. However, I ate the bare necessities and never spent more than $3.00 per week on groceries and avoided all other expenses. Rice was 55¢ for a five-pound bag that lasted me for two weeks. A loaf of bread was 19¢, and the sixteen or so slices were sufficient for my daily ration of two slices at lunchtime. Potatoes was 69¢ for ten pounds. A whole chicken was $1.23, and eggs were 22¢ per dozen. I never let anyone know my plight, and whenever they went to the cafeteria for lunch or a snack, I would make excuses that I had classes and leave. I ate once only on most days. I usually carried two slices of bread that I pinched from my pocket. A drink of water from the fountains and my hunger sufficed for the day until I could prepare some rice and fried potatoes in the evening. I walked the three-mile distance to school every day. In the winter, I walked in the ankle-deep snow and in the rain and thumbed a ride to classes on many days. The Canadian winter was bitterly cold, and the cheap winter coat and uninsulated winter shoes made the trips overbearing. By the time I arrived for classes on some days, my toes and hands would be almost frozen, and I had to stand in front of the heaters to thaw out for a while.

When I arrived in Canada, I was a clean-cut individual. I wore a suit on my first day to registration, dressed neatly, and had a haircut. I tried to keep up appearances, for this was my impression and expectation of a university student. It did not last for more than the first week, and soon I blended with the flow of things around me. Before long, I was beginning to witness a counterrevolutionary culture that was sweeping the nation and throughout campuses everywhere in Canada and the United States. I was caught up in the middle of this era of hippies, of young adults and students alike, venting their views in opposition to the "establishment" and "status quo." All the issues culminated with the Woodstock Festival that was held just a couple of months earlier. It seemed as if every conversation, every debate, and every squeamish idea rode on the principles of freedom of speech, freedom of assembly, and freedom of dissent. The motto was to be yourself and be whatever you want, and protests were the way to get you there.

In attitude, it was Peace and Love. Much of this was expressed on bumper stickers with slogans such as Make Love Not War or Peace or Groovy. In dress code, the desire was to look different from the general status quo. Jeans torn at the knees and colorful patches on the rear were the choice of many students. Long hair and a bandana were symbolic of togetherness, and smoking marijuana was commonplace. In arts, the graphics were incredibly intricate and often expressed on T-shirts and clothes of psychedelic colors. In music, the ultimate of expressions, the goal, was to harmonize and blend the perfect words with the perfect sounds that lend itself to pure bliss. All this culture had come together in the Woodstock Music and Arts Fair in August 1969 in upstate New York. Like only a handful of historical events, this festival and concert came to symbolize the cultural revolution of the 1960s and the baby boomers. With over 450,000 in attendance, it was four days of counterculture, illegal drugs, free love, sex, and open minds.

Conflicts cropped up all around me, and for the most part, I kept a two-sided facade on everything. On the outside, I went along with the flow of things and the new age ideology. However, on the inside, I never lost sight of my purpose or expectations. I let my hair grow because I could not afford a haircut, but that was the style. Without knowing any better, I had washed my two white shirts and colored shirts together at the local laundry, and all came out in psychedelic colors. I wore them anyway, not by choice, but it made me look hip and groovy. This was the style anyway. By the end of the year, I looked more like a bum and unrecognizable from when I just arrived. The room next to mine was being shared by two guys who always dressed in battle fatigue army uniforms. I became good friends with them in no time. Most nights I would find them and another half dozen or so of their friends sitting in a circle in the room. An awful smell emanated from the funny rolled up cigarette they were puffing and passing along.

"Hey, man," Tony would call out as I passed by his room. He would raise his thumb in a common gesture to symbolize that everything is cool.

"Hey, man," the others would join in at the same time.

"Hey, dudes," I would reply and move about my business of studying.

Tony and I had become good friends, and we would talk a lot about religion and philosophy. Sometimes I shared my rice and fried potatoes with him. I felt sorry for him when he looked weak and frail from the addiction he had developed. I was slow to catch on, but I learned that these guys were draft dodgers from the United States. They opposed the war in Vietnam and had moved out of the United States rather than fight a war they did not believe in.

I began to understand the reasons for the daily demonstrations on campus and the hippie culture that blanketed the campus activities. There were days when classes were cancelled because all the students assembled to listen to speakers denouncing the war effort in the United States. On May 4, 1970, the incident at Kent State University in Ohio sparked massive demonstrations at McMaster campus as students and activists vented their frustrations and anger. Two students and two bystanders were massacred when guards opened fire on a crowd of unarmed students denouncing the war in Vietnam at Kent State University. I joined the demonstrations and skipped classes. It was my first involvement in civil disobedience as a student, and my views on government and society were changed forever.

Sympathizing with their views, I always found many were too immature and naive to understand the world around them. Remembering the riots in my own country and the political turmoil there, I understood the mistrust the young generation had of their government and welcomed change by any means possible. What is to be expected of eighteen-year-old boys who were barely out of high school and then drafted into the army to be trained as killers of a people they had no quarrel with? They felt they were dispensable to the nation, and they refused to fight. Many sons of the wealthy and powerful people did not fight either. Later that year I found out that Tony had jumped out from the eighth-story balcony of an apartment building where he was visiting some friends.

He was high on PCP and thought that he was jumping into his parents' backyard pool. I understood the power of the designer drugs that were all around, but I never considered their usage, not even a puff. Smoking weed was cool, and wearing bell-bottom pants and beads were groovy. "Hey, man" was the common greeting, and no one cared that I was an Indian or different in any way. No one looked at me in a funny way or with a blank stare when I went into a bank or government office as if I did not belong.

No one laughed at the tear on the knees of my pants or the patch I had on to cover the tear near the back pockets.

Summer rolled along after a successful completion of my first year at McMaster. My grades were excellent, and feeling confident, I looked forward to better things to come. I owed the landlord for a couple months rent and desperately sought employment. The giant corporations such as Stelco, Dofasco, Proctor and Gamble, and International Harvester hired thousands of students each summer. Students of parents who worked for these companies were given first preference for jobs, and these companies pride themselves in serving the community and students alike. Most students worked to pay their own tuition, and I was no exception. My first job was picking tomatoes at a greenhouse in Winona, Ontario. The first day was the worst, when my task was to move a heap of cow manure with a wheelbarrow to the inside of the greenhouse. Long rows of ground were being prepared for the planting of beefsteak tomatoes. It was déjà vu all over again when the scent of cow manure penetrated my nostrils on that first day. It was a disgusting thought to say the least. Here I was in Canada and still can't get away from the smell of cow dung. The other two fellow workers got a real kick watching me struggle to control the wheelbarrow fully loaded with cow manure. I never flinched, and by afternoon, I had all the cow manure moved over. My arms and legs ached. Tired and worn down, I sat under a tree to await my bus ride home. Unknown to me, the owner of the greenhouse business was observing my work all day. He came over bringing a glass of lemonade for me. With his three-year-old grandson beside him, we had a nice conversation. We would have many more conversations after that, almost every day. He was a very kind Dutch man, and I learned a few things from him about life and hard work as he related his own experiences in Canada. The next day it was my other two fellow workers' turn to move the cow manure and to do the tilling.

All summer I picked off the buds from the tomato plants and rose bushes. This was done three times, and after each time, the plant grew taller. Then the buds would flourish from the bottom stems of the tomato plants all the way to the six-foot ceilings in a mature tree. Each day a tomato would ripen from the bottom, and each tree produced over fifty tomatoes. The roses were cut as soon as the first petals were about to open and sold to florists. In a vase of water, the petals continue to open with each passing day, and a bloom could last about two weeks. At $1.65 an hour, I had saved enough money by the end of the summer to pay my next year's tuition and some left over for books and living expenses and an airline ticket for my wife to travel to Canada. I remember my first week's pay of $68.00 and how happy I felt that Saturday afternoon.

Once again I made the most difficult of decisions to leave Nanda in the care of my mother-in-law. My wife joined me in Canada in July 1970. We planned that she would come over to work and support me while I was in school. Then Nanda would follow as soon as we got settled. Two blocks down from Main Street, at 10 Dundurn Street, we rented a room on the second floor for $10 per week. She did odd jobs as housekeeper for a few weeks and then as babysitter for our landlord for $15 per week. After we paid the rent, we lived on $5 in this tiny six-feet-by-eight-feet room. It had one continental bed, a card table with a one burner, hot plate, and a miniature fridge under the table. All our worldly possessions were kept in two garage bags that we stored under the bed. We were happy though, and I did well with my studies. On Saturdays, we walked the five miles to the Sears shopping plaza just to window-shop and sometimes to the botanical gardens in Burlington. We climbed the steep three-hundred-foot steps of the escarpment for a view of Hamilton Bay below. Two long years would pass for us in this tiny world. I endured because I knew that better things were in the horizon. Although I never told anyone, there was a picture of Nanda I received when she was about three years old that burned a hole in my soul. I had sworn that whatever it takes of me, she would never live in poor conditions again as soon as I completed my studies.

Nanda at age three, being cared for by my mother-in-law in Guyana.

Tragedy struck when my mother-in-law passed away suddenly on December 29, 1972. We did not have a dime to our name, and my wife wanted to return to Guyana for the funeral and take care of Nanda. I could never imagine the loss they felt and especially how Nanda had grown accustomed to her grandmother and grandfather. She was three and half years old now, and we longed to see her. There was no family member or friend that could offer me any financial assistance at that time.

I courageously approached Ivor Wynne, who was the assistant dean of students at McMaster University. It would be the first and the only time in my life that I had asked someone for help. It was a desperate act on my part.

"All I need is a loan from the university for a ticket to Guyana," I pleaded with the dean in his office after I had explained the circumstances. "I don't think I will be able to continue study," I continued. "She is just crying," I said. "I don't know what to do, sir."

"Well," the Dean said as he fumbled for some paper in his desk drawer. "How do you expect to pay back this loan?" he asked me directly. "Do you have any kind of security?" he asked as he leaned forward to scribble on the pad of paper on his desk.

"I don't have anything," I replied shaking my head. "But I promise to pay it back, sir," I said eagerly. "As soon as I start to work, I will pay it back," I assured him. "That's the first thing I will do," I pleaded. "All I can do is give you is my word on that, sir," I said again.

There was a long pause. He leaned back on his revolving leather chair and folded his hands behind his head as he pondered my remarks.

"Okay." Then he reached forward to scribble on the piece of paper on his desk.

"Go to this place here, and they will make the necessary travel arrangements," he commanded in his soft baritone voice. "Let me know how you make out," he said, looking out the window as he leaned back to fold his hands behind his head once more.

"Thank you, Mr. Wynne" were my last words to him.

He handed me a note with the address of a travel agent on Main Street within the downtown area. I was overwhelmed with his kindness and generosity and shook his strong thick hands warmly using both of mine to show my thanks and appreciation. I remembered seeing his pictures among the trophies that lined the hallway display cases near the bookstore. He was a football player for the McMaster Marauders and then played for years in the Canadian Football League for the Hamilton Tiger Cats. I was saddened when I learned that he had passed away later that year.

Ivor Wynne Stadium in Hamilton, Ontario, and home of the Hamilton Tiger Cats of the Canadian Football League.

In the early spring of 1974, I went back to the registrar's office to settle my account balance for the loan. I was working on my first full-time job for several months and had saved up $280, which was the amount of the loan for the airline tickets including the one for Nanda that I received from the travel agent.

"I am here to pay up my loan," I said to the clerk and handed her $280 in cash.

"Well, let me check your account," she said and went to retrieve my file.

"Oh, Mr. Ramsaroop, your account is up-to-date," she claimed. "You don't owe the university anything," she exclaimed.

"That's not right, ma'am," I remarked. "I took a personal student loan from Dean Wynne," I said to the clerk.

"Well, there is no record of it in your file," she assured me. "You don't owe the university anything," she assured me again.

I thought for a moment, but I could not move away from the window. I could have just walked away. The $280 staring at me on the counter was badly in need. It was the first hard cash I had in my hands in a long time. I could have used it to replace the twelve-inch black-and-white television we had bought from the Salvation Army a couple years ago. Nanda needed new clothes and shoes and maybe a bicycle also. There were several other students waiting in line and looking on. I could not move away and then my instincts took over.

"Just take this $280 anyway," I said to the clerk without any further hesitation. "I know I borrowed it from Dean Wynne."

"Just give me a receipt for it," I requested.

"Oooh," the clerk said with a sigh of sarcasm.

I sensed that she thought I was being silly or just an idiot. I walked away with a feeling of satisfaction and relief as if a heavy burden had been lifted off my mind. It would be years later that I finally realized the fruitfulness of this very simple deed. If I had not paid the $280, I knew it would have haunted my conscience for the rest of my days. For the many years that have passed since that time, I have always been very proud to have honored my word to Dean Wynne. There were many circumstances when I thought that my word was sometimes better than gold. I still have the receipt that I have kept like a treasure. Someday I plan to frame it on the wall and value it in the same way as a Van Gogh masterpiece. I will never know for certain, but I have come to the conclusion that the dean had paid for the tickets from his own personal funds. It was not a loan from the university, and that was the reason it never showed up in my records. I have always been humbled by this gesture of generosity. In my little ways, I have adopted this principle of helping others in need without regard for a payback. That same year I was delighted to read in the local newspapers that the football stadium in Hamilton was renamed the Ivor Wynn Stadium and home to the Hamilton Tiger Cats.

Nanda arrived in February 1973 after much kicking and screaming. She was missing her grandparents to whom she had become very attached. I saw her for the first time in more than three and a half years. I was in my final term, and graduation loomed in the horizon. Final exams were around the corner, and I adjusted to make it all happen. We moved to a two-room second-floor apartment at 212 Wellington Street. My wife took on a job as a sewing machine operator although it was illegal for her to do so. Written permission was required from the immigration authorities, and I knew she was not eligible since I was not yet a permanent resident. The rules were strictly enforced with stiff penalties including immediate deportation. However, we took the risk. We scrambled her social insurance number on the application and hoped no one would notice it. We made a determination that if there were any questions on its validity, we would say that it was just an error in typing. I took care of Nanda during the day. We enrolled her at Bartles Kindergarten School and received a waiver on the $25 per week fees because of my student status and inability to pay.

I was considered a charity case, but I knew that it was the influence of Sister Marie who made it possible. She was a nun I had befriended by a chance meeting one Saturday morning as I strolled past a Catholic church on Main Street. I missed all my classes during the last semester. Nanda would cry if I was not nearby and within her sight. I realized the losses that she had to undergo on the death of her grandmother and the separation from the close bond with her grandfather and now being taken halfway across the continent to a father who was a total stranger to her. She refused to walk the ten or eleven blocks to the school. Each day I carried her and stayed in the school yard near the door so that she could easily see me. Every now and then, she would come out to peek and make sure I was there. She adjusted quickly and adapted to all circumstances easily but not before I bribed her constantly with trips to the corner store for candy and chewing gum and then to the swings and monkey bars in the playground nearby.

I graduated cum laude in May 1973 with a Bachelor of Commerce degree majoring in economics and finance. I did not attend the graduation. It was the hippie thing to do at the time and partly because I could not afford the $25 rental charge for the gown and other expenses. Furthermore, it was the university's standing policy that no student could graduate until all fees and expenses were paid up in full. Knowing very well that I had an outstanding balance, I requested that the university mail my degree to my home address. Still, without a frame, it had been collecting dust for the past thirty-six years. I later read a news bulletin that the university had destroyed thousands of certificates from the era after students never bothered to pick them up. The idea behind this was simple. Many of these students or hippies as they were sometimes called considered their degree as just a piece of paper. It was the knowledge they gained that mattered. There were others like them throughout the country and especially in the USA who have since discarded their bandanas and hippie clothes for a business suit and a BMW. They became the yuppies who were running the businesses, the corporations, and the country from behind their once liberal ideas. I had become one of them and set aside my radical elements to embrace the very establishment that I once so reluctantly opposed.

An unexpected turn of events in the summer of 1973 disrupted my plans for the future. After graduation I secured a prestigious position with the Canada Life Assurance Company of Toronto as an Investment Analyst. I was scheduled to embark on a very exciting career. However, my job was put on hold due to uncertainties on the world stage.

The oil-producing cartel (OPEC) had created an embargo on exporting crude oil to the United States. With the slowdown of the economy and long lines at the gas stations, my employer was hesitant to extend my job opportunity until a later date. Disappointed and frustrated to find suitable employment in my chosen field, I had to seek alternative sources. I reluctantly took a job as an assistant manager with Consumers Distributing

Company, a catalog retailer headquartered in Toronto and with over two hundred showrooms around the country. It was a new experience for me, and I grasped the art of dealing with the public at large. After six months into the job, I had excelled to the point that my superiors had much confidence in my ability to manage the store. I had begun to like my work.

One routine workday I was approached by a customer, a young lady, who wanted to return a large glass punch bowl set with twenty-four matching small glasses. As expected, I always followed the company's policy and treated every customer as king.

"Do you have your receipt for the set?" I asked.

"No, I don't have one," she replied bluntly. "But I bought it here a year ago," she continued. She seemed agitated.

In the meantime I could see from the stains and dirt around the edges of the glasses that the unit was extensively used.

"Well, I cannot give you a refund for this set without a receipt."

Before I could explain the company policy in cases like this to the customer, she had picked up the punch bowl set from the counter.

"All you foreigners only come here to take the jobs," she blurted out in haste. In a second she smashed the punch bowl set on the floor in front me.

The sound of broken glass filled the air, and pieces scattered in every direction. Stunned by the incident, I was unable to move as I watched the young lady hurriedly walk out the store. I was more embarrassed than anything else as a dozen or so other customers in the store looked at me in dismay. The only thing I remembered after that was one elderly gentleman who came over and said, "Call the cops."

That afternoon, the only call I made was to my district supervisor to relate the incident and to offer my resignation. He pleaded with me to stay on. My mind was made up. Although I was a good salesperson, I did not want a job dealing with the public. My excellent work ethics had earned me some credibility with my supervisor, and I requested a transfer to the main distribution center in Mississauga, Ontario. I was assigned a clerical position in the returned goods department. I was not sure in what direction I was heading. From assistant manager to a clerk with a salary of about $8,000 per year did not look promising, especially when I was reminded every day that I have a coveted degree in my pocket.

Standing in front of one of Consumers Distributing showrooms in Ottawa, Ontario, Canada.

One of the first things to jolt me at my new job was how little I knew about the workings of the business world. These were the things we never studied in business courses. This was the practical world for me. I immersed myself in all its details from accounting to law and the intricate paper flow of international imports and exports. A few of the supervisors always found tasks for me to perform for them, which I did without hesitation. In time, I felt that I was being used as a patsy.

I saw myself doing detailed work while they were always walking around with their hands in their pockets. I did not complain but waited my turn.

About six months later, the company had announced that George Graff, one of the officers, was promoted to senior vice president of operations. Everyone knew of him for running a tight ship.

Many feared him also for his stern and heavy-handed ways in which he dealt with subordinates. Within the warehouse circles, some supervisors refer to him as Little Hitler. Everyone in management was on their toes when he announced that he was visiting the warehouse one Friday morning.

"Ram, make sure the return center is cleaned up," my boss had commanded over the phone. "George Graff is coming over," he said.

I had no idea who George Graff was and did not care. Later that afternoon, I noticed a large group of supervisors with a smartly dressed businessman in a three-piece suit making an inspection of the activities in the return center department. Soon afterward, my boss called me over the phone.

"Ram, George Graff wants to see you in his office right away," he announced.

My heart sank. *This is it*, I thought. I was sure that I was getting fired.

I gathered up all my personal belongings, especially the list of contacts I had made over the months who were in a position to offer me employment. The short drive over to the executive's offices at 62 Belfield Road in Rexdale seemed like an eternity. Many thoughts crossed my mind. Upon arrival at his office, George Graff motioned me to sit down. I listened attentively as he argued over the phone with someone from his bank about getting his dividends paid starting on the day the dividend was announced. I gathered from the conversation that the bank wanted to make the payments starting the next working day after the dividend was announced. It was a lot of money for him, considering that I had heard he owned over 500,000 common shares with the company. By nature of his aggressiveness, I was satisfied that he had convinced the bank manager to see things from his point of view.

"Wait here, I will be right back," he pointed his finger at me and left the office in hurry.

I eventually found out what had taken place when George Graff returned to the warehouse that afternoon.

Apparently, upon his tour of the return center, he inquired about various activities such as getting vendor authorizations, routing of deliveries, and especially the criteria to salvage merchandise that were subsequently reduced in price for sale at the clearance stores as red-tag or white-tag goods. This activity helped recoup millions of dollars for the company and padded the profit margin in a respectable way. Every time he had asked a question about the return center activities, the supervisors would say, "Ram takes care of that" or "Ram handles that" or "Ram does that."

That afternoon, George Graff had three of the supervisors reassigned from the return goods department.

"If Ram does everything here, then put Ram in charge," George Graff blurted out as he made a hasty exit. I eventually learned of the heated exchange of words from one of the supervisors present at the meeting.

"From here on, you work for me," George Graff said to me when he returned to his office. He left me to work out the details with his secretary. I never got the chance to say a word. I did not have to say anything.

It was months later after he had gained my trust that he recounted the situation.

"With you in the return center, I have one less problem to worry about," he assured me. It was an interesting conversation, and I was seeing the soft, gentle inner side of this man behind the iron shield from which he masked himself. He related one of his experiences to me, pointing out that I had reminded him of his first job, working as a stock boy for Acme Luggage Company in Montreal. This was shortly after he had immigrated to Canada from Hungary at the end of World War II. I listened attentively as he related his first experiences in Canada. Landing in Laval, Quebec, on a commercial freighter, he had to walk to Montreal in the middle of the winter. At nights he found sleeping quarters in the hallways of the YMCA. One day a few months later, a buyer was interested in placing a large order for a specialized luggage. None of the salesmen or warehouse staff could locate a sample of the luggage. The order was close to cancellation until George was called to locate the luggage. With dozens of different styles of luggage that the company manufactured, he knew where every piece was located within the cramped and limited warehouse facilities. George recounted the entire inventory to the manager and was able to retrieve the sample for the customer who eventually placed the order. This impressed the owner in such a manner that in time George Graff was promoted to a management position with the company.

Eventually, I learned many techniques of running a business from my conversations with George Graff. One day, it started casually about theft in the warehouse.

"So how do you think they are stealing over there?" he asked.

"Well, when loading the trucks, I suppose it is possible to drop small items by the sides and then pick them up later from the outside," I suggested.

I offered a few more explanations as he looked at me without expression.

"You think everyone who works in the offices are honest too, right?" he exclaimed.

I was startled. Then I realized that my idea of theft was confined to warehouse workers who physically handled the products. I felt silly.

"Let me tell you something," he said, leaning closer to point and waggle a finger in front of my chest. "The one who steals is always the one who has the most opportunity. Don't worry about the little guy at the bottom. It is always the ones at the top who steal the most," he continued.

"You mean people like in your position," I pointed out.

"Don't get smart now," dismissing my remark with a smile.

I marked his words, and for the rest of my days, I saw that statement played out in every facet of business and government. It became a fact of life.

In the twenty years I worked for Consumers Distributing Company and in private life afterward, I had seen it firsthand. Buyers, store managers, and vice presidents took bribes and made decisions that benefited their pockets. CEOs of large corporations became rich by stealing funds and manipulating stock options. Bankers and investment firms manipulate their clients' funds and benefited enormously. Government officials from small townships to the highest levels of federal government including some congressional members and senators have been involved in embezzlement and get-rich schemes. An avalanche of corporate scandals have been well documented in recent years. There were countless numbers. It rivaled the banana republics in many third world countries.

Only as recent as 2009, Bernard Madoff was sentenced to 150 years in prison after pleading guilty to federal charges of fraud and money laundering. He lured wealthy investors in a scam involving about 65 billion dollars. Only a small portion of that money was recovered. In 2002, the Halliburton Corporation improperly booked 100 million dollars in annual cost overruns. A judicial watchdog group filed an accounting fraud lawsuit against Halliburton and its former CEO and vice president of the United States Dick Cheney, among others. The energy giant, Enron Corporation, declared bankruptcy in 2006 when it was discovered that its officers boosted profits and hid debts totaling over 1 billion dollars. Charges filed involved bribing foreign governments to win contracts and making false claims regarding the company's financial health. Forced to close its doors, most employees lost not only their jobs but also their 401(k) investments, which were heavily invested in the company's inflated stocks. Other big names in the corporate scandal list include Merck, Tyco, Xerox, Bristol-Meyers, and Time Warner to name a few. The point is well-taken, and I am convinced that in business as well as politics, it's a dog-eat-dog world out there. George Graff was right.

Shortly thereafter, I had taken charge of the return center although I had no title and no office. For the most part, other than managing the return center, I became the troubleshooter for the senior vice president of operations and dispatched with the responsibility to resolve problems in all warehouse activities pertaining to the returned goods department. Suddenly, I felt the power of being in charge, and in a short time, I gained the respect of the buyers and many within the company. I was instrumental in setting the company standards for the return of damaged goods to the vendors by investigating and reporting on problems of product durability, safety, and quality assurance. I was the eyes and ears for all manufactured products sold through Consumers Distributing Company, being the first respondent when problems arose with a product.

The financial rewards were most welcome when George Graff authorized that I get paid hourly from the time I left home at five o'clock in the morning to the time I returned home that evening. On snowy days and slow-traffic days, I accumulated a lot of extra hours. The thirty-eight dollars per month in travel allowance was sufficient for the monthly payment on my brand-new Chevelle Malibu car. Soon afterward, I bought a town house at 10 Gatsby Square, Bramalea, Ontario, with the generous grant of $2,000 as a first-time home buyer from the Ontario government. It served as the down payment. Both my wife and I were working, and we were on sound financial grounds.

With all things going well, we opted for a second child, and Sharda was born on October 31, 1975, in Mississauga, Ontario. We were unprepared for her premature birth. With her low birth weight at three pounds and four ounces, she was kept in an incubator at the hospital for two months. I turned my thoughts to providing Nanda and Sharda with everything possible that I did not have as a child. I was on top of the world, planting my roots. I did not have a job that suited my qualifications, but I never looked back at it. Now I was happy. At work I walked around with my hands in my pocket most times. I was in control of my little world. I carried on with the lessons I learned from George Graff for the rest of my years.

"Good work always speaks for itself," he used to say to me. I realized that he did not care much about where I came from nor the color of my skin. He was more impressed with the work I did and the end results of my efforts. I liked that very much. It would be a decade later before I would encounter another person who treated me this way. It was a rare trait to find in people in those days.

Nanda and Sharda at play in the backyard of our new home at 15 Gatsby Square, Bramalea, Ontario, Canada.

One day, I started a conversation with an old Japanese man. None of the other supervisors wanted him because he spoke little English and he was not suitable to work in the fast-paced shipping department. The warehouse manager dispatched him to my department. He looked small and feeble, but that was deceiving. I would assign him a task of moving merchandise or to clean up an area. In no time he would be back standing next to me.

"Finish," he would say. "What do next?" he would then ask in a gentle manner.

Soon, it became evident that this gentleman could accomplish the task of four of my other employees put together. I was impressed with his work and used him to tackle some of the difficult tasks in the return center. I must admit he became my most favorite employee. He worked with the discipline of a samurai returning to his work routine exactly on time after coffee and lunch breaks.

Once, I saw him lift a nineteen-inch television set with little effort.

"Why do you work so hard?" I interrupted him one day.

"Oh, keep fit," he said and clinched his fists to show his biceps.

"What you do before?" I asked.

"I own laundry," he replied.

"What happen to laundry?" I was eager to ask again.

"Me sell for half million dollars," he said with faint smile.

"Wow," I uttered. Instantly I began to have a lot of total admiration for this old man. "So what you do with all money?" I questioned him with a touch of envy in my tone of voice. I was about to suggest that he stayed at home and retire to years of leisure and relaxation.

"I give to daughter," he said. He had a big smile. I could see that he felt proud.

"Oh, what daughter do?" I asked curiously and thinking of my own two little girls.

"She a lawyer," he said proudly again with a faint humble smile.

I could not speak for a while, and my thoughts raced to the successes of this Japanese man. With all my education and management position, I felt pale in comparison. I was clearly in awe, and I wished I was standing in his shoes. It was not the half million dollars in cash that he was worth, but I was struck about the proud manner in which he talked about his daughter being a lawyer. I could see the dazzle in his eyes. Later that day, I had to find out more about him and his exploits. It was the best piece of advice I ever got when I asked him how he got his daughter to become a lawyer.

"When she a baby, I say you be lawyer. As daughter grow up, I say you be a lawyer. When teacher ask daughter, what you be? Daughter say I be lawyer. Today daughter a lawyer. Like bonsai, to have tree, you must plant seed early in the spring."

I really liked that saying. It reminded me of my father and his proverbial sayings.

That afternoon, I could hardly wait to get home and to try out this theory with my own daughter, Nanda.

"What do you want to be when you grow up?" I asked her as she was enjoying her favorite Bugs Bunny cartoon shows on television.

"I don't know," she replied and shrugged her shoulders.

"Well, you going to be a doctor," I said and left it at that.

The next day, I asked the same question again during dinner and got the same answer.

"I don't know."

"You going to be a doctor," I said. This was the conversation I had with her for the next few days. I left her with the same comments every time.

I had planted a seed in her mind, and I was just nurturing the thought every now and then. It would not take long afterward, but when one day I asked her what she wanted to be when she grew up, her response was strikingly different.

"I want to be a doctor," she would say, and this was music to my ears.

Later that year, I found out that she had told her homeroom teacher that she wanted to be a doctor during a show-and-tell session in her third grade class. Sharda was only six months old by this time, but every moment that I had her in my arms, I would look her right in the eye and say, "You are going to be a doctor too, eh."

It is startling, but throughout elementary and high schools, Nanda and Sharda had no other ambition other than to be a doctor. It resonated in their science projects and courses outline. The seeds had sprouted, and two small trees started to blossom.

In the meantime, I was mindful of my family left behind in Guyana. Upon graduation from McMaster University, I made a short visit to Guyana in 1974 with wife and daughter. The economic situation in Guyana was deteriorating considerably, and daily life became harsh and unbearable for many throughout the land. Employment and opportunities for advancement became scarce for youths and young adults. My parents were struggling to sustain a living and more so with five of my unmarried brothers and sisters living with them. Of course, I helped with an occasional monetary dispersal while I was in Canada, but I knew that this alone was not sufficient.

It was my mother's request to me one afternoon that set my emotions into high gear. "Boy, see if you can help them out nah. Things ah really bad here in this country."

I knew what she meant. I was especially troubled knowing that they had no future and would never be able to make it on their own.

Returning to Canada, I immediately made application to sponsor Amos. I thought he had the best chances for success at the time. Then I brought my mother and father as visitors, and while in Canada, I made application for them to remain as permanent residents.

I was taking advantage of a loophole in the immigration laws. It allowed them to remain in Canada while the application was processing. It meant that when my parents received their permanent immigrant status, they would be entitled to bring across to Canada all their unmarried children under twenty-one years of age. In this way, Kamal, Datto, and Willliam would also be given visas for permanent resident status. With both my mother and father living comfortably with me in Canada, it was just a matter of waiting out a six-month period. Two months into the waiting period and my mother decided that she wanted to go back to Guyana. She was concerned about her children living alone in Guyana. I reluctantly agreed for her to return. It was sufficient that when the immigration department requested their presence to grant the permanent visa status, at least one parent must be present. Two months later my father created such a fuss about going back to Guyana that I agreed to his request with much disappointment. I was unable to convince him of the dire consequences of his foolish and obstinate action. I sympathized with him in that he became bored with the daily routine. The Canadian winter was upon us, and that meant he had to stay indoors. There were no activities that he could be involved with except watching television day and night. Recovering from a mild stroke and with vision problems, there was no way in which he could have traveled to the mall by bus or otherwise.

Six weeks after he departed to Guyana, I received a confirmation and appointment from the immigration department for one parent to be present for the issuing of permanent visas status. I was saddened by the loss of an opportunity for their future and that of my three youngest brothers and sisters. It was so easy and yet so far beyond reach. I would have to find another way. A year later Amos received his permanent visa status and arrived in Canada to live with me until he could get settled. Immediately, I convinced my supervisor to hire him as an assistant store manager, and soon he was on the road to success and financial independence on his own.

A nostalgic revisit to the School of Business at McMaster University Campus, Hamilton, Ontario, Canada (2007).

CHAPTER 7

Eye on the Prize

It is a wise father that knows his own child.
—William Shakespeare, Merchant of Venice

I did not realize the extent of which discrimination and prejudice had intruded the schools until I attended Nanda's *open-school night* at Greenbriar Elementary School. It was a rude awakening for me in many ways. For a while I was just subdued with disbelief, and before the evening was over, I was numbed and confused. In the depths of my thoughts, I could feel a slow anger brewing. It was not the feeling that discrimination was anything new to me. I was no stranger to racism and discrimination. It surrounded me for the most part of my life. Now I began to witness how it had permeated to the next generation. It was my children's turn, and that made the difference to me. Looking at the children's innocent faces, I wondered why it had to be this way.

It was never an easy situation to face people who harbored prejudice and racial hatred in their hearts, but in time I had learned to deal with it. It was the realization of it when an incident occurred that hurt the most. It was not name-calling or the violence which I mostly avoided at all costs; it was the realization of the small and subtle things that denigrated my very existence to a lower and unequal status. Sometimes, it was just the look in the eyes, the scorn of being ignored when it was my turn or denied outright without an explanation. Right up to this point, I always thought that this sort of thing was confined to the old south in the United States. Of course, I had studied and debated the subjects in my sociology and psychology classes while at McMaster University. At that time, it was more of an academic exercise for me, and although I knew that it existed, I thought most people were beyond this kind of behavior. Catching me off guard, I finally realized that it was deeply entrenched and prevalent.

Bramalea, Ontario, Canada, was the last place I expected to find hatred for people of color, but I was about to wake up to a sudden dose of reality. The worst part was that my innocent children were being subjected to this ugly and crude behavior. At least I never expected it from teachers. I held teachers in a very high esteem and as the pillars of society in any country. To say the least, this was not what I had in mind for my daughters. Of course, I had firsthand experiences in Guyana, a nation polarized by race and politics. However, the blacks and the Indians in Guyana coexisted peacefully, except during the national elections when the races were sharply divided and violence was the norm. I guess my expectations of Canada as a free and classless society were suddenly shattered.

We had moved to this beautiful and developing bedroom community on the outer fringes of Toronto. It was an ideal setting as I worked only seven miles down the road across from Toronto International Airport. I was so happy to move into our first home and leave the apartment-style living behind. Nanda and Sharda now had a backyard to play in, with a wading pool and a swing set. The schools were within walking distance, and both of the girls were enthusiastic about their new surroundings. I could not ask for anything more. Life was beginning to turn for the better with both my wife and I working at fairly good jobs.

In all my four years as a student at McMaster University, I can't remember a single occasion where I faced discrimination in any way. Maybe it was subtle and I did not recognize it or cared enough to know about it. Maybe it was because of my limited exposure within the university environment. Except for the academic circles of the university campus, there was little interaction with the Canadian public. As a student I posed no threat to anyone in the job market, and for four years I was almost invisible.

I thought the whole climate was different then, more tolerant, more open, and with less cultural rigidity. This was one thing I could say for the so-called hippie generation; race and color did not matter anywhere I went. Most of my classmates and friends were white Canadians. Very often, they would engage me in conversations and were eager to learn about my country and culture. I spent my first Christmas in the home of a Canadian family, the parents of my roommate. It was a pleasurable experience for me, and they were very happy to have me in their home.

Looking back, it seemed that the end of the war in Vietnam had spurred tremendous changes in the way people were looking at the issues facing them. The economic and political climate also fostered hatred. In the United States, the returning Vietnam vets were the scourge of society, and the media portrayed them as baby killers and dope addicts. There was no fanfare and no parades for them when they returned home to their families. In Canada, the immigration policy was relaxed, and waves of immigrants poured in from India and Pakistan. The oil embargo by the Arab nations against the United States created long lines at the gas stations, and many companies faltered in the economic squeeze. The economic slowdown put many Canadians out of work, and their economic woes were blamed on the new wave of immigrants. The Asians were made the scapegoats and were seen as a threat to jobs and were at the receiving end at the wrath of the white established Canadians. The civil rights movement in the United States spawned new attitudes among the upper-class whites. The upward mobility of blacks and Latinos created a definite threat to the diminishing middle class. The cities and neighborhoods became polarized by race riots, and conservatism was on the forefront of those who held the power. I had nothing to do with any of this but got caught right in the middle.

Rambling through the classrooms that evening, I felt proud and elated at the future prospects of a good education that awaited Nanda and Sharda. I was mesmerized at the facilities and the opportunities afforded all children in the public schools. The modern building with its elaborate classrooms and visual aid equipments brought much satisfaction.

I was especially happy that my children would share in this high standard. I felt satisfied for having reached this level in my life. My thoughts were flooded with memories of the poorly equipped and crowded schools in Guyana when I was a teacher and my own experiences in elementary school at St Patrick's Anglican. It seemed such a far cry from the hundreds of barefoot children crammed into rows of wooden benches. I talked briefly to some kids from Nanda's class as they introduced themselves. I inquired about how they liked their school and their teachers. All her classmates agreed that the school was great, but they all complained that they got too much homework from their teachers. This was odd, for I had never seen Nanda doing any homework. After school, she was engrossed watching Bugs Bunny, Tom and Jerry, or Speedy Gonzalez and other popular cartoons of the day on television. She always said that she had no homework to do. I remembered this well because as a former school teacher, I always gave my students a little homework to keep them occupied in learning and research activities.

Later that evening, I was able to chat briefly with Nanda's homeroom teacher and posed the question about not giving Nanda any homework to do. She explained that Nanda was a bright child and did not need to do any homework. I could sense that she was being evasive and skirted around the subject. Dissatisfied with her answer, I was more perturbed by the way I was brushed aside and the more detailed manner in which she attended to other parents. When I left the school that evening, there were only questions in my mind. I had begun to view myself in a different perspective. As the weeks and months passed, every situation became magnified and more disturbing to me. Coincidentally, there were articles in the local newspapers that highlighted a study that more than 60 percent of the people in the metropolitan Toronto area were prejudiced in some way against blacks, minorities, and especially immigrants. I translated this into 60 percent of teachers also. I was distressed about the whole situation. Now I realized why we were called names whenever we went to the Bramalea Square Shopping Mall. Youths would drive past us, sticking their heads out of their car windows, and yell "packies" or "you stinking packies."

At first, I paid no attention to the remarks and always dismissed them as directed against the Pakistani or Punjabi sheikhs who wore a turban. I always thought we were being mistaken for Pakistanis.

I slowly realized that some Canadians were unable to distinguish between Pakistanis, Indians, or West Indians. I was sure some thought that we were all alike. Every now and then, there would be an exposé on television and articles in the newspapers on someone who had faced discrimination in their lives. This was nothing new to me, although the subject matter always captured my attention. History has shown that the arrival of every new group of people or new wave of immigrants always faced the same wrath. This was time for the Indians and Pakistanis. Before it was the Italians and the Polish. Later it was the Vietnamese and the Hispanics. It was clear to me that some of the teachers were making a deliberate and unconscious effort to keep down the children of immigrants. I could sense that Nanda was just a body being processed through the school system. The subtle differences were noticeable, and the lack of personal attention that she received from the teachers was evident. I don't blame the general public for the prejudices that they displayed. I always thought it was more of ignorance on their part and a lack of exposure to people of other cultures.

One incident in particular angered me very much. Some of the youths would often play stick hockey on the street in front of my house. It was great fun to watch these kids play. It reminded me so much of my days as a youth playing softball cricket in the streets near my home in Guyana. One day, I came home from work to find one of the neighbor's kids sitting in the middle of my driveway. He was no more than thirteen or fourteen years old. I motioned for him to move aside so that I could park the car. I did not care that he was sitting there, but he did not budge an inch after I asked him to move twice. Then he had the nerve to say that this was not my house. A sudden rage came over me as I don't tolerate these situations lightly. In an instant, I had dragged him by the collar and seat of his pants and sent him flying to the street. He looked stunned and writhed in pain from the bruises on his hands and knees.

"Go tell your father to come see me," I shouted at him as he whined his way back to his house across the street. I was sure that most of the neighbors were looking on. I took out the baseball bat that I carried at all times in the trunk of my car, and I waited. More than half an hour passed before I cooled off and finally went in the house. No one came over, not the boy's parents or any of the neighbors. I continued to live on that street for another year without incident. Until the day I left Canada, I never saw that kid again. The stick hockey games continued but came to an abrupt end whenever I pulled into my driveway. Later I would learn that some of the very kids were harassing Nanda when she came home from school. I always believed that children learn behavior from their parents, and it's the root evil of all prejudices. I thought we were mistaken for Indians, who were stereotyped as docile and passive and can be taken advantage of. The kids knew little of us. The Indians and Pakistanis did little to enhance the image of their cultures also. They tend to huddle and to congregate in a small areas within the urban sprawl of most big cities. They were slow to learn and speak English properly in the public. More than often, I had observed that they participated little in the activities in the community. I remembered going to packed stadiums of hockey and football games and had never seen an Indian or Pakistani. This trend had continued for years to come, and I never could understand it. I remembered the first baseball game I saw at Yankee Stadium in 1982 between the New York Yankees and the Baltimore Orioles. In a packed, sold-out crowd of over fifty-five thousand fans, I dared my brother to show me a single Indian or Pakistani in the stands. Then I would give him a reward of a hundred dollars. Using binoculars and scanning the crowd for most of the game, he lost the bet. I scarcely saw them in restaurants and other public places that I frequented.

As for the Canadians, there was an identity crisis to start with, and the distinction between Canadians and Americans were frequently blurred. The television shows were mostly American in content, and most news programmers and sitcoms were dominated by American issues. Very often I would drive to the American side of Niagara Falls and to Buffalo to buy American beer, liquor, and cigarettes. From the advertisements hitting the airwaves, I thought Schlitz beer was the best brew at the time and Budweiser was king of the beers. I began to take a closer interest on Nanda's schoolwork and helped to reinforce her reading and math skills on my own. I could see the subtle differences and the simple guiding techniques of a teacher that were lacking on her behalf. It was the deciding factor that made up my mind to move to the United States. I thought that I had a better opportunity in the melting pot there. I was becoming restless too. The grass seemed greener on the other side.

The opportunity came in 1979 when my boss was promoted to senior vice president of the U.S.-based operations of Consumers Distributing Company. I requested a transfer to move and work in the U.S.-based operations in Sparks, Nevada. On his prompting, he eventually suggested that I take up a position in Edison, New Jersey, where my experiences were more desired. I was a naturalized Canadian citizen, but I also wanted to obtain U.S. citizenship. I knew how difficult it was to enter the United States without sponsorship. The most established way with top priority for visas was given to a family member who was a U.S. citizen.

I had no relations in the United States and no one to sponsor me. I was eager to acquire U.S. residency at any cost. At the back of my mind, I also knew that I would be in a better position to help with the immigration to the United States of my parents and other brothers and sisters.

Once again, I had made a difficult decision to sacrifice everything I had earned in Canada. I had no reservations to start over and to enter unsheltered waters. I had to take the chance. I knew that thousands of Guyanese had entered the United States as students or as visitors and continued to live illegally rather than go back to the deteriorating situation in Guyana. It was common for individuals to spend thousands of dollars to obtain forged green cards or make a business arrangement in marriage with a U.S. citizen to qualify for a green card. Later the marriage would be dissolved in a divorce. Every time I heard the government quote statistics that show that half of all marriages end up in divorce, I often wondered how many of these were the result of arranged marriages. Others hopscotched the islands as tourists to reach the Bahamas. Corrupt officers and employees of the airlines and travel businesses took bribes and kickbacks and then lent a blind eye to the ongoing illegal entry to the islands. From the Bahamas it was a quick but dangerous ninety-minute ride by a speedboat in the middle of the night to the shores of Miami. The whole process was known as backtracking, and for all those that came this way, it was worth the $10,000 price tag. I have heard that some had paid up to $30,000 for the privilege to get into the United States. I may have been caught up in the hysteria of the situation at the time to enter the United States, except that I was immigrating through legal means.

My hopes had developed into an insatiable longing to make sure my children were afforded a better education, and I had to achieve the means to get them there. I wanted to be financially secure and prepare for that moment when my children would attend a university, and I did not have to worry about their tuition and living expenses. I began to see myself in their shoes and my visions in their aspirations. All the little things that I did not have and all the bigger things that I longed for, I wanted to place on a platter at their feet for the taking. I saw the opportunities that were evident everywhere, and I admired the accomplishments of those immigrants before me who dared to seek them out. I too had an eye on the prize. The thought was profound and it came in many forms and took many shapes, but nonetheless, it was purely American. It was the American Dream. It presented itself to anyone who would seek it, and the rewards never failed anyone with an inclination for hard work and a determination to succeed. The rewards are sweet in its end. It grows in your soul slowly and never dies. My dream was to own my own home without the burden of a mortgage, to own a piece of America and send the kids to college. An education meant a job and continued prosperity throughout their years in America. After all, this was what liberty and the pursuit of happiness was all about. Then my dream was to live happily in my twilight years and pass on the dream to my children.

After living ten years in Canada, I became a naturalized citizen, and yet I felt like an outsider. My second daughter, Sharda, was born in Canada, but I could not foresee anyone referring to her as a Canadian if they saw her playing in the streets. Any European child right off the boat though would be referred automatically as a Canadian. It is my firm belief that people often see skin color first, and then the stereotype from their upbringing comes into play. The feelings toward immigrants were so far entrenched that it spilled over into downright hatred and violence. In Vancouver, an Indian student waiting for his train on the platform was pushed on the tracks and killed by the oncoming train. The only motivation of the two suspects was that he was an Indian. As the incidents of hate crimes became more prevalent, the government was prompted to make such crimes a felony, and stiff sentences were imposed. At least in America you know exactly where you stand in this giant melting pot. Discrimination and racism was part of the American landscape but was changing rapidly for the better. The U.S. government was in the thick with legislations that tore down the walls of racism. The efforts of Martin Luther King and his civil rights movement opened equal opportunities for all. I always have great reverence for Dr. Martin Luther King, and I am saddened that so many blacks still didn't heed his word. He was a great hero to them, but only a few put his teachings into action. I look forward to the day when professional black athletes in baseball, football, and basketball would observe his birthday by not playing a game on that day. Every time I am at a beach anywhere, such as Daytona Beach or Myrtle Beach or Jones Beach, I am reminded of the fact that only a short time ago, I would have to stay in a section designated Colored Only. That would have incensed me furiously and burn a hole in my soul. I doubted whether I would have been able to stand by and let it prevail. My belligerent nature would not allow it. Many times I wondered what I would have done if racist groups such as the Klu Klux Klan were to burn a cross in front of my home. I knew that some of those white sheets they wore to disguise and hide their faces would have turned red before it was over.

It took about six months for me to get settled in an apartment in New Brunswick, New Jersey. Unable to find a buyer for my house in Canada, I was ready to abandon it. I gave away some furniture and yard items that I could not use in an apartment so that I could just move on.

There were no regrets. My gut feelings were that better things lay ahead, and I always heeded my gut feelings. On the very night while the truck was being loaded for the move to the USA, an offer was made to buy the house. I accepted it, knowing that I sold my house at a loss. After ten years in Canada, I was leaving everything behind to start over in the United States. Sometimes, I wondered if it was my courage or just my stupidity.

We lived at the University Towers Apartments that I like to refer to as Cockroach City. From the outside, it was a beautiful high-rise building with redbrick town houses on one side. Across the highway was a waterfront park with tennis courts along the Raritan Canal. Immediately behind was the Cook Campus of Rutgers University, which was within walking distance if Nanda wanted to study there. It was my choice. It would have been the ideal setting and cost-effective too with no room and board or travel expenses to worry about. We endured three years here. New Brunswick was a completely black neighborhood with much of the city in decay.

One of the first things to shock me was when I went to enroll Nanda at Highland Park Middle School just across the river.

"How can I help you?" asked the secretary very politely.

"We came to enroll my daughter here," I said. "This my daughter Nanda. "Here are her transfer papers. We just moved here from Canada" I continued.

"Hi there, welcome, she is so cute," the secretary said and busied herself scrutinizing the transfer documents.

Glancing out the window, I was pleased to see children dotting the school yard in idle conversations or at play. I knew Nanda and Sharda would love their schools here in Highland Park.

"What is your address, sir?" the woman asked.

"Commercial Avenue, Apartment 4D, New Brunswick."

"You mean you live in New Brunswick?"

"Yes, ma'am."

"I am sorry, sir, you can't register your child here," she said sternly.

"Why not?" I asked.

"You have to register her in New Brunswick," she continued. The smile was gone from her face in an instant as she pushed the transfer papers toward me.

"But I want her to go to this school," I protested pushing the transfer papers back toward her.

"Well, you live and pay taxes in New Brunswick," she snapped back.

"What difference does it make where I pay taxes, I pay the same equal taxes like everybody else."

"Well, that's the way it is, you have to register her in New Brunswick," she dismissed me without any further comment.

In the meantime another clerk following the conversation came over. Leaning over the counter, she politely told me that I have to live in Highland Park in order to register my daughter in any of the Highland Park school systems.

"That's just the way it is," she explained. "There is nothing more we can do."

My heart sank to a very low level in that moment. I could feel the tension as the bubble of my high expectations exploded. This was unfair, and it would eventually be the cornerstone of much of my views concerning education in this country. It's wrong when parents anywhere in the United States cannot send their child to a school of their choice. I saw it as the reason for the uneven education systems between poor black neighborhoods and rich white neighborhoods. I know of no place in the United States that can be labeled as a neighborhood of rich black people. Highland Park was predominantly white while New Brunswick was predominantly a black neighborhood with a small percentage of Hispanics. It is a fact that rich neighborhoods have better schools due to the tax base. What then has happened to "Equality and Justice for All" etched in concrete at the Lincoln Memorial in Washington DC? The shock to me was that I was trying to escape the burdensome weights of race in the schools in Canada only to be thrust right back in the thick of it. I felt defeated. It was a kick in the stomach.

Faced with this dilemma, I was forced to enroll Nanda at Lord Sterling, an all black elementary school in New Brunswick. Nanda excelled immediately upon enrollment, but I always thought the standard was lower than comparable classes in white neighborhood schools. Mr. Payne, the principal, recognized Nanda's ability and encouraged her in all areas. Mr. Payne reminded me a lot of Mr. Archer, one of the teachers at St. Patrick's Anglican School in British Guiana. Nanda contested in the city spelling bee contest. I felt comfortable with her performance and the homework that was assigned to her each day. Sharda was still in kindergarten.

As a family, we had a fairly rough time in the beginning while living in New Brunswick, but I knew it was only temporary and would soon pass. I had decided to make a brand-new start with new goals. We were barely making ends meet and constantly scraping with rent payments, car payments, and a few little luxuries we could afford. It was a big step down. In spite of the hardships, I had no regrets of leaving Canada behind. What I did not realize at the time was that my problems were beginning to compound.

Not even two months had passed after settling down to my new job that George Graff resigned from the company as president of the U.S. division. He had a disagreement with the owner and chief operating officer as far as the circumstances circulated. It was the last time I had heard anything about him. There were no good-byes, and from the grapevine I found out that he had returned to Toronto where he bought a car-wash business to service all the vehicles used by the post office in Ontario. My position in the company became uncertain. I had the option of returning to Canada since my status in the United States was a temporary worker on an L-1 visa. Fortunately, there were a few other associates in high-level management positions on L-1 visas as well, including the newly appointed president. Later that week, I consulted with Dick Zemp (the vice president and controller), who was also a Canadian. He assured me that Consumers Distributing Company would apply on my behalf for permanent resident status (green card). I had pleaded my case convincingly, relying on the fact that the company brought me to the U.S. operations and it was the company's responsibility to sponsor my application. I protested without success, when it was decided that I was responsible to pay the two thousand dollars the New York law firm of Barst and Mukamal charged for processing the application. I could not afford the fee, and in lieu of my excellent standing with the company over the years, Consumers Distributing loaded me the amount with deductions taken from my paycheck for the next two years. I had set a president. Dick Zemp noted that I was the first and only employee to whom the company made a personal loan. I was especially pleased with that gesture. Now it was just a matter of waiting two years for the application to process. Being in the United States with an L-1 visa meant my wife was not allowed to work. That presented another hurdle.

The situation was further compounded when in 1981 thousands of Cubans were exiled from Castro's jails and President Jimmy Carter allowed the Mariel boatlift bringing thousands to Miami.

It was reported that most of these Cubans were convicted criminals and mentally unstable. About the same time, I had contacted the immigration department in Newark, New Jersey, regarding the status of my immigration papers. The officer told me that my immigrant visa among others were put on hold because they were swamped with paperwork processing the Cuban refugees, and my visa could not be approved for another two years.

I was entering the country legally, with all the necessary documentation with the application filed with a respected law firm from New York. I had a job and was paying my fair share of taxes, yet I had to wait at the back of the line. It was certainly unfair and all because the Cubans came over on a boat. To add insult to injury, the Cubans received assistance from the government in the form of housing, food, and job training. They could work legally the next day, and my wife had to wait for another two years until the visa was approved.

It was like walking on eggshells for two years while I waited for my coveted green card. If I had lost my job, I would have to return to Canada.

So I walked the extra mile and became an extraordinary good soldier at work. I worked extra hard and kissed up to my bosses to be in the limelight. As manager of the returned goods department, I was very happy with my job, and the financial rewards were excellent. I refused several better-paying jobs and several promotions in order to remain in close proximity to home. I had decided that this was where I wanted to grow my roots permanently. I was more interested in maintaining stability for the children's sake. They were growing up now too.

Why did I have to go through this all over again? I used to question myself. What did I do to deserve this? I used to say to myself. Why is it that nothing seems to go right for me? I used to say in frustration. Then a voice within me would remind me of my past accomplishments, and I would dismiss it as being the fruits of my *karma*. When I had satisfied my ego that all good things usually come to those who wait, my thoughts would move on to the next level and to a winding path full of hope and desires. I wondered if I had made mistakes along the way, and every time, there were more questions than answers. For the most part, it was my hunches and gut feelings that kept me going. I believed that a man's fortune changes with time. I decided to be patient and wait for a break.

In the meantime, it was by accident that I came into contact with Laxie, whom I had not seen for more than twenty years. He was living in Queens, New York, where a sizeable number of immigrants from Guyana took up residency in what would eventually become known as *Little Guyana*. I never found out by what means he came to America, but I knew he was legally in the country, living with his wife and children. It was Laxie, who pointed me to the strategy of getting around the illegal immigration status that so many faced. Other than his wife, Laxie maintained an apartment for his girlfriend, who was illegal in the country. He had arranged with a Puerto Rican fellow who was a United States citizen to marry his girlfriend, and then the Puerto Rican would apply for his wife to be granted legal green card status. It was merely a formality as they continued to live separate lives. The monetary arrangement was $2,500 at the time of marriage in order to get the marriage certificate and then $2,500 when the green card was obtained. It was simple and completely legal. I thought this was clever, and from what I heard through the grapevine, it was the customary practice among thousands from the West Indies, India, China, and Europe. Within months I ventured into the scheme to assist my younger brothers and sisters to get into the United States. It had become a costly affair for me, but I was willing to spend thousands of dollars of my hard-earned cash on their behalf. I knew that they would never have been able to afford any decent living on their own. It meant a lifetime of rotting in impoverished Guyana, and that would have been a sore point on my conscience. Furthermore, it was my mother who insisted that I lend them a helping hand when I had returned to Guyana to take care of my father's funeral arrangements and burial in June 1981. Returning to the United States, I embarked on a deliberate effort to get them across. With the help of Amos in Canada, we sponsored my mother as a parent to Canada, paying all expenses. Since only William was under sixteen years old, he was able to accompany her on the same sponsorship.

With regard to Prem, Kamal, and Datto, I made arrangements with friends and business associates I had known to get all three of them married to U.S. citizens. In the case of Prem, the young lady was the daughter of a Baptist preacher. It was the preacher who performed the wedding ceremony at one of my friends' home in New Jersey. I paid him $2,500 for the privilege and was sorry that he passed away a few months later before I could pay him the balance owed. I would learn that money talks when the price was right, even for a man of the faith. In the case of Kamal and Datto, it was Amos who was instrumental in bringing them to Canada as visitors. Then I arranged flights for the grooms to Ontario, Canada, where the marriage ceremonies took place. Fortunately, the wedding ceremony was solemnized by one of my former pupils from Reliance S. H. School. I was surprised but pleased to learn he was ordained as a Hindu priest in Ontario and licensed to perform marriages. Being a close friend of Amos, his fees were not an expensive proposal, but the more than five thousand dollars each for the grooms and all travel expenses was more than I could afford.

Armed with the marriage certificates, it was countless hours waiting in lines at the immigration department to file the applications for immigrant status. Then, when the green card was obtained, it was more expenses for the divorce process and then many more hours to process all the paperwork. The case involving Kamal was more disturbing and very difficult for me. The boy was a brother of the fellow who had married Laxie's girlfriend. It had come to light that Laxie was refusing to pay the last installment of twenty-five hundred dollars to him because the Puerto Rican wanted to move in and live with his girlfriend. Whenever we got together, I listened as Laxie complained furiously that the Puerto Rican had planned to expose the whole affair to the immigration authorities if he was not paid the balance due him immediately. He was insisting that he live with the girl he married. On several occasions, their arguments boiled over into serious threats to each other.

A few months had gone by when I received the devastating news that Laxie had passed away suddenly. His family members claimed that he had a heart attack, but I had my suspicions otherwise. No sooner than this had occurred, I got scared of the whole incident and made no objections to awarding the other brother with any of his requests. He pestered me every week on the status of the divorce because he wanted to get married to the girl with whom he fell in love. To appease him and make him wait out the time for the immigration papers to work through the process, I gave into his demands for a Seiko watch, television set, Canon camera, and Panasonic VCR among the lump sum cash at the end. Looking back years later, I did not mind the tremendous strain on my meager salary or the risks that were involved. It robbed my own family and especially my daughters of some basic necessities while we lived in this apartment building that I liked to refer to as Cockroach City. My intentions were clear for I never wanted anything in return as I had said to them in the beginning. My only consolation for my generosity and sacrifice was that my mother was very pleased to see that her children were happy living here in the United States, especially since they have been able to establish successful lives of their own.

As a couple of years ticked by, I continued to keep my eyes on the prize. Highland Park was across the river, and I had a commanding view of the luxurious houses and parklike setting from the apartment in New Brunswick. I spent many hours gazing over toward Highland Park and dreamed of living there. This was a predominantly white neighborhood with the majority of residents being Jewish. The Highland Park High School had the reputation of being among the one hundred best high schools in the country. It was impressive although I did not know this at that time. Every day I would pass through Highland Park on my way home just to look at the school environment. I had canvassed the surrounding towns in Middlesex County and settled in my desire to buy a house in Highland Park.

I was surprised when some of my coworkers and friends tried to discourage me.

"Highland Park?" they will utter in total amazement. "Why do you want to live there?"

"What's wrong with Highland Park?" I would ask.

"Well, if you want to live among the Jews," they would frown in resignation.

I did not understand the resentment so many people had for the Jews. I did not know much about their plight in the United States, and up to now, I had very little associations with Jews. My only knowledge was the atrocities they suffered in Europe during the Second World War. There were certainly no Jews in British Guiana where I grew up. I was actually impressed with the lifestyles of the Jewish people in Highland Park. The houses were highly valued with manicured lawns and excellent schools. There was next to no crime in the town, and most Jews were family oriented. On Saturdays they walked to the synagogues with children well dressed. They all seemed happy as a family. This was what I had in mind for my family and a school and a nice safe neighborhood free from crime. Most of all I liked the close proximity of Highland Park to my workplace and its small-town image.

If there was such a thing as luck, then luck was on my side. The only other explanation was divine intervention for the events that occurred next that changed my fortunes. It was the turn of the tides for me and my quest to realize the American Dream. I always believed that I was beginning to receive the rewards for the good tidings my parents had performed throughout their lives. I had read somewhere that according to Hindu teachings and philosophy a man's wealth is in his children. What a man does in his lifetime, the rewards will be bestowed upon his children. I strongly believed in this concept and followed it religiously.

I am not a religious person by any means, and I had rarely stepped past the front door of a church or temple. However, I am a devout believer in the simple truths of life. I followed in the more spiritual values that presented a realistic concept to life and its meanings. "Whatsoever a man sows, he shall reap" was one of them. All my days I did the right thing and endured the seeds of my labor. There were the many times when there were hardships and things were not going well that I questioned the wisdom of God. What have I done to deserve the years of constant struggles? When will the good light shine in my direction? I could have gone to church and prayed. What is the difference if I just prayed at home? Jesus prayed in the garden of Gethsemane all by himself. I believed in this omnipresent God and called on the names of all his prophets. I called on Jesus and Lord Rama and Lord Krishna and Lord Sewji and Gautama Buddha and Mohammad and the God of all Gods. I asked nothing for myself. All I asked was for my children to get a higher education. Foremost was my burning desire for Nanda and Sharda to go to high school and eventually college and to a better life. That time had come for my prayers were answered.

One afternoon I dropped in at the Century 21 Realty Office in Highland Park to make inquiries. The realtors gave me a scare and more things to worry about. The salesman inquired about the price range of the house I wanted to purchase.

"About forty to forty-five thousand," I said. I had a glimmer of hope that he had properties within that price range in the area.

"Hahaha," the salesman burst out in uncontrollable laughter. I felt like a fool sitting there.

"Forget it," he said.

"There are no houses in this area in your price range."

"Why don't you try the New Brunswick area?" he suggested.

The conversation went no further, and when I left, I could still hear the laughter as a couple of other sales associates joined him in a huddle. I began to wonder if I would ever be able to live in Highland Park. My hopes of sending the kids to school there were dashed for the time being. I always clung to hope and waited for the tables to turn. It was my firm belief that nothing stays the same and it was only a matter of time. Every day, I reminded myself that good things always come to those who wait.

It would be three weeks later when I accompanied an Oriental woman to view a house in Highland Park. The woman who had made the offer to buy the house did not qualify for a mortgage, and the house was on the market again. Without seeing the inside of the house, I offered to buy it immediately for the asking price of $45,000. On October 1, 1982, we moved into our modest two-bedroom, two-story home at 237 Dennison Street in Highland Park. Directly across the street is a Jewish synagogue.

We did not have curtains on the windows and hung sheets over them, but it did not matter. The bathroom and kitchen were turn-of-the-century design, but it did not matter. The basement was of dirt floor, but it did not matter. All that mattered was the excellent school system. Nanda started grade seven at the middle school, and Sharda started grade one at Irving Elementary School. Nanda had a late start and some difficulty in adjusting to the higher standards of academic work but caught up quickly. When she started at the high school a few years later, the first part of my dream was underway. The convenience of the high school was within a three-block walking distance from my home. I had read in the borough's newsletter that 85 percent of students who graduated from Highland Park High School went on to four-year colleges and 15 percent to two-year colleges. These were excellent odds in my favor, and I kept my fingers crossed. Every day I would pass by the high school on my way home from work only to be reminded how Nanda and Sharda would have the privilege to attend. This would fulfill my dream for them to take the opportunity for a higher education.

My home at 237 Dennison Street, Highland Park, New Jersey, where my wife and I have lived the American Dream since the fall of 1982.

Every day I kept my eye on the prize. It was very simple at first. After high school, I envisioned that Nanda and Sharda would go on to college and hopefully Rutgers University, which was just across the river. In the years to come, the mortgage would be paid off on the house, and eventually I would own a piece of America. This was my American Dream, and I tried to do everything I could to stay on that course. My actions were deliberate. I wanted stability first and foremost. I refused to take on new offers for better-paying jobs as my skills as a warehouse returns manager were in great demand. General Electric Company, Sunbeam Corporation, and Service Merchandise offered me higher salaries to lure me to their operations. Although I considered them, it meant relocating outside the state of New Jersey, and I was reluctant to uproot my children from their stable environment and the friends they had cultivated. I knew firsthand of the problems that can result from sudden changes and thus shunned the opportunities to climb the corporate ladder. Upgrading to bigger and more luxurious housing went to the wayside also. There were times when I regretted my decisions, but in the end I was better off staying in Highland Park. I was reminded by one of my father's sayings, "A slow cent is always better than the fast dollar." From this I took considerable consolation. So I stayed on in my little house, my little castle. In the years to come, the roots went deep here, and I never found another reason to move anywhere else. I became superstitious about this house, and it remains to this day. Luck shined on me and my family and in more ways than I wished for. As my economic situation became better, I wanted to sell this house and move to a bigger house with more amenities such as a garage, but I felt I would lose the memory of those good years there. Then there was a feeling within me that the luck this house brought me would then run out, and the fear of not wanting to go through hard times again made any suggestions to move futile. Not even a dozen of the king's men or a dozen of the king's horses could move me. My ascent to achieve the American Dream was slow but steadfast. Like the saying goes," All good things come to those who wait."

It was an idle conversation I had with one of my coworkers that made me reflect on some of the things I had done. He related how he had worked so hard all his life to give his teenage daughter all the privileges and comforts of life. Yet he had nothing to show for it. His daughter became disrespectful, and her troubled behavior caused him much heartache. I could see the depressed look in his face.

"Ram, how did you do it? What's your secret?" he asked.

"I really don't know, just lucky I guess."

That question followed me like a shadow over the years. My reliance on keen observations and my own experiences raising two daughters have taught me a few valuable lessons. It has long been every parent's dream for their child to become a doctor. I was no different. When asked, it seems that doctor comes first, not lawyer, not engineer or scientist. I am sure there are volumes written on the do's and don'ts on how to prepare a child to become a doctor. I can only offer these simple suggestions that dispel some of the myths. From the literature available and the advice of educators and college counselors, I was led to believe that a child had to have some exceptional ability and a high IQ to enter the medical profession. I beg to differ from what I observed from the application process and the selection criteria of the medical colleges. My firm beliefs were that there are millions of parents who never consider medical school as an option for their sons or daughters because their children are considered as average students. I am sure one can find many doctors who will confirm that at some point they were just an average student. Both Nanda and Sharda started out as average students in high school. They did not display any extraordinary talent or any exceptional level of intelligence. What they possessed were old-fashioned family values with the incentive to persevere and succeed at any endeavor.

In my opinion, a child's drive and self-motivation are much more important factors. Here the child's personality comes into play. A doctor is a caring person and must deal with a multitude of different situations every day. Life and death rest in a doctor's hands and at every moment on the job. A child cannot become a doctor because the parents want the child to be a doctor. Even doctors cannot get their own children to take up the medical profession. One cannot wait until career day in high school to decide. It is easy to look around and find no president, no senators or congressmen or some of the richest people in the United States who have had a child who went to medical school. It is not that simple, and it does not happen overnight. I know I was on the right track when I planted the idea early in their minds and watch it radiate in every activity they involved themselves.

Some values are taught while others are learned. Kindness, respect for others, integrity, and tolerance are some of those values I tried to instill in the upbringing and character while growing up. They are of the utmost importance in a doctor's skills. A doctor treats patients and always sees the person as a patient first. There is no room for cultural bias and hatred that is so common in society today. The best doctors never fathom such feelings. A doctor is a people person.

Summer activities are just as important. Admission offices look carefully at what students did with their spare time during the summer months. A student with a 4.0 average may not find this important and may spend his or her summers surfing the waves of Waikiki, camping the Great Smokey Mountains, or backpacking through Europe. There are many stories of students with superior GPAs whose applications to medical schools were rejected in favor of students with a lesser GPA. Medical schools look for students whose summer activities complement and reinforce their goal to become a doctor. Volunteer work at a local hospital goes a long way in making an indelible impression on anyone. While in high school, Nanda was a volunteer at St. Peter's Hospital in New Brunswick and a coordinator in the parks and recreation department for youngsters.

It is different with every parent, but one crucial element in a child's development is the home environment. It is the atmosphere in the home that creates the child. A child only spends eight hours per day in school, but it is said that two-thirds of what a child learns is from the home. I have had no quarrel with that statement. What I tried to do was to provide safety in the home and without fear of anything or anyone. It allows for freedom of expression. Drawing from my own experiences, I recognized the *generation gap* as they refer to it in the 1980s with my own children. I had seen the start of the new age of electronic gadgetry, computers, video games, and the bombardment of new sounds in music, new styles of dress codes, MTV, and the development of the Internet. It was enough to drive any parent crazy. I must say that I never interfered with their likes and dislikes as long as they did well in school.

"As long as you get As in every subject is all I want to hear," I used to say.

"Don't be the best, just try to be in the top 10 percent."

Then I would relate some stories about my days in school as a contrast. After a while, I was sure I sounded like a broken record. I was sure of it because they would always say, "We have heard that before." One summer I returned to Guyana taking Nanda and Sharda for a summer vacation. They saw firsthand the school I attended and the harsh living conditions in which I grew up. I am sure that experience reinforced their commitment to do much better, considering that they had a better opportunity here in the United States. However, the rewards for their hard toil at the end of each school year were sweet. Every year we embarked on a vacation to a different city in the United States. In some years we sailed the seas in few first-class cruises through some of the most exotic islands in the Caribbean. I am sure it reinforced the fact that high school and then a college education was top priority for them. My expectations were surpassed.

On June 30,1989, we received confirmation from Boston University that Nanda was accepted into their six-year medical program with explicit acceptance into medical school. We had closely watched our mail for this long-anticipated reply since her initial application in January. From that afternoon our lives were changed forever. I must have been dazed because I kept scanning those few words over and over, three or four times just to be certain. I still did not believe it and handed the letter to my wife to read it out loud so that I could catch every word and that there was no mistake. Then it sank in; yes, Nanda was accepted into medical school at Boston University. We had a doctor in the making. Until this letter arrived, I don't think anything had ever compared closely to that moment. I had that certain feeling of fullness at heart and euphoric jubilation. I kept staring at the letter, and my wife rushed to phone Nanda with the good news. I had not felt this way since I passed the PTA exam in 1962. Without a doubt, I have had many successes and had accomplished many things since my days as a school teacher. Yet no single moment brought about such a rush as these brief few seconds. If there was ever such a thing as walking on cloud nine, then this was it. That was how happy I felt, peaceful and serene. The daily stress at the workplace and the financial burden that worried my very thought just vanished that very moment. I was never the same person again. I felt like I was being transformed into a realm of a new dimension. Everything began to look different, and my perspective of events around me changed in the way I saw them, a more satisfying way. I walked proud, and even when things were not going right, my thoughts always veered away to a future when there would be a doctor in the house. Then everything seemed all right, and the pep in my step would be there again. I was on the verge to realize the American Dream. All I had to do now was wait and let time run its course.

I can only imagine how ecstatic Nanda was too. All her hard work and dedication, all her tireless efforts and resiliency throughout her youthful years finally paid off. She was a well-rounded student and excelled in everything she attempted. Academically, she ranked eighth in her senior class standing and earned a scholarship to Boston University. In sports, she played softball and field hockey for the varsity team and was involved in music and was editor of the high school's year book. Because of her excellent performance in biology in her freshman year at Boston University, she was invited to become an undergraduate teaching assistant in that course, which she did as a volunteer. At the end of her second year, she was accepted into medical school in Boston University's Modular Medical Integrated Curriculum (MMEDIC). Every year fifteen outstanding students from a pool of students nationwide are selected to undergo an integrated curriculum in liberal arts and preclinical modules of instruction. Students are granted explicit acceptance into Boston University Medical School and must follow a definite course outline and maintain a high grade point average. This program allowed students to plunge directly into medical courses while in their third and fourth years of their undergraduate degrees and thus a gradual transition into the School of Medicine Curriculum. Students in the MMEDIC program were better equipped to pursue their medical degrees, and in most cases, they outperformed their counterparts accepted in the traditional method. They became better doctors. The odds of Nanda getting into medical school were staggering. At Boston University she was one of a class of 135 students accepted from an applicant pool of over six thousand students. Later, I came to realize that to become a doctor, the most important step was to get accepted into a medical school. The rest would come, and I was confident that Nanda would do well in her studies. I had no doubts about financing her medical education. I was ready to spend every penny I had, and I eventually did spend every penny I had without second thoughts.

Soon afterward my attention turned to Sharda's activities. I wondered if she too could get into medical school. What an accomplishment that would be. I could only hope and wait. She was growing up in the shadows of her sister and six years her junior. She was naturally a bright child, and although she emulated Nanda in most ways, she carved out a personality of her own. She was more quiet and reserved. I noticed that she never wanted the same styles of clothing and preferred to differ in her lifestyles and tastes in music, movies, and general habits. I knew it was hard for her to grow up in Nanda's shadows, especially when we praised Nanda and showed some parental bias a lot of times. It was never intentional. I am sure there was jealousy although she never showed any signs of such. I wanted her to be jealous for I always thought maybe it would serve as a motivating factor. I wanted her to aim high, to achieve at the same level. When her time came, we bestowed the same glory and adulation on her. One thing was very clear; Sharda always wanted to be a doctor. I had planted the idea very early on. I took the advice of the Japanese gentleman I had encountered at my job in Canada and followed the principle devoutly. It worked for Nanda. I reasoned that it would work for Sharda also. At show-and-tell classes in the early grades, Sharda would always say that she wanted to be a doctor when she grew up. This was music to my ears. I can't remember her wanting to be anything else in all our conversations, not a teacher, not a lawyer, or anything else. In one of her science projects in grade four, she presented the workings of the human heart complete with a plastic model that acts like a pump. Tubes representing the arteries and veins carried a red dye liquid to and from the heart with instructions on how it worked. I was amazed at how meticulously she had assembled the project mostly on her own. It was a pleasure to hear the kind reviews from the passersby at the science fair.

By the time Sharda entered Highland Park High School, her path was very much laid out like her sister. She played softball and field hockey for the varsity team. She played the flute in the high school's marching band and took dance lessons in ballet and modern jazz. Every Fourth of July, I watched proudly as she passed with her marching band down Main Street in the annual parade through Highland Park. Academically, her grades were excellent, and she concentrated in the science subjects. Graduating in 1993, she ranked third in her class. Her efforts to gain admission to a university were more concentrated and more focused than on a few colleges. This was made easier too with the experiences we had accumulated during Nanda's excursion some six years ago. By now the college experience was becoming a familiar scene to Sharda. Some of the mystery that surrounded college courses and dormitory living were more transparent from the countless visits we made to Nanda at Boston University. She received admission to premed at Rutgers University, Washington University, Ohio State University, and an excellent financial package at Boston University with over $16,000 per year in grants and scholarship.

At Michigan State University, she applied to the medical scholars program, which accepted ten outstanding high school seniors each year from across the nation. The MSU College of Human Medicine recognizes outstanding high school achievement and early dedication to medicine by offering conditional College of Human Medicine acceptance to each medical scholar. Medical Scholars fulfill medical school admission requirements through the nationally respected MSU premedical program. Because they have been accepted to the College of Human Medicine, medical scholars can enjoy their rich and diverse undergraduate experience, free from concern about the traditional medical school application process. Sharda was called for an interview, and I accompanied her, taking the Amtrak train to East Lansing, Michigan. It was February, and temperature was close to zero. We could not walk a hundred yards without feeling completely frozen. Although the interview went well, I was not thrilled about her prospects of attending Michigan State University. She was turned off by the bitter cold weather and the never-ending scenery of farmland. We did not bother to take a closer look at the campus any further and scurried home on the next train. I thought her mind was leaning toward Boston University, and that would have been very satisfactory to me. My wife was happy too for it would mean frequent trips to Boston with both daughters there. I had purchased a condominium in Brookline within walking distance of Boston University and a short drive to the medical school at Boston City Hospital. Nanda still had two more years in medical school, and then I was hoping that she would do her residency at Boston City Hospital. Both Nanda and Sharda would live in the two-bedroom condo, and their life would be somewhat comfortable. I could not help the comparison with my days at McMaster University in a little room. Everything was falling into place. At least that was what I thought.

Two weeks later, there was a phone call from the Dean of Admissions at Michigan State University. Sharda was not home, and I took the call. The dean informed us that Sharda was accepted as a medical scholar, and she wanted to know if Sharda might accept the spot. Before the dean could finish the sentence, I had said yes a few times. I tried hard to be cordial and keep from jumping up and down. It was the crowning moment of my life. I was so overjoyed; I had to run up and down the stairs just to relieve some of the energy that was building. I knew Sharda would have accepted too, but I did not take a second to think about it and accepted the offer on her behalf without any reservations. This was a moment of monumental proportions for me, and I reflected to savor every second. Suddenly, it dawned on me that all that I ever wanted was at hand. I have two daughters, and both would be doctors. I was sure that I would never experience another happier occasion in my lifetime. It became doubtful that there would be anything that could top that moment. My dream was coming to pass, the American Dream. This was the prize at last, and when they both become doctors, *nirvana* would be at hand. My emotions were numbed and at awe of Sharda. My thoughts could not fathom or imagine what it would be like to be accepted into medical school immediately after graduating from high school. The odds were enormous. When she was accepted into medical school, she was one of a class of 116 students from an applicant pool of 3,696 students. As a medical scholar, she received a scholarship of $4,000 per year. Together with additional grants and student loans, Sharda was able to finance her education for the eight years she would spend at Michigan State University. It was easy for her to be convinced that a bird in the hand was worth two in the bush. She quickly rejected the offer from Boston University since there was no assurance that she would get into medical school there. That summer, we toured Michigan State University to find the most beautiful campus among the big ten universities. The lush lawns, sprawling academic buildings, and student residences dotted the landscape with the majestic Spartan Stadium and other sporting facilities as its showcase. The campus reminded me of my days at McMaster University and how little student life at a university had changed.

With both Nanda and Sharda in pursuit of their MD degrees, my wife and I were as happy as could be. We were content to be modest about the prospect of two doctors in the family. At work I spoke very little about my children, not wanting to sound off as if I was boasting or anything of that nature. I knew my wife was proud to announce it to all her friends. It was a good thing though, and she commanded respect and was revered by all her coworkers. Even the president of the company paid his respects to her many times on chance encounters at the workplace and would always ask how the kids were doing. I only said anything if I was asked directly. It was a rare occasion when anyone from my extended family inquired about their welfare. I was more superstitious. I reminded myself of one of Aesop's famous fables about the woman going to the market with a basket on her head full of eggs. She had dreams of selling all the eggs, and with the money in hand, she would buy a dress to wear. Then she would show everyone how pretty she looked and would dance in this way. As she was swaying her body, the basket fell, and all the eggs were broken and her dreams shattered. It was a valuable lesson she learned: *don't count the chickens until the eggs are hatched.*

It was two years to Nanda's graduation and eight years to Sharda's graduation from their respective medical schools. Nothing seemed to have mattered to me anymore, and I lacked the motivation to pursue other goals. Nothing seemed to have bothered me in any particular way. Bad news whisked by me like water off a duck's back. Consumers Distributing was closing its U.S. operations, and I was about to lose my job after twenty years of loyal service. But that did not bother me as it should. I knew that I could always find another job. I had the ability and willingness to do anything even if I had to become a janitor. Buried in the thought that my daughters would be doctors someday, I resigned to the feeling that my life was over. All my energies were focused in this direction only. The part I was destined to play in my karma had come to an end. There was the unexpected turn of events in one of life's mysteries that would also play out around me. This I had to learn the hard way. One must be mindful of what one wishes for, I had heard someone say, because you never know when your wish would be granted. Years later it had come to pass that I eventually took on a temporary position as a janitor at Robert Wood Johnson Hospital while Sharda was performing her medical resident training there. It afforded me free medical coverage. Here again my work ethics would stand out. I had frequent conversations with the dean of the medical school, but it landed me in trouble. Fearful of my close relationship with the dean, my inexperienced boss, half my age, terminated my services on cost-saving grounds explaining that her department was in budget shortfall. However, I knew she was more concerned that I would expose the theft and unsanitary practices of some employees. It was a blessing in disguise for I successfully embarked on property acquisitions in Florida.

There were many, including my family members, who thought that I was wealthy and had a lot of money. I never understood this. If someone asked for anything, I would always say, "What do you think, I got a tree growing money in the backyard?" Even Nanda and Sharda thought that I had a money tree in the backyard. What they did not realize was that together with my wife, we had a comfortable income. We worked hard and steady and saved most of our income. I made a few extra dollars from a flea market business I undertook between 1986 and 1990. Afternoons and weekends I fixed and prepared slightly scratched and dented items for sale, which I purchased by the truckload from a friend I came to know from Pennsylvania. It was a marvelous experience for me, and I did well trying to wheel and deal in a world of cutthroat competition and the haggling with irritating bargain hunters bent on getting a deal for a dollar. It was satisfying to go home with sales of over three thousand dollars on some weekends and to have Nanda and Sharda help count the money. Now I know why they thought I was rich. Furthermore, I hardly spent any money on house-ware appliances or jewelry.

As manager of the returned goods department, I conducted warehouse sales to the general public on behalf of the company under the supervision of the president. I was in charge of the whole operation from setting up the displays to pricing and supervising the staff. I benefited from the very low price I was able to buy the items I needed, and naturally, I got first choice of the pickings. Everything, from televisions, stereos, video recorders, and lawn furniture to watches and jewelry, I bought at a bargain, and I did buy a lot of stuff. When Nanda and Sharda went on to college, all they had to do was take what they needed from the stockpile in my basement of microwaves, record players, and kitchen wares, among others. This was another reason why they thought I was rich. My basement looked like a K-Mart store to them. All I did was take advantage of a good situation. I was at the right place at the right time. This was my payoff for the long hours and hard work I put into the preparation and making the sales event successful. I remembered the one weekend we had sales of over $250,000. I was required to have a police escort with me all the time as I counted and safeguarded the cash receipts. That evening, my company's president asked me to take the cash home and to bring it back for the bank deposit the following Monday morning. That was the trust the company and the president had in me. However, I did not take the chance, and I eventually called the Brink's Security to collect and deliver the cash to a night depository at a bank. After ten years of purchasing my house, I paid off the mortgage. Although I had not realized it at the time, it was monumental for me to have owned my own home and thus a little piece of America.

It was a sad day for me in October 1993 when Consumers Distributing Company closed its doors and handed over a meager severance pay. I had spent twenty years there, and it was my only full-time job since graduation from McMaster University. Life continued in any case, and in no time I had found another comparable job but with next-to-no-fringe benefits. I had to work my way to the top again. I had only one thought in mind. Whatever it took, my children must complete their education. I could have retired or invested in any business enterprise I chose. I had enough to live comfortably for the rest of my life somewhere in Florida. I contemplated buying a farmland just so that I could ride around on a tractor and do some ploughing and keep a cow and a horse and a few animals as pets. I gave this up when everyone started to laugh. My ultimate plan was to move to Bora-Bora in the Tahiti islands and live out a simple life as an islander with no modern conveniences. It would be just like my early days in Guyana. All I wanted was a little thatched hut right on the beach overlooking the lagoon with its aquamarine waters, shimmering over the pearl white sand. I imagined sleeping in my handmade Indian hammock under the shade of coconut trees, sipping rum and coconut water, and listening to the enchanting guitar strings of Polynesian music as the rest of the tourists passed by in awe. A bicycle to ride around the island would have been sufficient, and the luxury of a satellite dish hanging on the coconut tree to watch HBO Movies on television would be a welcome gift. Then, when Nanda and Sharda were on vacation from college, they could visit to enjoy snorkeling and diving among the shimmering aquamarine waters of the coral reefs. I could have lived the good life in exotic Polynesia, a dream that I am still pursuing. Everyone is still laughing.

Instead, reality always came back to awaken me. I was reminded every so often of the enormous costs of a medical school education. As it so happened, I had no choice but to invest in two medical students at the same time spanning a period of sixteen years. Surprisingly, I ended up spending every dollar I had earned. There were no regrets. My only desire was for them to enjoy their college years because I considered it the best years of their lives and to live and study in comfortable surroundings. My own experiences living hand to mouth each day compelled me to spend all that I had to pave the way. My motto was that it was only money anyway; here today, gone tomorrow. However, the making of a doctor was forever priceless. It has been every parent's dream to have a child as a doctor. I don't know what the odds are to have one member of a family as a doctor, but to have two doctors in the same family, I am sure it must be staggering. I took comfort in that fact. It was a long and dusty road to the ocean.

Nanda Ramsaroop MD graduated from Boston University in May 1995. After completing her residency training in internal medicine at New York University at its Bellevue and Tisch Hospitals in Manhattan, she joined a group practice at the Long Island Medical Center in Lake Success, New York. Nanda resides in Minneola, Long Island, New York.

Sharda Ramsaroop MD graduated six years later in June 2001 from Michigan State University. She completed her residency training in internal medicine at Robert Wood Johnson Hospital in New Brunswick, New Jersey. Then she pursued a clinical fellowship program at New York Presbyterian Hospital of Cornell University in New York City. She has since joined the house staff as an assistant professor of medicine and attending physician in the Division of Geriatrics and Gerontology.

It was a proud moment for all of us when a year later, Sharda was honored by receiving the prestigious Physician of the Year Award for her hard work and dedication to patient care. I chalked it as one of my most proud moments. Sharda resides in the Upper East Side of Manhattan, New York City.

Nanda D. Ramsaroop MD

Graduation day at Boston University, School of Medicine, May 1995

Sharda D. Ramsaroop MD

Graduation day at Michigan State University, College of Human Medicine, June 2001

CHAPTER 8

The American Dream

Wisdom comes with age.

—A proverb

I have come to realize that my experiences were the best teachers on the nature of life's mysteries. There is no substitute for a firsthand experience, and this has been the basis of my understanding of the interactions of everyday events that play out in our lives. Since my years as a primary school teacher, I have always been a keen observer of the forces around me that shape the circumstances that propel the way we live and behave. One of the most prolific of these has been the far-reaching consequences of poverty and how pervasive it has always been around the world. Like the waves of the ocean, it rolls continuously in a never-ending cycle. Its power is always beyond our challenge. Reflecting on my own childhood memories, it had become easy for me to understand this phenomenon and how growing up in needy conditions created certain basic needs. In due time, these needs developed into strong desires. It was these desires that created my dreams. Without a doubt in my mind, I can say unequivocally that it was these dreams that became the driving force from within me. This powerful force captivated my will to achieve, and consequently, it became the key to my successes in life. Without dreams, life is no more than a log adrift in the open oceans. There is a lack of purpose.

There are men and women in all walks of life who have stories to tell. Most have dreams of something that they want in their lives. Many never realized their dreams. There are those who have had humble beginnings and acquired great wealth. Countless others with little opportunity have risen to esteemed positions of stature and recognition. Some had just a simple passion and acquired a deep satisfaction when it was accomplished. In others it was merely an idea that had been brought forth by their efforts. There are as many dreams of successes as there are Americans, and each dream is unique in its own merit.

But what is *the American Dream?* Does personal success or the accumulation of large material wealth mean that one has realized the American Dream? People acquire personal successes in almost every country. One can find wealthy people in the poorest of nations. Men and women with positions of power and prestige can be found living in every corner of the globe. Is personal success and wealth the American Dream? Why is the American Dream unique only in America? Why is it that a billionaire living in America is living the American Dream whereas a billionaire living is India is not? I have often wondered if I have reached the stage where I can say that I have realized the American Dream.

How can I fathom the thought that I am living the American Dream? Exploring my thoughts and searching for the answer to that question has been a grueling task for some time now.

The term *the American Dream* has been used so loosely by so many that I am almost convinced that the concept has lost its true meaning. Its meaning has noticeably changed over the years, and it depicts different things to different people. It stirs up varied emotions all the time. Here were a few of the responses I got when I asked some people on the street what their concept was of the American Dream:

- "I am free, and I can do whatever I want."
- "It's enjoying life to the fullest without the government on your back all the time."

- "In America, I can send my children to nice schools and get them well educated."
- "No doubt about it, it's owning your own home and living like a king."
- "In America, everybody has a chance to work hard and become rich."
- "Hey, I know one guy who only came to this country one week ago, and he bought a lottery ticket and won a million bucks. That's the American Dream, baby."
- "Man, I get my vacation every year and just go sit at the beach. Last year I took my family to Disney World, had a great time."
- "It is living in a home, having a nice job, and enjoying life with my children."

Dan Rather in his book *The American Dream* said that the American Dream is simply "well what Americans dream of."

With all due respect to a writer and journalist of such great caliber, I always thought that statement was too much of a simplification. There is certainly more to it than that. Although I do not disagree with it altogether, I have had my own idea of what constitutes the American Dream. It was this idea that spawned my efforts over the years. It is deeply rooted in the American culture, and it can only be understood in a historical perspective.

The American Dream as I have come to know it has its roots in the early 1950s. Although the term was used earlier, *the American Dream* was fabricated and reinforced in this era, and thus its concept has remained uniquely American. It is easy to see why when we consider the climate of events and put them in perspective.

The Second World War (1939-1945) consumed all Americans, and it thrust this nation into a bloody conflict after the Japanese bombed Pearl Harbor, Hawaii, on December 7, 1941. The United States government was quick to respond. Americans of Japanese descent on the West Coast were interned in concentration camps and their personal properties and homes confiscated. One must be mindful of the fact that these Japanese were American citizens by birth. What American Dreams did the thousands of Japanese American children living in these concentration camps have at this time? I asked.

With Adolf Hitler on the war path as his army invaded and occupied nations through Europe and elsewhere, the Germans were hated, the Russians were looked upon with suspicion, and the Japanese were scorned. Americans of African descent were still second-class citizens, but they were requested to give their lives fighting for their country in the battlefields in Europe and the Pacific. Many did so gallantly with great distinction and honor for their country. Yet what American Dreams did millions of African American children living in a segregated America have at this time? I asked.

Up to this point, immigrants in the United States were mainly whites from European countries who assimilated readily into the general population. It is often assumed that they came for the American Dream. The records show that most came for the economic opportunities and to escape the harsh and oppressive governments in their own countries. At the turn of the century, the immigrant population was still poor and outcast. Where they came from were poorer in places like Ireland, Italy, Sweden, Poland, and other areas. They came for the economic advantages available in America, although it was often claimed that they came for freedom. It was not for freedom that they came. It was for a chance to find work and earn money. Later the entire family followed. Freedom came later when it was inherent that they fight to preserve the wealth that they accumulated. What American dreams did the millions of immigrant children living in the ghettos of most American cities have at this time? I asked.

There was no doubt that many came to America for the freedom to express their religious beliefs. Scandinavian and German immigrants of the mid-1800s settled in the Midwest as farmers. In the late nineteenth century,

Southern and Eastern Europeans came to work in the factories. Jews fled religious persecution while Asian immigrants crossed the Pacific to find work in the American West. What American Dreams did these immigrants and their children have at this time? I asked.

Before the start of the Second World War in 1939, the country was beginning to recover from the Great Depression. With the exception of a small percentage, most Americans hardly had an opportunity for success. The dust bowl in the southwestern states devastated the landscape and disrupted the food supply. Citizens with little to eat crammed the soup kitchens in urban areas, begging for scraps of food. What American Dreams did millions of Americans standing in line for a bowl of soup have at this time? I asked.

In the roaring twenties, only the rich and the famous enjoyed life in America. With alcohol prohibition as the law of the land, mobsters and gangs ruled the inner cities with officials corrupted by drugs and crime. What American Dream did a man on the street have at this time? I asked.

Going back a little further in time, we found a divided America. The 1896 Supreme Court decision in Plessy vs. Ferguson upheld the constitutionality of a Louisiana law requiring whites and *colored* persons to ride in *equal* but *separate* railway cars. The ruling sanctioned segregation in public schools based on race. America was a divided nation, and the scars were evident in every social gathering. Signs such as Colored Entrance and Whites Only hung in most public places. In every rural town or city block, whites resided on one side of the township and blacks on the other. What American Dreams did a Negro family have in this era? I asked.

Before 1926, even white American women in this country did not have the right to vote in any form. The United States of America was a country created by men, its laws were made by men, and only men governed this country until then. In a culture of men only, what American Dream did a woman have at this time? I asked. Yet women comprised about than half of the population.

Scenes like the above kept me wondering over the years.

Beyond those years, it is hard to see what American Dream existed for a large part of the population when slavery was the rule of the land. There is no doubt that whatever successes and wealth accumulated were vested in the hands of a few. They had the overriding power. What American Dream did these slaves have at this time? I asked.

There are some who would say that the founding fathers had the American Dream in mind when they founded this nation and wrote the Constitution. Yet others have pointed out that these very founding fathers were more inclined and acted to protect their holdings in land and ownership of slaves. It would take a century and more to correct the inequality and injustices in the Constitution through amendments to protect a vast majority Americans that were left out. What American Dream did the founders of this nation have at this time? I asked.

Now, after the Second World War, everything in the American landscape began to change. In the beginning there were problems, and the outlook was not so promising. The American Dream was not so apparent. The cold war with the Soviet Union cast a dark shadow in America, and the territorial disputes between North Korea and South Korea plunged the United States into another conflict. President Harry Truman ordered the development of the super hydrogen bomb, and U.S. Senator Eugene McCarthy of Wisconsin launched his investigations to weed out communists and subversive elements of the population. In his senate hearings, he made reckless allegations. Anyone who criticized the government was considered an enemy and traitor and was branded a communist. People feared to speak or engage in organizations that would brand them as communists. Many lives were ruined needlessly. He trampled the First Amendment rights of many American citizens. This was the climate in the country, and I wondered if anyone ever thought about the American Dream when this communist purge was being carried out by our government with help from the long arm of the FBI.

Things began to change for the better when President Eisenhower took office in 1953. He concluded the war in Korea and set in motion a climate that unified the country. America began to grow and prosper. What Americans had were great ideas and individuality. We were our own thinkers and entrepreneurs. Many succeeded in their ideas.

In 1954, in Brown vs. the Board of Education, the Supreme Court unanimously rejected the *separate but equal* rationale. Its ruling struck down the laws of twenty-one states that had racially segregated public schools. It all began with Oliver L. Brown, a resident of Topeka, Kansas. In 1950, Brown tried to register his seven-year-old daughter Linda at a new school closer to their home. Her application was rejected, and that decision was challenged all the way to the Supreme Court. When the Supreme Court reversed the decision, there began the birth of a new America. It definitely started the process for the civil rights movement.

My favorite artwork by Norman Rockwell. A print hangs in my living room wall between the graduation pictures of my two daughters receiving their medical degrees. It shows a student's courageous steps entering a newly desegregated school, escorted by US Marshals, after the Supreme Court had ordered an end to unequal and inferior education. After more than four decades this scene still grips my imagination.

Most dramatically, it helped to turn around the conscience of the nation. The progress was remarkable in that many blacks were now able to attend universities of their choice and play in sports with any college team while others rose to the ranks of managers and CEOs of many companies. In this time of change, the nation was shocked with incidents of racial outrage. In Mississippi, a fourteen-year-old boy visiting from Chicago was brutally murdered for whistling to a white woman at a local corner store. Emmett Till was shot, and with barbed wire tied to his neck, he was dumped in the Mississippi River where he was found days later. When his mother laid him out in an open casket in Chicago, five hundred thousand people walked past it to view his mutilated body. At the court trial later, the whites celebrated the not-guilty verdict when the all-white jury acquitted the accused husband of the woman to whom the boy had whistled. This was because the prosecutor claimed that the mother could not identify the body and that the body was not that of Emmett Till. Blacks could not testify at the trial for fear of their lives. Willie Reed, the only eyewitness to the event, was hospitalized with a nervous breakdown after his testimony. The federal government did nothing, and Edgar Hoover of the FBI ignored the situation altogether. It was ugly, and people were disgusted for it brought out the racist nature of the South.

"The life of a Negro in Mississippi is not worth a whistle," one of the European newspapers reported. People everywhere were outraged by the incident. It can be argued that the death of Emmett Till openly sparked the birth of the civil rights movement in this country. About three months later, a black woman named Rosa Parks refused to give up her seat and go to the back of the bus for a white man in Montgomery, Alabama. Her arrest became the rallying symbol and a driving force that propelled the civil rights movement that was spearheaded by Dr. Martin Luther King and others. The result was the Civil Rights Act of 1964 and the Voting Rights Act of 1965 that constituently guaranteed every American the same opportunities for the first time in the history of the United States. Dreams were now possible for every individual regardless of race or color or economic strata.

In the early 1960s, John F. Kennedy launched his bold dream to land a man on the moon before the decade was over, and the entire nation rose to his challenge. America was one nation moving forward together. It was this unprecedented outlook for the future that spawned the American Dream as I have come to know it. There was the sense that everyone in the country had an opportunity to fulfill their dreams. Ambition and hard work were rewarded, and only the sky was the limit. This was the climate in which I found myself when I came to the United States. This was the environment in which any American was able to set goals for themselves. Only when there was personal satisfaction that the goals were achieved could one claim the American dream. Thus, it is the individual who decides on his or her American dream regardless of the dream. The common thread is that all Americans are equally afforded the same opportunity in education, employment, the military and government, among others. This remains the foundation of the American Dream. Equal access to all the resources that this country can afford became the norm. Hindrances of any kind were possible to overcome as the laws that stood in the way were changed.

The economic facts tell the whole story. The United States produced most of the world's manufactured goods since its factories remained intact after the Second World War. The United States produced more than two-thirds of the world's manufactured goods. Large corporations such as General Motors, Westinghouse, and General Electric had turned out the wartime machinery for the war effort and now turned their factories for the production of consumer goods. In comparison, all Europe was devastated. There was little unemployment in the United States, and personal income jumped. Each individual and each household had tremendous purchasing power in a short time. The wartime production of automobiles, household appliances, and basic consumer goods created a great demand for them. The GI Bill of Rights created an unforeseen prosperity and a generation of educated, ambitious veterans. Suddenly, a large segment of the population had money in their pockets to spend. It was the birth of the middle class, and they formed the backbone of the country. The blitz of advertisements on print media and especially on television that were readily available to most households spawned a network of consumerism that gripped the nation. There was a rush to buy the latest model cars, and Americans' love affair with the automobile was born. Credit was readily available, and the latest household appliances became fashionable for all to acquire. To *keep up with the Joneses* became the norm. Parents raised large families and competed to promote and pass on this prosperity to their children. The security of permanent jobs enabled families to purchase homes in the suburbs and grow roots in the community. A college education became affordable to their children. It was the dream of each parent to pass on this wealth and education to each successive generation. They wanted to pass on the luxury lifestyle they had created. They wanted their own children to buy a house and raise families of their own.

Within this backdrop, each generation fought to preserve and pass on what they had inherited. This became the American Dream for all to achieve. To preserve meant a personal involvement in the political scene and the freedom to exercise the right to vote in an election for the leaders of the government. In this way, freedom and democracy were protected under the Constitution. This a country of laws which each individual must obey and which is guaranteed by the decisions of the Supreme Court. Imagine what happens when the president does not comply with the laws. There is always recourse whether through the courts, the Senate, or the Congress. This is our right to participation in the political process. The right to vote preserves this process in the smooth transition of power in each successive government. This is the inherent American Dream. Imagine what happens if you accumulate great wealth and the government could just take it away. Imagine if you have no recourse to claim it back. I have witnessed it in my own country and many others.

The world is dotted with countries like this ruled by dictators and governments with no regard for its people or their property. This is why I came to the United States like so many millions before me and the many more millions that will come after me. This why the American Dream is uniquely American. We inherit certain rights that are guaranteed by the Constitution. We adapt to these rights, and Americans die every day to preserve and protect these constitutional rights. This was the climate when I set foot in this great country. It was pervasive, and it grew on my soul. This was the dream I had in mind. First, it was personal success through an education and the accumulation of wealth. Next, homeownership became the key toward achieving my American Dream. Paying off the mortgage and owning a piece of America without the burden of debts was the final straw in my quest. Finally, raising a family and providing the resources for my children to achieve their goals of a college education became paramount. This is what I struggled to preserve over the years and which I have passed on to the next generation of my children. This is what I knew as the American Dream.

A few summers have passed now, gone in a whisper. I enjoyed my leisure lifestyle between doing little at my home in New Jersey or driving my tractor around on my farm at my mountain retreat in upstate New York to engage in gentleman farming. In the winter months, it's always a quick escape to the warmth and sunshine of my house and wildlife sanctuary near Daytona Beach, Florida. The savings, pensions, and small fortune from my real estate investments are more than sufficient to live comfortably. There is nothing for me to complain about except that I have a few concerns for the next generation of my children and grandchildren. My only recourse is that I can offer bits of advice to anyone who would listen. With my background, I am now confident that I know a few secrets and the roadway to the American Dream for I have realized mine.

As an immigrant to the United States, it is apparent that I have valued certain things in a different light from an American born and bred here. My views on the issues reflect my experiences and accomplishments. At the same time, I have cherished some of the things that are often taken for granted by most Americans. However, I share the core values of the rich heritage and deeply rooted culture of this great nation. Over the years, I have become part and parcel American although it may not be so apparent. To bear this out, I have realized that there is one undisputed fact about America. This country grows on you. It grows on everything you become. It grows on your soul from the very moment you set foot on its soil. This is the nature of America regardless of who you are or where you have come from. However, it does take some time, and for some, this may take many years. But it will eventually overtake you in a wholesome way. It has been three decades for me, and my roots have grown deep. Its history and culture have been pervasive on me to the core. They undercut my thoughts and behavior and all those things that are good and decent about a man. I know this to be true for I have not escaped its wrath.

I remembered the many years when the American flag flew effortless in the wind in front of my home. My brother had given it to me one summer after returning from a tour of duty in the Middle East with the U.S. Navy on board the USS *Guadalcanal* (an amphibious assault ship).

I felt proud and elated every day I looked at the flag for which I would give my life to defend and protect. Since I was a little too old to join the armed forces, I was happy that my brother joined the U.S. Navy and gallantly represented our family in the name of freedom and democracy.

Tattered and torn into threads by the wind, its bright red, white, and blue colors have faded, and I have to keep it indoors to preserve it from the elements of the weather. I still treasure it for all its glory. I supposed that I could have gone to any Wal-Mart store to buy another flag. Then I felt that it would not have the same meaning. It would be worse if it was stamped Made in China. Something did not feel right to me with just any other flag. I had wanted to send the tattered flag to General Tommy Franks, who had just led the U.S. forces to topple the regime of Saddam Hussein. I would have liked to exchange it for the flag that he had behind his desk, and I am still hoping that one day I will get another American flag with some significance to freedom. It would be an honor.

America is no longer what it used to be when I arrived on its soil. Today, I sense an uneasiness in this country among its people. I wonder where we are heading in this twenty-first century. I wonder about the American Dream and whether it will still be there for the next generations of my children and grandchildren. Although it is still well-defined and reachable, I have seen signs that a downward slide has begun. In my view the American Dream is slipping away for a vast majority of Americans. The foundations that made the American Dream so accessible to all have begun to wane. It is becoming much more difficult as the time we live in undergoes dynamic changes. We are beginning to weaken the very things that made this country great. There is no doubt that America is still the greatest country on earth. Its massive economic strengths and military might are still second to none. We have been to the moon and now reaching to the stars, yet things are beginning to sour right here on this land. The evidences are all around us as the undercurrent of social and economic factors change the direction in which we are heading. What kind of America will my grandchildren inherit? I asked.

When I look around, I see a nation in agony. I see decay in its cities and streets. I see distress in the eyes of its people. Where is the America I had come to know? I was always proud to say "I am American and this is God's country." I relished its culture and values that were uniquely American. I carved out a piece of America and called it mine and basked in the glory of it. This was not so long ago, a little less than three decades. Now, I long for those days. Most people will agree that our views and opinions are shaped by our varied news media outlets. Something has gone wrong here. Following the news of the day on television and the daily print media has become extremely painful. There is not a peaceful day anymore. To know what I have in mind is simply to turn on the cable networks' news broadcasts on

MSNBC, Fox News, and CNN and listen for a few hours through several programs. Soon, one gets the feeling that the world is coming to an end. There is no consensus, and every issue gets divided along the established viewpoints of either the Democrats or the Republicans. Most of what is now considered news is merely contradictory arguments, and I find it rather depressing.

There has been a shift from actual news events in the country to frivolous gossip mongering in the same manner as supermarket tabloids. I missed the six o'clock local news followed by the half hour international news by veterans like Walter Cronkite, Dan Rather, and Tom Brokaw. There was more depth to the coverage with a wider sweep of the issues. The news was believable, and I had a sense that I was very much informed on the events of the day. Experienced correspondents and seasoned journalists stationed around the country and around the world gathered the news and reported from the field. Experts in their field were interviewed for their opinions and advice on the issues of the day. It was a time when the viewer trusted the journalist for bringing out the truth based on facts. It was investigative journalism. Of course, there are some that still exist, and the quality of reporting is excellent, but these journalists have dwindled in number. Bob Schieffer and Bob Woodward are among the last few that seem to find the right sources for their stories. Their in-depth coverage are worth noticing, unlike the clowns who shout out their biased messages every day on Fox News and then are rebutted on the other networks. I am yet to see someone with the same caliber and insight of such journalists as Eric Sevaroid of the 60 Minutes broadcast. Every Sunday evening at seven o'clock, I usually stopped all my activities to listen to his take of the day. Harry Reasoner and Howard K. Smith were of equal standing as journalists on the other networks. Nowadays, the news broadcast is more about sixty-second headlines and sound bites. There seems to be too much attention and time spent on celebrity mishaps and scandalous behavior of government officials. There have been many of these from O. J. Simpson and Michael Jackson to Britney Spears, Paris Hilton, Tiger Woods, and former president Bill Clinton. The list goes on and on with no shortage of new players.

The varied talk shows, as some have referred to them, have become boring and redundant. In order to fill the time with the twenty-four-hour news cycle, each host regurgitates an event of the day with a slightly different twist. They compete for ratings and popularity to make a mark for themselves and their career. Listening to the hosts and commentators, all that is heard is anger and ridicule, and the real issues get lost in the muddle. They masticate a story like beating a dead horse. There is usually little news from the rest of the world. It seems that the ideas and issues that rest on the minds of Americans are shaped by what is heard and seen on television. Everyone says the same thing on every talk show. Anyone who disagrees with the popular views at the time is chastised. Foremost is the obvious media bias on the coverage of politics and government. CNN condones the liberal politicians with guests of liberal points of view. Fox News creates viewpoints that slant the issues in favor of the Republicans and conservatives with critical views toward the Democrats. Why tune in to Fox News when I know exactly what the guests or talk show host will say? The talking points dwell on subject matter that is critical to anything with a liberal point of view. The aim is always the same—create controversy, condemn and raise fear. Consequently, I have had to tune out Fox News as a source for news of the day. I am unable to understand how intelligent men and women working for Fox News cling to only one side of a story as the absolute fact. The danger lies with their loyal following of listeners who share the same viewpoints. The frightening part is that these very people form a voting bloc that must be reckoned.

Too often, journalists look to the experts and seek out their advice as if they are the only ones who know the truth. Too often, the so-called experts are dead wrong. What are we to do when even the experts disagree and have different versions of the same issue? They fight and argue like little third graders in the school yard. The same freedom that we practice is the same freedom that we step on when the facts are not borne out in their entirety. For democracy to work, we must know the facts. Many journalists criticize and report on issues without knowing the facts. This is when I usually step back and resort to the old common sense. Sometimes I have found that the truth is as clear as night and day. It looks right back at you, but you must look for it first. As it turned out, I was fortunate that I kept one eye opened all the time. It was the primary reason I succeeded in my own way.

It begged the question. How did we get this way? Over the last decade, I can point to several reasons.

The Supreme Court decision to award George W. Bush the winner of the 2000 presidential election results was the start of the slide. It was a disastrous decision. The Constitution guaranteed the right of every individual to vote with the specific intention of that vote to count in any election of office bearers. If there was a problem with voting machines or the way the vote was being interpreted and counted, then there should have been a statewide recount of the votes polled. True democracy is what separated the United States from the rest of the world. When the Supreme Court intervened to decide the winner, it gave the appearance that the election was similar to any third world country. Why did we have to stoop to this low standard? With the voters' decisions set aside by the courts, it meant an assault on the basic rights of the people to choose. Who can say what motivated any of the Supreme Court justices in their final decision? They are only human, and regardless of what many may think, these mortals are no different than any of us. They are persuaded by many factors other than finding equal justice. A conservative judge would most likely vote on the conservative side of the issue while a judge with liberal viewpoints would vote on the liberal side of the issue. There is no mystery here.

The country has to sustain with several bad decisions lately. Of particular concern to me were the laws governing eminent domain.

I followed a case in Piscataway, New Jersey, for years, where a family fought bitterly to keep the farm that they possessed for generations. Many times as I passed by on weekends, it was a joy to see dozens of young children learning to ride horses. This was part of their business. The battle was lost when the court decided in favor of the township in the name of eminent domain. Although the plan was to build a shopping mall, the farm remained undeveloped and in decay. The same issues have played out all across the land where unscrupulous developers were able to take away properties from landowners through bribery and corruption of the individuals in charge.

In the name of freedom of speech, the Supreme Court sanctioned the use of advertisements in election campaign finance laws. It gave the approval for groups to run ads of any type. More than two billion dollars were spent in these so-called Swift Boat ads in 2006 to depose and defame opposing candidates. It did not matter that some of these ads were outright lies and deception to sway the voters. Democracy is at stake here, and it is reminiscent of elections in third world countries.

In early 2010, in a five to four decision, the Supreme Court handed down another landmark decision. It removed restrictions on the amount of money foreign corporations can spend on candidates running for an elected office or any political party. A century of long-standing regulations limiting campaign funding by large corporations has been set aside as the Supreme Court suddenly decided that this practice is unconstitutional and a violation of free speech. This ruling now opens the floodgates for undue influence in the electoral process by special interest groups. In simple terms, it is easy to see how money alone could determine the outcome of an election. America is for sale, some have claimed. It is only a matter of time when some corporation or billionaire from a foreign country could step up to determine who would be president of the United States because that corporation or billionaire has unlimited funds to bankroll the candidate's election efforts. It is just another assault on our democratic process.

Furthermore, I wondered where we were heading when the Supreme Court decided to tighten the screws on freedom of speech in the schools. Today, schools can limit the use of certain words such as wearing a T-shirt with a personal message and even request the removal of certain religious symbols or jewelry. Muslim girls who must cover their head and faces as their traditional mode of dress have been asked to remove them. More frightening is the unwarranted search of students' lockers and personal belongings on suspicions for illegal drugs based on the whim of a teacher or student. What has happened to our constitutional rights against unreasonable search and seizure?

In most cases, the decisions have been a five to four vote. Unanimous decisions from the Supreme Court are now far and few between. It is a testimony to the deep divisions in this country along ideological grounds, the divisions that sustain the way we are forced to live our lives. This is why I disagree with the way judges are selected to the Supreme Court. It has become more of a personal choice of the president rather than an objective search, and the best qualified candidates for the court are usually left out of the process. I think it should be an elected office, and the people should have a chance to decide by means of a vote. It is time that we consider a time limit to their tenure since health is affected by age, and the judges should be subjected to an independent health examination in similar fashion as the president. Who can say when dementia sets in as age progresses? We are leaving to chance the decisions that will influence our lives and the lives of successive generations when we have judges with no time limit to their tenure. I will never believe that all the decisions of a Supreme Court judge are based on competency.

As the eight years of the Bush administration ticked away, there was a deliberate attempt to move the country in a new direction after the terrorist activities of September 11, 2001, with the bombing of the World Trade Center in New York City. The goal of protecting the citizens of the

United States from further terrorist activities guided the government's actions. National security issues became a priority. Although the decisions of the government to go to war in Afghanistan and Iraq were not popular, I was rather supportive because I trusted the officials in the beginning. The president in taking office swore to uphold and defend the Constitution, but it was soon forgotten as the administration embarked on their own personal agenda. What is the average American to do when none of these decisions were questioned by the free press? In hindsight, it became clear that the Bush administration trampled the constitutional rights of its citizens. The Geneva convention was tossed aside, and power brokers like Vice President Cheney sanctioned the use of torture on individuals suspected of terrorist activities. We were doing exactly what we have always denounced in countries with a communist ideology and nations ruled by ruthless dictators. In so doing, we lost our moral high ground, and other nations lost their respect for the American president as leader of the free world. As a result, heads of states in some countries challenge the policy decisions of our president. I am embarrassed of the many derogatory terms that were used to describe President George W. Bush, such as being called an idiot, stupid, a Nazi, a devil, and a warmonger among others.

This trend continues as our next president Barack Obama is on the receiving end of not-so-respectful terms such as a terrorist, a Muslim, a liar, and some racial slurs due to his African heritage. Those Republicans or conservatives who did not vote for him ridicule and use offensive language to attack him on a personal level that has fostered racism and wedged a division among the American people. There are many journalists and talk show hosts that don't even refer to him as President Obama. The *Jewish Voice* magazine that was distributed in my neighborhood put out a full page advertisement saying that we take a small-time criminal from the crime pits of Chicago, and now we get a big-time criminal in a big White House. What crime did this man commit? It is offensive to say the least, but this is the state of politics in this country today. It is certainly a far cry from the days when presidents had fireside chats to inform the nation and when families gather around their television sets to listen attentively the president's remarks. The point here is that like him or not, voted for him or not, he is still the president of the United States of America. He won the election by a majority of votes in a true democratic process. This is what democracy is all about. The president represents all Americans, and we should always show our respect in decorum. We must hold our self to this high ideal or democracy as was intended by the founding fathers; otherwise, democracy will take a backseat to special interests sectors.

My ultimate concern was the assault on my freedom and civil liberties. In particular, it was the Patriot Act that was enacted by Congress in response to the terrorist attack which ignited a real fear in me. Suddenly, I found that I could be labeled a terrorist by anyone—a neighbor, a friend, a family member, or a total stranger. This is all it takes and with a phone call to the FBI, I could be whisked away in handcuffs to a terrorist detention facility in Guantánamo Bay, Cuba, and held indefinitely without a trial. My wife and children would not even be told of my incarceration. Under the Patriot Act, my home could be searched without my knowledge and any item taken, including seizing my property and freezing my bank account. It gave the government the right to collect information on the books I read, my e-mails and Internet sites visited, the subjects that I studied, the items I purchased, and such things as my medical history and finances. The act permits a vast array of information gathered on U.S. citizens such as phone wiretaps, and this information can be shared with the CIA. Thus, the law puts the CIA in the business of spying on Americans without a warrant, contrary to its charter. Most disturbing to me is that the act permits indefinite incarceration of immigrants and other noncitizens without the government having to show that they are in fact terrorists. It conjured up images in my mind of the Soviet Union during the days of Joseph Stalin and Nazi Germany during the reign of Adolf Hitler.

Knowing the sweeping powers that the Patriot Act affords law enforcement officials, my entire outlook changed. It curtailed my movement in some public places and the use of certain words in a conversation that would label me as a terrorist. Air travel was avoided altogether as I had seen reports of many travelers of Indian, Middle Eastern, and Pakistani origin escorted out of their flight because a white passenger in the same aircraft feared that they may be terrorists. I have had many instances where I received suspicious stares at a shopping mall or was followed by security guards. In other instances the courtesy to me was absent at the cash register or courtesy desk compared to others.

On one occasion, I was on my way to the post office. Two young men and an elderly individual were canvassing for their candidate during the primaries for the 2008 presidential election. I stopped to look over a colorful brochure they were handing out, and soon they had engaged me in a lively conversation.

"He is the best man to be our next president," one of the young men boasted.

"He is the kind of man that looks out for people like you," the elderly gentleman pointed out.

"People like me?" I asked inquisitively.

"Can you make a donation?" the young man intervened.

"Any amount is acceptable," the other young man pleaded.

I could sense that they were very eager to convince me of their point of view. Instinctively, I could not resist my urge to teach them a lesson. I had done it to others many times before, so I wanted to give these fellows a lecture that they may not quickly forget.

"Let me ask you something," I said as I pretended to take out my wallet.

Then I continued without interruption. "When you look at me, what do you see? An Indian or a Pakistani? Maybe you are guessing that I am probably from Bangladesh.

You don't have to answer that because I am sure you are confused. Now let me give you an idea about myself. You are looking at an individual from Guyana, and since you may have missed out in your studies of geography, that's in South America, not Africa.

I have been in this country for thirty years now, and before that, it was ten years in Canada."

Then I pulled out my daughter's business cards from my wallet, and I continued to lecture these three fellows. By now they were listening attentively, and a few other passersby had stopped to listen to the commotion.

"Here is a card of my eldest daughter," I pointed out as I handed it to one of the younger fellow. "She is a doctor."

"Wow," he exclaimed and passed the card to the others.

"And here is a card from my youngest daughter," I said proudly.

"Wow, both of your daughters are doctors," the older gentleman remarked.

"You can keep those," I remarked. "Now, I have been here for thirty years. I hold a degree in Economics from one of the best universities in Canada. Have you heard of McMaster University? I don't work anymore because I have no need to work at a job.

I have real estate properties in New Jersey, New York, and Florida that are worth more than a million dollars. I live right here in Highland Park about two blocks down that street."

Pausing for a few seconds to let all that information be digested in their minds, I asked, "And all you see is my skin color? All you see is that I am probably an Indian?

All you see is that I am an immigrant? How come you don't see me as an American?

When do I become an American to you? Do I have to wait fourteen thousand years for evolution to take place and my skin to turn white? But you will consider someone like that fellow walking down the street over there an American. He may be here illegally or just got off the boat from Russia or England or Israel, and yet he is American and I am not.

"Think about it fellows, and sorry I cannot give you a donation. My support is for Barack Obama."

I left as they were in stunned silence admiring my daughters' business cards.

It is regrettable that I have to resort to conversations of this nature, but I always prefer to make that point. I am not bothered by it anymore. My intention is to put a pause to the situation and make the other person think again. Hopefully, the next time they will see people for who they are and not to judge by ethnicity or the color of their skin. Because a person of color is different is no indicator that the person is just another immigrant. I know very well that this is not a big deal because immigration will continue to be a dominant issue. The stereotype will continue, but I am committed to do my little part to lessen the burden for the next generation. The term *illegal immigrant* has conjured up much fear in this country and is perpetuated almost daily by television personalities like Lou Dobbs for years until he was subsequently terminated from his news broadcast on CNN. It means Mexicans to him as if only Mexicans are here illegally in the United States. I understand his concerns about our border security in the southern and western states with Mexico. It is a calamity. Certainly, the Mexicans are on top of the list, but I am sure there are millions of illegal immigrants from the Soviet bloc countries, Western Europe, Asia, and Africa? Are there no illegal Jews from Israel in this country? I have never heard any television reporter claim that there are illegal Chinese in this country. Why is it that I have never seen a Help Wanted sign on a Chinese food store? Illegal immigration had become a major issue.. The government seems unable to stop the flow. I often wondered if these illegal immigrants would ever have the opportunity to realize the American Dream. How they would get the chance is yet to be seen. It was not so long ago when I arrived and had my immigration papers scrutinized for a valid visa, medical certificates, and availability of funds. I had to apply for a permit to accept employment. Today, it seems immigration to the United States is out of control. Anyone can just walk across the border from Mexico and Canada.

It is estimated that there are over fifteen million illegal immigrants in the country, and the government is willing to tolerate the situation. I am not at all concerned about immigration. People from poor countries will continue to gravitate to the United States to take advantage of the opportunities available here. The demand for cheap labor will insure the influx, and the economic benefits to the businesses that demand cheap labor will maintain the cycle. When I arrived in the United States about thirty years ago, the population was around 144 million. Today, it is more than doubled to over three hundred million. The problems facing many on social services, housing, education, and health care are far reaching, and the American dream for the vast majority is in doubt.

Considering the trend of recent years and the direction that we are heading, I can point to three distinct scenarios that have definitely contributed to the decline of the American Dream. First and foremost is the breakdown of the family as a household unit. Second, it is the faltering economy with its global tentacles. Third, and to a lesser extent, it is the decline of religion in our daily lives. All three of these factors have had a direct impact on every facet of the American culture. In my view, these factors transcend the opportunity of every American. It is these factors that underscore the difficulty for many of the next generation to realize the American Dream. Let me explain what I have in mind based on my insight and observation over the years.

With regard to the family, it is a largely forgotten fact that the home is the basic foundation of any society. The home is where the groundwork for learning and the building of individual character, values, goals, morality, self-control, and loyalty. It is the family from which the youths get their nourishment of the virtues of obedience, respect for authority, and respect for the property of others. The breakdown of the family is the heart of the breakdown of the society in which we live. This trend is underway. The role of the father is eroding. Divorce is on the rise, and it is estimated that one out of every two marriages fail. More and more children are brought up by a single parent, usually the mother. Men play around and stay away from home on business trips. Our good lifestyles have encouraged loose and easy morals. The fine edge of character has been blunted. Sexual affairs outside the marriage have become acceptable. It has intruded every facet and even to the highest levels of those we hold in high esteem.

Among the most notable in recent years was that of our president Bill Clinton. His sexual affair in 1998 with a young White House intern resulted in impeachment and a trial by the senate that paralyzed the nation and weakened our resolve. Dan Burton, a senator, at the same time was a fierce critic of Bill Clinton. He admitted to having an extramarital affair and fathered a child out of wedlock. Henry Hyde, another critic of Bill Clinton, admitted to an extramarital affair. To top it off, Newt Gingrich, the Speaker of the House, bitterly criticized Bill Clinton, proclaiming family values while he was having an extramarital affair. He resigned in disgrace after admitting to his sexual affair. These men were hypocrites at their best.

More recently, Eliot Spitzer, the governor of New York, resigned in 2008 after he was exposed for spending tens of thousands of dollars on escapades with prostitutes despite the fact that he was married with kids. John Edwards, senator and presidential candidate, taunted his family upbringing and character, fighting for the little people as he called them. He admitted in 2008 to having an affair out of wedlock with one of his campaign staff at the same time his wife was fighting a bout with cancer. Mark Sanford, the governor of South Carolina, had an affair with a woman from Argentina in 2008 and lied to his staff and family about it. Tiger Woods, the great golf legend and one of the most prolific sports figures in this country, found himself in difficulties after admitting to scandalous affairs with more than a dozen women. The list goes on and on with such names as senators Gary Condit and Mark Foley, New York Mayor Rudy Giuliani, New Jersey Governor Jim McGreevey, and others. This is nothing new since it is a known fact, although not reported fully at the time, that even John Kennedy and Franklin Roosevelt had sexual escapades during their presidency. The list is endless when it comes to celebrities and sports personalities. I can only imagine the scale of the issue as we count downward to the general population from school teachers to priests and the average American. Scandalous behavior graces our news daily. What message does it carry to the younger generation? It goes to our core values, and in the end, the family bears a heavy burden. When the culprits are caught, they rush to apologize and beg for mercy with their family at their side. In a short time, it's forgotten and life goes on as if it never happened, but the strain on that family never ends. The children suffer the heaviest burden, and they must carry it to adulthood and to the next generation. I cannot imagine the shame these children must bear throughout their lives.

We have allowed the discipline of our youths to lax, and most parents are indulging and pampering their children. America has become an affluent nation, and that in itself created its own problem. Children have become obese and lazy. Spare time after school is spent on playing video games, watching television, or surfing the Internet. This diminishes their creativity. I have seen kids from the first grade walking home from school with cell phones clinging to the ears. They don't talk to each other or stop to watch for ongoing vehicular traffic before crossing the road. There are no verbal exchanges of the day's activities, and the close friendship, togetherness, and laughter are mostly absent. Children have become loners, and those that do not measure up are ridiculed. Since the role model of the father has declined, children look to celebrities and sports heroes as role models. This is sad as some of these role models are themselves deficient in one way or the other. These are the youths who would become the adults of tomorrow. What is there to look forward to from these youths? It is no wonder that this generation suffers from a culture awakening. I am sure that some high school or college-bound students in this era have not known a world without the Internet, flat-screen television, cell phone, GPS, iPods, BlackBerry, and a host of other electronic gadgets at their disposal.

Today, millions of Americans have no high ideals or purposes for themselves. We are so wrapped up in our personal pleasures that few are willing to make sacrifices or endure any discomfort. Our material successes have dampened our resolve and willingness to make sacrifices. The resilience of the people, which was once the strength of the nation, has become a liability. Other nations such as India and China are beginning to overtake us. What has happened to the Greatest Generation that Tom Brokaw talked about in his book? We built the atomic bomb and walked on the moon. Where has that spirit of American ingenuity gone? The oil-producing nations are holding the American consumer hostage as we become dependent on oil consumption. We are willing to pay between two and three dollars per gallon for gasoline at the pump, yet millions will not give up their gas-guzzling sports utility vehicles for more fuel-efficient vehicles. Where is the outrage?

I consider modern education to be the bastion of the American Dream, but something has gone wrong here. We spend billions of dollars into the education system, but it has not been the answer and has not produced what was hoped for. An education system is supposed to disseminate knowledge so that we have the capability of solving the nation's problems. Instead, the education system itself has become the problem. The *U.S. News & World Report* (September 2009) claimed that we have 25 percent of the best universities in the world. Yet 30 percent of the over three million students who start their college career in 2009 will drop out after the first year, and nearly half of the students will drop out before they earn their degree. The problem lies with the high schools that do not adequately prepare students for the rigors of college level work. In the Detroit school system for example, it was reported that only 58 percent of high school students graduated in 2009. Statewide, the graduation rate is 76 percent. What happened to the rest of the 24 percent of students who did not graduate, I wondered. What remained was a lost opportunity for the American Dream.

Stories abound of high school seniors unable to read and comprehend a college entrance questionnaire. We are lagging behind other countries in mathematics and the sciences. What I have seen over the years as a warehouse manager were high school and college graduates who could not read write or spell to function on the job. They were unprepared to earn a living. As a warehouse manager for over twenty years, it was always a struggle to train and develop the abilities of my employees. Many had to be disciplined over simple directives and observation of the company's rules. I had to constantly oversee their activities at every turn to prevent screwups and errors that would have put my job in jeopardy. Creative genius in youths has certainly dwindled. Subjects such as geography and world history are no longer taught in the schools. We had invaded Afghanistan and Iraq, and yet some students could not find those countries on a world map. When I am asked what country I am from, I usually say Guyana. Many have confused it with Ghana in Africa. How awkward is it for me to explain that I am not from Africa. The most recent initiative of the "No Child Left Behind" program launched by the government has been a total failure. With the program underfunded, more than three million children were left behind. The College Board reported in 2009 that the SAT scores have dropped 72 points for African American students.

We seem to be living in a time where anything goes. Every idea and anything trivial becomes commercialized to earn the mighty dollar. Billboards litter the highways, and neon signs light up the city streets. Our advertisements scream and shout at materialistic goals at every turn. No one can escape the commercials on television shows, televised sports events, and even the news broadcasts. Companies spend millions competing for a few seconds of airtime on Super Bowl and World Series games to get their message out. It's all about pleasure seeking and self-indulgence. It is okay to drink this beer, smoke a particular brand of cigarette, take this vacation, wear this style of clothing, or pop this medication for ailments. I know of families spending a hundred dollars to buy a certain brand of sneakers for a child but will not spend two dollars to buy a book or school supplies for the same child. Cities and towns spend millions to build new baseball and football stadiums but cannot find the meager sum needed to fix crumbling schools. For instance, in 2009, two new multimillion-dollar baseball stadiums opened in New York City for the New York Yankees and the New York Mets while a new football stadium opened for the New York Giants in New Jersey. The point here is that our priorities have changed, and we are following the wrong path. We are living in crazy times.

On the national scale, the character of the nation has changed. Our government has become too large. There is too much government intervention in every frivolous facet of our daily lives, yet it is completely lacking where real action is required in areas of health, education, food safety, drug addiction, and child abuse. Many Americans will never believe that over fifteen million children in the United States go to bed hungry every day. On the other hand, Americans have become too dependent on the government to solve their problems. Every time there is a downturn in their lives, it's always a rush to blame the government. There are some who say that we are becoming a welfare state with a host of social and economic programs in place from subsidies to farmers and bailout money to failed businesses to extended unemployment benefits and child-care subsidies. We have a soaring national debt that puts a tax burden on the next generation of our children. Compounding the situation is the fact that the population is aging with fewer younger workers to carry the tax burden. I can envision the curtailment of some services that we have taken for granted in this era and the impact it would have on the American Dream in the future.

The second scenario which in my view has impacted the American Dream rests with the economy. The quality of life of a nation rests with the economy. As the economy of this country takes a nosedive, the American Dream becomes much more difficult to achieve for a vast majority of Americans. Here again our priority has shifted from a self-sufficient nation to a dependent nation. The backbone of this country lies with its middle-class citizens. Since the 1950s and for over fifty years, the middle-class was the driving force for the demand of goods and services. In turn they worked the manufacturing sector, producing those goods and services. They paid their fair share of taxes from which the United States government financed our military might and superiority. We developed an elaborate infrastructure and exported manufactured goods and technology to the rest of the world. Since the year 2000, there has been a steady decline.

Today, the number of families who can call themselves middle-class citizens have dwindled considerably. The disparity between rich and poor has widened. This affected the tax base, and we have had to increase our borrowing from other nations to maintain our high standard of living. The national debt is now in the trillions of dollars. It is so enormous that most Americans cannot fathom the burden on the next generations or how to pay for it. It is a shame that the government must now borrow funds from China to pay the interest on the national debt. It stifles our economic policies, and the role of our government is held hostage to it.

Several factors have contributed to our economic decline over the years. Let me start with President Ronald Reagan and his executive order that weakened the trade union movement in this country. Employers were no longer required to negotiate with their employees. Employers were now free to close factories without recourse from the employees or the government and to move their operations elsewhere. Many companies relocated to cheaper labor markets and discouraged unions to bargain for the employee. By the end of President Bill Clinton's administration, this trend accelerated with an unstoppable force. The North American Free Trade Agreement (NAFTA) with Canada and Mexico sucked out the jobs. The same goods that were being produced by American workers in American factories were now produced by cheaper labor market in Mexico and Canada. Factories closed their doors in droves, and millions of Americans were left unemployed. To compound the matter, we opened up free trade relations with China, India, and other cheap-labor markets. Americans benefited with cheaper goods available for purchase, but the nation paid a heavy price for it in lost wages. The national economy suffered from a diminishing tax base. The buying powers of Americans decreased and with it the demand for goods and services. Sales in the automotive industry slumped significantly, and giants like General Motors, the pride of America, declared bankruptcy, putting millions out of work.

Anyone can take a look at a Wal-Mart store and find more than 90 percent of the items for sale were made overseas. I am particularly saddened to see American corporations like General Electric, Proctor Silex, Black and Decker, Mattel, Tyco, Fisher Price, and dozens of other companies who moved their operations to China, India, and various third world countries. In America, we no longer produce television, toasters, irons, microwave ovens, and a multitude of electronic and textile products. I am unable to find a shirt made in the USA anymore. I had become accustomed to buying Van Heusen and Arrow shirts made with 100 percent fine cotton that had the perfect slim fit for me. Today I have to contend with shirts made in India, China, and a long list of third world countries from Guatemala and Bangladesh to Vietnam, Egypt, and Hong Kong.

In the meantime, there has been a steady decline of the manufacturing base in this country. Factories failed to compete in what became a global economy. Manufacturing operations rushed to other nations to produce the same consumer goods that were produced in the United States. The lure of free trade, a less stringent tax code, and cheaper labor costs contributed heavily to this decline. We are no longer the champion producing the goods that were the backbone of our economy, from heavy steel and automobiles to electronics, toys, and textile products. The middle-class Americans, who once produced them, have dwindled and with them the tax base. This was the economic strength of America.

Deregulations of the banking and financial institutions since the 1990s have had disastrous consequences. Coupled with greed and a total disrespect for the laws, this country grappled with an avalanche of financial scandals in recent years. A few well-documented cases of fraud, bribery, and corruption involved the CEOs and top management officers of corporations like Halliburton, Tyco, Xerox, Merck, Bristol-Meyers, Time Warner, and Enron. The financial woes forced layoffs, and thousands of workers suffered a loss of good paying jobs. In the financial markets, stock prices tumbled as a meltdown followed primarily from losses made by bad loans and unregulated investments. It resulted in the greatest financial collapse since the Great Depression of the 1930s. The severity of the situation required an immediate intervention by the government and an infusion of funds to keep several large banks and financial firms from going bankrupt. The effects were widespread, and even the auto industry felt the squeeze. I always remembered the slogan, What is good for General Motors is Good for America. Even General Motors teetered on bankruptcy, and that alone is an indication of the state of America.

So what are we left with today?

The most recent indicators show unemployment at a national average of over 10 percent and over 16 percent in several states like Michigan. The financial markets and the banking system are teetering on collapse in the worse depression since the 1930s. Millions of Americans have lost their jobs. The housing sector is in crisis with significant decline in the average home values. Millions of Americans have lost their homes to foreclosure, which is at an all-time high throughout the country. Many states, townships, and municipalities find it difficult to maintain the same level of services because of budget shortfalls. Businesses have had to cut back or close down altogether from a lack of demand for their product or services. Striving communities where factories once stood have begun to experience decay with abandoned homes and empty shopping malls. Cities like Detroit, Flint, and Cleveland, which were not so long ago the show places of glimmer and prosperity, are now ghost towns in utter decay. The end result is the strain on families as many struggle to survive and make ends meet. Parents cut back spending on needy services or endure without health care coverage. Others delay spending on their children's college education because they cannot afford the high cost of tuition, and the cycle continues to the next generation. The American Dream is receding in the distance for millions of Americans.

Nowadays, I find this is a stark contrast to my years toiling with Consumers Distributing Company in Canada and then in the United States. Working for more than twenty years, I cannot remember having to worry about the security of my job and from where my next paycheck would be coming. Companies in this period of time operated on a different philosophy, to make a profit for the shareholders. Profits were normally ploughed back into the company toward expansion or better working conditions for the employees. In this way, companies operated successfully for many decades. The CEOs were paid a salary based on their performance. Employees like myself were servants of the company, and in my case, I always worked in the best interest of the company. The company was regarded as my bread and butter, and I always gave 110 percent. I could see the future of my American Dream within my grasp in terms of owning my home, sending my kids to college, and retire with dignity and financial independence. Three decades and a generation later was all that it took to turn the tables on the American Dream. In these modern times, it is apparent the younger generation must face an American landscape with more diverse and tougher problems.

Longevity with a company counts for nothing anymore. It is becoming sparse to find employees with long years of service with any private company. The option for management is to cut costs and trim budgets. CEOs find every possible way to improve the profits margin because they themselves get a large chunk of the profits in bonuses and incentives. This is at the expense of employees with no regard for the consequences. Take the case of my wife, for example. She was forced into accepting a retirement from Hanover Insurance Company after twenty-eight years of loyal, dedicated service. Certain benefits that were considered normal over the years were discontinued, such as health care coverage, life insurance, and 401(k) retirement saving plan among them. The company opted to a cheaper labor market in India, where workers do a substandard work for a fraction of the costs with absolutely no benefits such as sick pay, vacation, or pension. This is the scenario that is being played out all across this country today. Although it is not a strain for us since we have already accomplished our dreams, it was certainly devastating to younger employees with young children or large families. It shatters the American Dream for the millions who have lost their jobs in this fashion in the last decade. I still think that a secure job is the gateway to the American Dream, but I now realize how difficult and illusive it has become. Who is looking out for the American worker? Certainly, it is not the government or the trade union movement. The American worker is now powerless against business corporations, and so it has become apparent that for those families affected, the American Dream is more difficult to achieve.

Finally, religion is the third factor that underlies the erosion of the American Dream, which in my view is worth mentioning. The extent of religion in our lives cannot be measured in real terms, but like the undercurrent of the oceans, unseen from the surface, it is always there. I am not sure what weight it lends itself, but if history has taught us anything, then it should be duly noted. Inclined to believe that God is looking over this country, I am saddened that religious fervor in our lives has lost its luster. From its inception by the first settlers, Americans were a God-fearing people. Thomas Jefferson was inspired to note that we are a people endowed with alienable rights. America is a Christian nation founded on Christian principles. In God We Trust is printed on its currency notes, and we sing "God Bless America" in its praise. America earned its greatness from it adherence to qualities and principles from a religious philosophy. Hard work, sacrifice, community involvement, and a spirit of brotherhood have now taken a backseat.

Religion in this country is in a state of confusion and turmoil. The Catholic Church has been bombarded by scandals up to its highest levels of authority including the pope and the Vatican. Millions of dollars have been paid out to settle cases where homosexual priests have molested young boys in their congregation. Parents are afraid to send their children freely to church, always keeping a watchful eye over them. The average layman shows weakness in spiritually. Churchgoing has become a once-per-week half-hearted effort. Faith ministries and evangelists have become big businesses, and these have not been without corruption and scandals either. The result is that the family as a unit suffers from a lack of high morals with twisted behavior. Compassion for the less fortunate seems to have dwindled in our society with little concern for the over fifteen million children who go to bed hungry every day in this country. I have seen pet owners who shower their dogs and cats with care but frown at charities collecting spare change at the street corners to feed the hungry and homeless.

Lately, there has been a movement away from God, a movement toward greed, selfishness, and hatred. There seems to be a culture of unwarranted behavior from simple lack of manners to outright disrespect to others. Some are just plain nasty. One does not have to be a behavior expert to observe that much of this anti-social behavior has its roots in religious values. Religion has always been the basis of good morals. With religion playing a lesser role in our daily lives, I am convinced that we undermine the essence of our greatness.

The observation of Christmas is a prime example of this decline. Nothing is more prevalent than the celebration of Christmas in this country. It rivals the great traditional honor bestowed to Thanksgiving, Fourth of July, President's Day, Memorial Day, and Labor Day. These pale in comparison to the pomp and pageantry of Christmas. When I first came to the United States, I had never felt before such peacefulness in a people filled with generosity, friendliness, and the close bond between families. Sending a Christmas card to everyone with whom I had an acquaintance was such a joy, and buying a token gift for coworkers, friends, and family was always the norm. In recent years, I have witnessed a marked degradation of the Christmas spirit. It has become one gigantic economic bonanza for retailers. The onus seems to be on sales volume with merchants hacking anything from jewelry, toys, and clothing apparel. In the midst of this frenzy, some behavior has gone out the window. Pushing and shoving to be first in line or getting a scarce parking place takes on a tone of indifference. In many stores, the term *Merry Christmas* has been dropped from the vocabulary as some feel this is offensive language. The nativity scene has been banned from public display so that it does not offend some individuals. I understand the reasoning behind it, but I will never understand the intolerance. It's only Christmas in a Christian nation.

So what does religion have to do with the American Dream, some would ask. Plenty is my answer. A lack of religious beliefs has left many devoid of compassion. This is troubling from the point of view of immigrants seeking the American Dream. With challenges of a different culture, language problems and the scorn of being born of a different race pose many barriers in achieving the American Dream. Sometimes it was just a simple matter of showing courtesy and kindness. I remembered the many times when all I wanted was to be given a fair chance and an opportunity to show my worthiness and talent. Kindness and compassion only comes with a religious upbringing. Some of the best people I have met were ordinary citizens with some form of religious faith. Some of the worst were also religious zealots but with one difference, a lack of education. Americans must take heed and return to the lessons of God and once again a people that hold forth the laws of God. If not, we will destroy in the end what we have as a nation of people. It makes me long for the old days when everyday events were simple and dreams were easier to realize.

Having said all of the above, what direct effect does it have on the American Dream? I know that every day in this country, there are millions of Americans who are striving to realize their American dream.

My concern is that we must look to tomorrow and the next generation of Americans, a nation that will comprise my grandchildren. I wonder what kind of America they would inherit and whether the American Dream would be within their reach.

There are defining moments in everyone's life. I am sure of it. They are those brief moments in time that are game changing. It sets off a new course of action that cannot be explained rationally. Suddenly, you change direction without reason although you know it is convincingly the right thing to do. One such incident touched off a storm in me. Sitting idly in the waiting room at North Shore Hospital, Long Island, New York, I was eager to find out the sonogram results of my daughter's baby.

"So, are you going to be a father soon?" a young girl asked from across the room.

"Oh no, no, it's my daughter who is having the baby," I babbled in reply, completely startled by the comment. "Looking forward to being a grandpa," I said gleefully.

"That's nice. I am just waiting on my sister. This is her third child."

"Congratulations. What do you do?" I asked.

"Second year student at Adelphi," she remarked, turning the pages of a sports magazine she was perusing.

"Well, stay in school," I said. "It's a tough world out there."

"Yeah, that's all I ever hear from anyone," she said sarcastically.

After some small talk about how I struggled to get through my years at the university and putting my two daughters through medical school, she posed a question to me that still haunts me to this day.

"People always tell me how much they accomplished," she pointed out. "It is always that they did this or they did that. I hear it all the time from my own parents. How he had to walk miles to school each day in the snow and had to work two jobs to help put food on the table. I have never heard anyone say what they have learned. What can I learn from you?" she asked.

Suddenly, I was taken aback by the question. Startled, I felt I was jolted by a lightning bolt. Folding my hands to prop up my chin, I wrestled with the question. Then, being quick on my thoughts, I commented.

"Don't fall in love or get married until you finished your college education, and don't worry about having fun and going to parties, drinking, and gallivanting like the rest of your friends today. After you get a good job and money in your pocket, all the boys will come chasing after you, and then life will be good because you will be independent. Then you can do whatever you want, you will have wide choices."

She smiled.

Realizing that I hardly said anything that this young college student could learn from me, I began to regroup my thoughts. Reflecting on my years past, all my conversations with young people, family, and friends were always concentrated on how things were during my days as a student and how I had overcome certain hardships. I began to realize how futile my stories of the past have been. It was always about how I did this and how I did that.

Now, I felt small as if the hurdles I jumped were immaterial and irrelevant. What is it that I can now tell the youths of the next generation? What are some things about life and its mysteries that I can impart? What can anyone learn from me? Then the thoughts of my future grandchildren engulfed me. What kind of world would they inherit? What can I teach them, or better yet, what can they learn from me to realize the American Dream?

Not being of any kind of a certified expert, I can only offer the following advice. I am confident it will stand the test of time. The American Dream will always be there and within reach for anyone with a desire to succeed. Children born and bred in America have an added advantage, especially those coupled with an upper- and middle-class status and the professional aptitude of their parents. In the case of my children and the next generation of my grandchildren, I am confident that I have set the stage for them to realize their American Dream, whatever that may be. I am inclined to believe that children of blue-collar workers and at a lower spectrum of the economic ladder will find it much more difficult to reach their goals. It will take much more in terms of hard work and dedication with some degree of luck and an opportunity. There is one sure way of achieving the American Dream, short of winning the lottery. It is through an education. Growing up in poor conditions should never be a hindrance to an education. My recommendation to the youths of tomorrow is to concentrate in school activities, read voraciously, and make use of the public library and all its resources with a dedication to succeed at their chosen endeavors. Those born in poverty will have to struggle to survive, but there will always be those among them with some degree of ability and talent which will enable them to break out. The key here is motivation. The desire to achieve is always strong in the less fortunate.

Immigrants to this country would always be part of the American landscape. Since immigrants make up the core of its citizens, the future prospects are good, although the path to the American Dream seems much more difficult in these modern times. One advantage of new immigrants is that there would always be the desire to live better lives than from their country of origin. Immigrants usually take risks to venture into the unknown. It will be no different than the risks I took. A different language and, in many cases, a different accent or custom will pose challenges. Nonetheless, they will adjust and become American citizens and respectful of the laws and traditions of America. As a consequence, the political aspect of the land will allow them to progress as much as they decide for themselves. This would be their call to the American Dream. This inherent factor would serve as the motivating force that will propel immigrants to achieve their American Dream. The prospects are still as good as when I set foot on this land of opportunity. God bless them all, and God bless America.

Made in the USA
Middletown, DE
05 June 2017